P9-DMH-320

VERMONT COLLEGE
MONTPELIER, VT.

WITHDRAWN

WITHDRAWN

A Synoptic Philosophy
of Education

ARTHUR W. MUNK

A Synoptic Philosophy
of Education

*Toward Perspective, Synthesis,
and Creativity*

ABINGDON PRESS NEW YORK • NASHVILLE

A SYNOPTIC PHILOSOPHY OF EDUCATION

Copyright © 1965 by Abingdon Press

All rights in this book are reserved.
No part of the book may be reproduced in any
manner whatsoever without written permission of
the publishers except brief quotations embodied in
critical articles or reviews. For information address
Abingdon Press, Nashville, Tennessee.

Library of Congress Catalog Card Number: 65-13146

SET UP, PRINTED, AND BOUND BY THE
PARTHENON PRESS, AT NASHVILLE,
TENNESSEE, UNITED STATES OF AMERICA

370.1
M966s

Dedicated to my grandsons
John Caldwell Munk & Jeffrey William Munk

15135

Preface

This book has been in process for many years. Along with what I have learned elsewhere, I have drawn heavily upon nearly twenty years of classroom experience. Most of this time was spent trying to introduce undergraduates to those great teachers of mankind known as the philosophers.

Instead of being a narrow, specialized venture (whose number is legion), in keeping with the chief need of a time of unparalleled danger as well as opportunity, what follows constitutes an attempt at *comprehensiveness, unity,* and *wholeness.* Consequently, while one aspect of the basic aim is, of necessity, *critical,* the other and *most significant* is decidedly *constructive.* If mankind is to find its way out of the confusion resulting from the spread of science and technology, the collision of cultures, two world wars, and the advent of the Nuclear Age, a basis for unity in education as well as in political affairs must be found. This demands *creativity* of a very high order along with *perspective* and *synthesis.*

Although—unlike the usual textbook—controversial issues are faced frankly and reasonable solutions are suggested, at the same time a real attempt is made to avoid dogmatism. In accordance with this attempt, by means of the extensive footnotes and the annotated bibliography, the thoughtful student is encouraged to undertake further investigations of the basic problems.

Parts of chapters III, VI, and XIII really involve an expansion of an article of mine entitled "Educational Philosophy for Today." This article appeared in the July, 1961 issue of *The Philosophical*

Quarterly—an organ of the Indian Institute of Philosophy and the Indian Philosophical Congress. I am grateful to the managing editor, Professor G. R. Malkani, for his kindness in allowing me to use this material. I am also grateful to Dr. Herman E. Wornom, General Secretary of The Religious Education Association, for informing me that I could freely use my article "A Synoptic Approach to Religious Education." This article is reprinted in part in chapter X from the May-June, 1958 issue of *Religious Education*, by permission of the publisher, The Religious Education Association, New York City. Mention must likewise be made of the fact that part of what follows was delivered as a series of lectures to teachers at Claflin University during the summer of 1957.

While helpful suggestions have come from many sources, I am especially indebted to the following: Professor Panis Bardis (a sociologist, author, and former colleague at Albion College), the Reverend James E. Leach (a specialist in religious education), and to my son, J. B. Munk (an attorney in the State of New York). I am also grateful to Miss Dallas Dee Andersen (a major in my department and an honors student) for her assistance in typing and proofreading the index. That this volume may—in some little way —help both teachers and students in their quest for a philosophy of education *adequate* for these perilous times is my hope and wish.

ARTHUR W. MUNK

Contents

PART ONE: *The Meaning and Scope of Education*

I. *Education: Its Nature and Significance* 15
   1. What Is Education? 15
   2. Man's Precarious Situation 17
   3. The Need of Perspective 18

II. *Education in Historic and Global Perspective* 20
   1. The Dim Beginnings 20
   2. Our Debt to Antiquity 22
   3. Medieval Contributions 30
   4. The Modern and Contemporary Scene 33

PART TWO: *Perspectives for Synthesis*

III. *Education and Philosophy* 43
   1. The Nature of Philosophy........................ 44
   2. The Significance of Philosophy of Education............ 47

IV. *The Strife of Systems* 50
   1. Pragmatism and Experimentalism 51
   2. Progressivism 55
   3. Essentialism 57
   4. Authoritarianism 65
   5. Other Types 76
   6. Conclusion 82

9

V. *From Diversity Toward Unity* 83
   1. Purpose and Method 83
   2. Weaknesses and Contributions 84
   3. Conclusion: Contrasts and Similarities 109

VI. *The Question of Goals* 112
   1. Why the Concern for Goals? 112
   2. The Current Aimlessness 113
   3. In Search of a Criterion 114
   4. A Critique of Ten Important Goals 116
   5. Aspects of an Adequate Goal 130
   6. Two Possible Objections 137

PART THREE: *Perspectives for Creativity*

VII. *Creativity: Its Nature and Significance* 141
   1. Scope of the Inquiry 141
   2. What Is Creativity? 142
   3. Creativity, Intuition, and the Unconscious 145
   4. The Need of Creativity 151

VIII. *Obstructions to Creativity* 152
   1. Factors in Modern Cultures 152
   2. Factors Within Our Schools 155
   3. Four Obstructive Dogmas 159
   4. The Four Dogmas Examined 162
   5. Conclusions 174

IX. *Toward Creativity in Science* 175
   1. Science Yesterday and Today 175
   2. The Nature of Science 176
   3. Historic Relations 180
   4. Limitations and Dangers 182
   5. Science as Indispensable 187
   6. Scientific Creativity for the Future 189

X. *Toward Creativity in Religion* 191
   1. The Nature and Significance of Religion 191
   2. Historic Relations 193
   3. The American Dilemma 197
   4. The Religious Outlook 200
   5. The Problem of Religious Education 205
   6. Can Religion Again Become Creative? 210

XI. *Toward Creativity in Philosophy* 216
   1. Eclipse of Philosophy 216
   2. Creative Tendencies 221
   3. The Cost of Philosophical Neglect 223
   4. Toward Greater Creativity 225

PART FOUR: *Conclusion*

XII. *Education in This Age of Transition* 233
   1. A Turning Point in History 233
   2. The Crisis in American Education 235
   3. The Greatest Single Need 236

XIII. *Aspects of a Synoptic View* 238
   1. A Realistic Idealism 239
   2. A Daring Experimentalism 242
   3. Specialization Without Fragmentation 244
   4. Authority Without Authoritarianism 246
   5. Freedom Without License and Anarchy 248
   6. A Universal Outlook 250
   7. The Educator's Role Today and Tomorrow 251

Annotated Bibliography 253

Index 259

Part 1

The Meaning and Scope of Education

I

Education: Its Nature and Significance

A creature totally devoid of education, even though belonging to the human species, would be something less than a man. Lacking any development whatsoever of its *basic* capacities, it would be animalistic. The chief motive of all the great educators, in fact, has been to save man from animalism through the development of his creative and distinctly human aspects. "I lived like a beggar," said Johann Pestalozzi, "in order to learn how to make beggars live like men."

At its very beginning the educative process was very informal. Nature, in truth, was man's first teacher—a very stern teacher indeed. Yet, in spite of all her harshness, through dangers and rewards, sufferings and satisfactions, she succeeded in awakening her pupil's vast creative capacities.

1. What Is Education?

Viewed in the broad perspective of its long history, education really involves two significant aspects. The first may well be termed the transmissive and receptive, since it constitutes the impartation of the traditions, skills, insights, and accumulated values of the past. Without this precious legacy, the individual would be even more helpless than his most distant ancestor long before the dawn of history. It can also arouse in the pupil a consciousness of his dependence on society: that he is a part of the great stream of human life as it has flowed richly down the ages. Nor can there be any doubt that, without this feeling on the part of its members, society soon faces the nemesis of atomism and anarchy and inevitable destruction. Moreover, in a day when all living cultures are in contact and when the historian, the anthropologist, and the archaeologist have shed so much light on so many forgotten episodes of the human drama, there is virtually no limit to the amount that an alert student may appropriate.

Yet, important as this factor undoubtedly is (particularly in times such as these when an irresponsible individualism threatens to run riot in the West), standing alone, it can easily lead to sterility. When educators are spellbound by a blind, unthinking reverence for the past, the result can only mean a stifling of the creative impulse. Witness the deadly effect of this phenomenon on Chinese and Hindu culture, and on Medieval Europe just prior to the Renaissance. Interestingly enough, in contemporary America, in spite of a certain rebellious attitude whenever any attempt is made to restrict their pleasures, the dominant mood among students—so far as the great issues are concerned—is a kind of blind conformity to society.[1] This is a bad omen indeed.

The second aspect of education may be designated as the active and creative.[2] While the first finds its source and center largely in society, the second, though profoundly sensitive to social influences, wells up more or less spontaneously from the development and free play of the highest capacities of the learner himself. It is the mind itself coming out of its shell and wondering, curiously observing, examining, and daring to venture beyond the frontier into the dangerous unknown. There is no fear of

1. See Philip E. Jacob, *Changing Values in College* (New York: Harper & Row, 1958), pp. 120-22. On the loss of vision due to affluence, see also Arnold J. Toynbee, *America and the World Revolution and Other Lectures* (New York: Oxford University Press, 1962), pp. 103-53.

2. Throughout his *Aims of Education* (New York: New American Library of World Literature 1949), Alfred North Whitehead stresses this aspect.

experiment, of novelty, and of adventure. In Part Three of this book we shall deal with this factor at length.

In the final analysis, any educational scheme which aims at wholeness must include both the transmissive and the creative aspects. While lack of the first would make continuity impossible with all the dire consequences which this would entail, lack of the second would stifle progress. Society would become frozen, ossified, totalitarian. In short, education, in the very highest sense of the word, means nothing less than the marriage of the transmissive and the creative aspects; for, after all, they are really complementary rather than contradictory.

2. Man's Precarious Situation

Toynbee has warned that the greatest threat to civilization during these perilous times comes not from afar, but rather from the barbarians bred in our midst.[3] The assassination of President Kennedy verifies this warning. Moreover, when one hears of the brutality associated with efforts for racial equality, one trembles for the future of democracy. For many years a great sociologist has also called our attention to the dangers inherent in our "sensate culture" [4]—dangers which are steadily becoming worse.

Ironically enough, since one extreme tends to produce its opposite, there is also the ever-present threat of totalitarianism. The lesson of history seems to be that, frightened by chaos, sooner or later the poor human animal, in search for a phantom security, naturally turns in the direction of authoritarianism. Lasting solutions of pressing problems require sustained efforts in terms of synoptic thinking, long-range planning, and effective action— challenges which Homo sapiens, ever in search for short cuts and quick remedies, never relishes.

Finally, the nuclear crisis is still very much with us. While man's

3. In *A Study of History*, Arnold J. Toynbee, abridgment of Vols. I-X by D. C. Somervell (2 vols.; New York: Oxford University Press, 1947), I, 419.

4. See Pitirium A. Sorokin, *The Crisis of Our Age* (New York: E. P. Dutton & Co., 1941). To make bad matters worse, most Americans are so conditioned by the prevailing hedonism that they are hardly aware of these dangers.

situation has always been precarious, today, perched as he is on the very rim of hell, his position is desperate. To escape destruction will require far greater vision and creativity than he has ever shown before.

3. The Need of Perspective

In his *Civilization on Trial*, Toynbee makes the interesting distinction between what we actually see and what we might see.[5] What everyone actually sees is his own particular nation, which may be relatively young. This finite god, in fact, tends to take up the entire horizon. What everyone might see, however, is the whole drama of man on this planet together with the contributions of all races, civilizations, and nations. In an age that is at once nuclear and global, nationalism and tribalism could make a swift end of us. Hence, even aside from all idealism, from a cold pragmatic point of view, our great need is perspective.

Moreover, it is interesting to note that in the face of impending danger, the thoughtful naturally look hopefully in the direction of education. In their efforts to meet the crisis in Greek life occasioned, on the one hand, by the disintegrating effects of Sophist relativism and, on the other, by the terrible Peloponnesian War, Socrates, Plato, and Aristotle turned in this direction. Likewise, in a desperate endeavor to save his little country from annihilation at the hand of the Roman tyrant, Jesus began his great campaign of mass education.

Few would question this ancient belief that man's last, best hope lies in education. Back in 1926, in his Nobel Prize winning book, *Education and the Good Life*, Bertrand Russell even went so far as to insist that "Education is the key to the new world." [6] It is doubtful that he would be quite so optimistic today.

Important as it undoubtedly is, education is far from being the

---

5. (Paperback; New York: Meridan Books, 1958), see especially pp. 136-37.
6. (Paperback; New York: Avon Book Division of the Hearst Corporation, 1926), p. 51.

panacea for every human ill. Not only is it being questioned widely today, but even its best friends are far from agreement concerning its meaning, its nature, and its ultimate purpose and goal. Nor must it be forgotten that, in the final analysis, everything depends on the *kind* of education. The kind of education sponsored by dictators could give civilization itself the kiss of death.

One may, of course, with good reason contend that all the totalitarian forms are mere pretenders and that, as such, they are wholly unworthy of being classed as educational. They are most certainly hopelessly deficient so far as the vital creative factor is concerned. In view of this fact, it might be better to call them forms of training rather than education.

At any rate, at this juncture, it may be best to follow the method of Plato. For, as in his *Republic,* in his attempt to portray the nature and significance of justice, he found it advantageous to place it in the larger context of a just society. In order to be understood in the fullest possible sense, the effort must likewise be made to view education in the widest possible perspective. This means that we must take a glance at the process as a whole as it has developed historically. This we propose to do in the next chapter.

II

Education in Historic and Global Perspective

Since this is a philosophy of education, what follows in this chapter constitutes nothing but the most general survey of certain very significant aspects of the history of education. In no sense is it to be regarded as an adequate treatment of the history of education.[1] In short, our purpose is *perspective*.

1. The Dim Beginnings

Surrounded by dense, dark forests in which lurked monstrous beasts of prey, subject to nature's caprice in a thousand ways, visited by the mysterious forces of sickness and death, and devoid of any effective means to strike back, our primitive ancestors were in great plight. In spite of all these handicaps, a few of them responded with an astounding creativity and thus, unknowingly, laid the foundation of the cultural structures of the future. Primi-

1. What follows is based upon the following authorities which students will find profitable for a more detailed account: Frank Pierrepont Graves' monumental three volume work, *A History of Education* (New York: The Macmillan Co., 1909, 1910, 1915); Thomas Davidson, *A History of Education* (New York: Charles Scribner's Sons, 1900); James Mulhern, *A History of Education* (second edition; New York: The Ronald Press Co., 1959); Frederick Eby, *The Development of Modern Education* (second edition; New York: Prentice-Hall, 1952); A. D. C. Peterson, *A Hundred Years of Education* (paperback, second revised edition; New York: Collier Books, 1962); Adolph E. Meyer, *The Development of Education in the Twentieth Century* ("Prentice-Hall Educational Series" [second edition; New York: Prentice-Hall, 1949]); and J. Donald Butler, *Religious Education* (New York: Harper & Row, 1962).

tive man, in fact, made at least three outstanding contributions.

The first constitutes the priceless legacy of language. No one knows or will ever know just how or when man first began to speak. The many theories that have been advanced do not concern us here.[2] At any rate, the importance of language is beyond dispute. Without it effective communication would be impossible; and without this factor education could never have developed. Be it said, then, to the credit of primitive man that while the perfection of language had to wait until the great civilizations, it was his genius that laid the foundations long before the dawn of history.

These early men must likewise be given the credit for laying the foundations of the arts and sciences. Neanderthal Man was probably much more intelligent than was once thought: not only did he make beautiful tools, but he also buried his dead and hence possessed and made use of religious concepts. In his achievements he was surpassed, however, by the Cro-Magnons—whom Montagu calls "the Apollos of the prehistoric world." [3] This remarkable race especially excelled in artistic ability.

Whatever the men of the Paleolithic Age may have learned, either through insight spurred on by necessity or through sheer chance, those of the Neolithic (c. 10,000-3,000 B.C.) tried to improve. They not only polished their weapons and tools, but also made pottery, constructed rude houses and boats, domesticated animals, began the art of surgery, and developed much more complex religious concepts and practices.

Finally, Stone Age Man made the first crude venture into education. Most of it was, of course, incidental to the terrific struggle for existence. As a result it was as informal and incidental as it was crude. Gradually, as tradition and the knowledge gained accumulated, the tribal ceremonies also began to occupy a very

2. On these theories, see Ashley Montagu, *Man: His First Million Years* (second edition, paperback; New York: New American Library of World Literature, 1957), pp. 102-103.

3. *Ibid.*, p. 61.

prominent place. This brought the shaman or medicine man into a special position of influence and power. Indeed, he is really the forerunner of the teacher as well as of the priest and the physician.

2. Our Debt to Antiquity

While the first faint gleams of civilization seemed to have appeared at Jericho over ten thousand years ago,[4] the first two great civilizations were the Sumerian and the Egyptian. They were followed by others such as the Hindu, the Sinic, the Babylonian, the Greco-Roman, and the Syriac. In keeping with our purpose, a summary of their vast contributions under four general heads must suffice.

First of all, there is the invention of the alphabet which made written records possible.[5] The invention of writing has, in fact, been hailed as the greatest single event in history. Moreover, libraries were established as early as 2,000 B.C. in Egypt.

Second, there are the immense contributions of the ancient world to the arts, to philosophy and religion, and to the sciences. The ziggurats of Sumeria, the pyramids of Egypt, the palaces of Babylon, Assyria, and Persia all bear eloquent witness to the remarkable progress in architecture; while the mere mention of names such as Phidias, Praxiteles, Sophocles, and Euripides brings to mind that glorious age of Athens when the arts reached a standard of excellence that has never been surpassed.

There is also the development of philosophy. Although there were glimmerings in Sumeria, in Egypt, and elsewhere, it began in earnest in the profound speculations of those Hindu thinkers who speak to us through the Upanishads, and it reached its highwater mark among the Greeks in Socrates, Plato, and Aristotle. Mention must also be made of the universalism of the Stoics and

4. For some interesting observations on Jericho, see Arnold J. Toynbee, *Reconsiderations*, Vol. XII of *A Study of History* (New York: Oxford University Press, 1961), pp. 318-21, 335.

5. On the origin and development of writing, see Mulhern, *A History of Education,* pp. 65, 69-70, 73; and Albert A. Trever, *History of Ancient Civilization* (New York: Harcourt, Brace & Co., 1936), I, 28, 32-33, 41-42, 102-3.

of their influence upon Roman law. Nor can the great religions be forgotten. Later, in dealing with the great teachers of the ancient world, we shall return to philosophy and religion.

There were likewise outstanding scientific advances. Astronomy, mathematics, and medicine had their beginnings in the temples of Egypt, Sumeria, and Babylon; and the gifted Greeks added something to almost every science in the catalog. Several of their philosophers even anticipated the theory of evolution.[6]

Third, it is to these ancient peoples that we owe the school—the formal education—in the full sense of the word. William E. Hocking's thesis that religion "is the *mother of the Arts*"[7] is well illustrated by the fact that the schools of both Egypt and Sumeria were in the hands of the priests in the temples.[8] Yet, in spite of this, these schools were primarily practical and professional.

No nation has ever regarded the teacher with greater reverence than ancient China. The basic purposes were largely practical: the development of character through discipline and a knowledge of the classics, and the preparation of the most gifted for the government service. In ancient India, however, while practical affairs were not forgotten and while some notable contributions were made even to science,[9] the chief aim was religious, that is, preparation for the life to come—absorption in Brahman.

So far as the Greeks are concerned, while the Spartan system was militaristic to the core, the Athenian, though primarily designed for citizenship, was much more liberal. Ultimately, in truth, it aimed at nothing less than the development of the whole man. Moreover, with the rise of those wandering teachers known

6. See Trever, *History of Ancient Civilization*, p. 513; William Cecil Dampier, *A Shorter History of Science* (New York: Macmillan Co., 1944), pp. 16-33; and Giorgio De Santillana, *The Origins of Scientific Thought* (paperback; New York: New American Library of World Literature, 1961).

7. William Ernest Hocking, *The Meaning of God in Human Experience* (New Haven: Yale University Press, 1912), pp. 14-15.

8. See Graves, *A History of Education*, I, 34-35, 49; and Davidson; *A History of Education*, pp. 37, 39, 53.

9. For notable Hindu contributions to the sciences, see Mulhern, *A History of Education*, pp. 101-2.

as the Sophists, a youth, if he could afford it, might receive instruction in almost any subject.

When Plato established his Academy, the foundations of Greek higher education (as well as of our future Western higher education) were laid. Later the other leading philosophical groups also established schools; and, finally, it was out of a coalition of these philosophical institutions with what was known as the Ephebic College that the University of Athens gradually took shape. During the Hellenistic Age the University of Alexandria, with its famous library, was established, and, since it was dominated by Aristotelianism, scientific research flourished side by side with philosophic speculation.

The early Roman schools had certain distinct characteristics of their own. Yet, ironical as it may seem, with the passage of time, they came to be dominated by Greek culture and ideas. "Captive Greece took captive her rude conqueror, and brought the arts to Latium."

The Hebrews, like the Chinese and the Greeks, had a profound respect for education, especially after they had encountered tragedy after tragedy. The Talmud goes so far as to say, "A town without schools and school children should be destroyed." Although there were schools of a sort among the Hebrews long before, in the formal sense they did not come into existence until after 500 B.C. Even then they were chiefly for the training of religious leaders. Later attempts were made to make a certain amount of education compulsory for all Jewish children. Be that as it may, Hebrew education is important for two reasons: its primary aim was moral and religious; and, in spite of the stress on memory work and on rigorous discipline, it was illuminated by an astounding amount of practical wisdom.[10]

The fourth and greatest contribution of ancient times is that long line of teachers who have exerted and continue to exert such

10. On Hebrew education, see Graves, *A History of Education*, pp. 110-37; and James Hastings (ed.), *Encyclopaedia of Religion and Ethics*, V, 194-98.

a vast influence. Since it is impossible to consider them all, we shall deal only with the most outstanding.

Next to Jesus of Nazareth, Gautama Buddha (born *c.* 560 B.C.) has probably had the greatest influence. He had a keen analytical mind which enabled him to cut through the superficial notions so prevalent in the India of his day. Coupled with this passion for truth were a concern for men and a compassion which has perhaps been surpassed only once in history. Buddha, like Socrates and Jesus, tried to clarify his teachings by means of the question-and-answer method. He also made use of stories drawn from actual life situations.[11]

Confucius (*c.* 551-479 B.C.) was particularly concerned about the sad state of his country. Everywhere he saw moral and spiritual decay. His remedy was to lead men back to sound moral principles. In his teachings one finds both the Golden Rule and the Golden Mean. Moreover, since he urged men to pursue "the investigation of things," there is also an empirical note in the teachings of the great sage. For him, as for many other great teachers, the goal of education is the development of the whole man. From the *Analects* we learn that he taught by means of thought-provoking statements that brought questions, by means of pithy sayings grounded in the wisdom of the past, and, most effectively of all, by the power of his own example. Though he probably died thinking that he had failed, he had, in fact, succeeded beyond measure: that is, he impressed an intimate circle of gifted young men so deeply that they kept his ideas and ideals alive until that memorable day when the Emperor himself made the Confucian system the very core of Chinese education.[12]

This brings us to Socrates (*c.* 470-399 B.C.), the "Father of Philosophy." Like Confucius had been in China, he was deeply

11. On Buddha, see John B. Noss, *Man's Religions* (revised edition; New York: Macmillan Co., 1956), pp. 155-180; and E. A. Burtt (ed.), *The Teachings of the Compassionate Buddha* (New York: New American Library, 1955).

12. On Confucius and Confucianism, see Noss, *Man's Religions*, pp. 338-98, and H. G. Creel, *Chinese Thought from Confucius to Mao Tsê-tung* (Chicago: University of Chicago Press, 1953), pp. 25-45.

moved by the moral and social decay which was eating at the
very foundations of Greek life. The irresponsible individualism
and relativism of extremists among the Sophists particularly provoked his creative response. Along with his charm and wit, his remarkable self-control, his devotion to truth, and his moral courage, he is known for the famous dialectical method which, interestingly enough, influenced the Marxists as well as Hegel. This
method is based upon the conviction that reason alone (in terms
of a penetrating analysis followed by a strenuous effort at a comprehensive synthesis), rather than sensation, constitutes the road
to truth. Concerning the vast influence of Socrates, Warbeke in-
forms us that not only was he the source of many schools of
Greek philosophy, but also through his greatest followers—
Plato, Aristotle, and the Stoics—he has had and still has a powerful effect on both man's ethical and theological thinking.[13] Similarly, Sir Walter Moberly points out that it was Socrates, as over
against Thrasymachus, who championed that point of view so
essential to modern man's survival; namely, that power must be
made fully responsible by the recognition of the existence of a
universal and objective moral law to which it must be, always and
everywhere, subject.[14]

Plato (c. 427-347 B.C.) is perhaps the greatest, the boldest, and
the most original educational theorist of all times. To begin with,
his aim is lofty. It involves the harmonious development of the
whole man—with special stress on man's highest capacities. In
his commonwealth all the children are to be given a real chance
to prove themselves: that is, through a series of tests, the ultimate
aim of which is *perfection, excellence*.

In Plato's educational scheme the religious education of the
children must be based upon a theology that is ethically sound:
God, unlike the gods in Homer, must be conceived of as the perfect example for man's highest aspirations. In broad outline his

---

13. John M. Warbeke, *The Searching Mind of Greece* (New York: Appleton-Century-
Crofts, 1930), p. 132.

14. In *The Crisis in the University* (London: SCM Press, 1949), pp. 128-29.

plan is somewhat as follows: during early childhood education by means of carefully chosen stories, play activities,[15] and good example; up to seventeen or eighteen the beginnings of more formal education but with a minimum amount of compulsion and considerable activity; then two years of military training; at twenty examinations for all, with the survivors continuing their studies at a much higher level; after further selection at thirty, the chosen few will spend the next five years in an intensive study of dialectic and ethics; from thirty-five to fifty this group of geniuses will gain practical experience through occupying minor posts in public service; and, finally, the best, having survived all previous tests and being in possession of the vision of the "Good," will be the philosopher-kings spending their time in study and in conducting the highest affairs of state. Thus it is clear that for Plato education is basic; his whole superstructure rests upon it. Even in his *Laws*, a watered down version of his utopia, the minister of education is the most important officer in the state.

Unlike his master, Aristotle (384-322 B.C.) was much less boldly speculative and much more empirical and precise. There is hardly a science to which he did not make a contribution. Although Charles Darwin praised Linnaeus and Cuvier as his "two gods," he confessed that "they were mere schoolboys to old Aristotle." At any rate, he was much more formal than Plato—reminding us of the traditional college professor.

Like Confucius (whom he resembles in many ways)[16] and like Plato, Aristotle was a perfectionist and a self-realizationist. He was especially concerned that due attention be given to those capacities which most decidedly distinguish man from the beast. Among these reason is paramount. Aristotle was very suspicious both of athletics and of utilitarian types of education. Instead he favored a liberal education as a means toward the enjoyment of

15. Here he anticipated progressivism; see the *Republic*, VII, 536.

16. This became especially evident to this writer some years ago, when one of his majors wrote his Honors Thesis on these two great thinkers.

leisure;[17] and, while he undoubtedly went to extremes, in view of the increasing amount of leisure which civilization affords and the need of refining our modern barbarians lest they destroy every semblance of law and order, we must take him more seriously.

Perhaps no philosopher has presented more explicitly the conception of education as a function of government. Moreover, although (except in a narrow domestic sense) women were excluded, it was for all citizens. Interestingly enough, there is a dualistic element in Aristotle's conception of education, namely, in the distinction that he made between the education of the body and the irrational soul, on the one hand, and the education of the rational soul, on the other. The truth of the matter is that, while the former could more properly be called training, the latter (even though he is not as clear as he might be) is education in the fullest and highest sense of the word—that is, what we call liberal education.

Finally, there is Jesus of Nazareth. Although, as in the case of Buddha, he is enshrouded in myth so that—following the wake of Rudolf Bultmann [18]—demythologization has become a primary concern of many New Testament scholars and theologians, certain facts about his life and teachings seem to be clear.[19] To begin with, it is certain that, like Confucius and Socrates, Jesus was deeply concerned with the plight of his people.[20] Restless as they were under the heel of the Roman tyrant, there was the ever-present threat of suicidal revolt. Moral and spiritual decay were also evident. Confronted with this situation, Jesus became convinced

17. His views of education are given particularly in Book VIII of his *Politics*.

18. On demythologization, see especially the following: Rudolf Bultmann, *Jesus Christ and Mythology* (New York: Charles Scribner's Sons, 1958), and his *History and Eschatology* (paperback; New York: Harper & Row, 1962); and also Schubert M. Ogden, *Christ Without Myth* (New York: Harper & Row, 1961).

19. On this point, see L. Harold DeWolf, *The Case for Theology in Liberal Perspective* (Philadelphia: The Westminster Press, 1959), pp. 65-70; and on the importance of "the Jesus of History," see also Henry P. Van Dusen, *The Vindication of Liberal Theology* (New York: Charles Scribner's Sons, 1963), pp. 41-46.

20. See Vladimir G. Simkhovitch, *Toward the Understanding of Jesus* (New York: The Macmillan Co., 1933). This still remains one of the most illuminating books on the subject.

that his mission—as the fulfiller of Moses and the Prophets—was to proclaim the kingdom of God.[21] While he was certainly influenced by the current apocalyptic expectations,[22] it is safe to say that this concept of the kingdom meant for him God's new order based upon the two great commandments (Matt. 22:34-40), on the Golden Rule (Matt. 7:12), and upon the ideal of humble human service as the mark of true greatness (Luke 22:24-27).[23]

The methods of Jesus as a teacher are interesting. First and foremost, he was usually positive rather than negative. Again, in his skillful use of the stimulating technique of question and answer together with a penetrating analysis which prepared the way for his own higher synthesis, he reminds us of both Buddha and Socrates. Like the Prophets of Israel and the philosophers of Greece, he was also very critical of tradition and mere rote; and, since he was never afraid to raise controversial issues, he was profoundly creative. Not unlike Plato, Jesus was likewise the artist and the poet. This is evident both from his love of nature and from the rich figures of speech with which he sprinkled his teaching. His use of hyperbole or rhetorical overstatement, often with a most delicate and subtle coloring of humor, is also striking (Matt. 7:4; 23:24). Above all else, however, he was the master of the parable. Dickens declared the parable of the prodigal son "the most touching passage in all literature." Along with this, there is also his remarkable versatility: he was as much at home with a group of ignorant fishermen as with the most learned men of his nation.

Furthermore, Jesus avoided the false dualism of learner versus subject matter. Both the learner and the precious truth to be

21. On the centrality of the kingdom, see John Bright's *The Kingdom of God* (Nashville: Abingdon Press, 1953), pp. 197-98; and also Ray C. Petry, *Christian Eschatology and Social Thought* (Nashville: Abingdon Press, 1956), p. 46.

22. For a moderate view, see DeWolf, *The Case for Theology in Liberal Perspective*, pp. 178-81.

23. On Christianity's "vital essence," see my article, "Is Christianity Adequate For These Times?" in *The London Quarterly & Holborn Review*, July, 1963, pp. 221-24.

learned are important and demand due respect. Finally, he also made use, like the Old Testament Prophets, of dramatic action. Cases in point are the washing of the disciples' feet and his triumphal entry into Jerusalem. Even though he failed in his attempt to save his people from well-nigh complete destruction, through his teachings and his splendid courage and compassion— a courage and compassion that did not flinch even at the prospect of the most horrible of deaths—he released a power for good that has never been surpassed. With Jesus we bring our discussion of our debt to antiquity to a close.[24]

3. Medieval Contributions

To understand and appreciate the Middle Ages properly, and especially the early period following the fall of Rome and often referred to as the Dark Ages, one must always keep clearly in mind the stupendous problems which had to be solved: the preservation of the ancient learning and the taming of the bar- barians. Anyone who has read Augustine's *City of God* can un- derstand how profoundly people were shocked when Alaric captured Rome in A.D. 410. To some, indeed, it looked like the end of the world. In short, it meant nothing less than the beginning of the Dark Ages. Though the darkness was by no means total so far as Europe as a whole was concerned, yet after Odoacer in 476 (the traditional date of the fall of the Roman Empire) put an end to the Roman line of emperors, cultural disintegration became al- most total in the West. Men who were completely illiterate sat on the throne of the Caesars. Basically then, the problem was the colossal one of building a new civilization on the ruins of the old.

24. Due largely to the present concern with theology and the Christ of experience, there has been little written on Jesus as a teacher. Surprisingly enough, even such books as J. Donald Butler's *Religious Education,* and Marvin J. Taylor (ed.), *Religious Education: A Comprehensive Survey* (Nashville: Abingdon Press, 1960) contain virtually nothing. The same also applies to Howard Grimes, *The Church Redemptive* (Nashville: Abingdon Press, 1958). Therefore, the above is based largely on the two older books: Herman Harrell Horne, *Jesus, The Master Teacher* (New York: Association Press, 1920); and Charles Foster Kent, *The Life and Teachings of Jesus* (New York: Charles Scribner's Sons, 1913).

Whatever the shortcomings of the Christian church may have been, and they were many, still it rose to the occasion. Through its monasteries, like so many lighthouses in this vast sea of barbarism, it did much to keep learning alive. By copying the ancient manuscripts by hand, the monks, in fact, produced libraries. This gave rise to the saying, "A monastery without a library is like a castle without an armory." At the same time, heroic representatives of the church such as Ulfilas, Patrick, Columban, and Boniface undertook the gigantic task of Christianizing and civilizing our savage ancestors.[25]

As Graves has pointed out, it was during the sixth century that those four factors met which were destined to become the most significant in Western civilization, namely, the Greek, the Roman, the Christian, and the German; and while they existed side by side for a time, they gradually fused during the course of the following centuries.[26] Without the laying of these foundations, the superstructure of modern Western civilization could never have been built.

There can be no doubt that this process prepared the way for modern philosophy and modern science. At the very beginning of the medieval period, Augustine developed a system which constituted a synthesis of Platonism and Christianity;[27] and Platonism in this Augustinian form remained dominant until the time of Albertus Magnus and Thomas Aquinas—with whom a mild type of Aristotelianism began to assert itself. The emphasis of the medieval theologians on law and order, together with the more empirical orientation which Thomism supplied, opened the way for those speculations which eventually led to the scientific revo-

25. See Kenneth Scott Latourette, *A History of the Expansion of Christianity* (2 vol.; New York: Harper & Row, 1937 & 1938), I, 171-238; II, 22-149.

26. Frank Pierrepont Graves, *A History of Education During the Middle Ages* (New York: The Macmillan Co., 1910), pp. 1-2. This really constitutes the second volume of his *History of Education.*

27. This process began long before Augustine. It can be traced back to Justin Martyr (*c*. A.D. 100-160), and even to the New Testament itself. Moreover, since Christianity sprang from Judaism, its ultimate source is Philo (30 B.C.-A.D. 50).

lution.[28] Due credit must also be given to Moslem philosophers such as Avicenna (980-1037) and Averroës (1126-98), who exerted an enormous influence on Christian Europe. Finally, with the appearance of such thinkers as Roger Bacon and William of Ockham, there can be little doubt concerning the wave of the future.

There are certain aspects of the medieval spirit which have special relevance for the present situation. Chief among these is the problem of the place of religion in the curriculum. Religion was certainly dominant during the Middle Ages; and, so far as higher education was concerned, theology ranked as "the Queen of the sciences." Moreover, in spite of all our attempts at secularization, the religious question is still with us. It has, in fact, become so important that an entire chapter must be devoted to it.

Closely related is the medieval concern for metaphysics and a rational *Weltanschauung* (world view). Inadequate as the medieval world view undoubtedly is, yet, since the mystery of existence will continue to intrigue thoughtful men, and since the attempt of the logical positivists to destroy metaphysics has failed,[29] we shall have to come to grips with the relevance of philosophy and metaphysics to any modern scheme of education. Somehow, if he is to avoid catastrophe, modern man must find a philosophy of life that makes for more wholeness and unity than the prevailing, predominantly analytical philosophies allow. Whatever his faults, the scholastic at least saw life in terms of a meaningful whole.

Similarly there is a grain of truth in the schoolman's stress on authority. While it is impossible to accept an authoritarian church or the rigid, ascetic, disciplinary schemes which ruled the schools,

28. On the relation of science to medieval theology, see Alfred North Whitehead, *Science and the Modern World* (New York: The Macmillan Co., 1937), pp. 18-19; and on the empirical element in St. Thomas, see Jacques Maritain, "The Humanism of St. Thomas Aquinas," in Dagobert D. Runes (ed.), *Twentieth Century Philosophy* (New York: Philosophical Library, 1947), p. 297.

29. For an excellent critique of Logical Positivism, see Errol E. Harris, *Nature, Mind and Modern Science* ("Muirhead Library of Philosophy Series" [New York: The Macmillan Co., 1954]), pp. 274-351.

still modern relativism and irresponsible individualism—if not worse—are just as bad. The resulting anarchy may, in truth, drive us into the waiting arms of totalitarianism. It may well be that the medieval doctors can teach us something concerning the majesty and authority of truth and the necessity of at least a minimum of discipline, if we are to achieve both self-realization in the very highest sense and excellence.

Finally, it must be made clear that the modern school system is a more or less direct outgrowth of the medieval. First there came the Catechumenal and Catechetical followed by the Cathedral Schools and a large variety of others. Among these was the famous Palace School established by Charlemagne which, under the direction of Alcuin, tried to spread learning throughout the kingdom. Later came the great universities beginning with the University of Bologna. Many of these, such as Heidelberg, Bologna, Padua, Oxford, and Cambridge, survive to this very day and function as vital centers of learning and culture.[30] Hence, viewed in this larger perspective, the educational contributions of the Middle Ages, in spite of certain obvious limitations and weaknesses, are nothing short of stupendous.

4. The Modern and Contemporary Scene

Since modern and contemporary educational achievements are well known and since consideration shall be given to current educational philosophies in the chapters which follow, we can afford to be brief at this juncture. Perhaps, in the light of our basic purpose, it is best to summarize the chief characteristics and accomplishments in terms of certain outstanding movements.

First of all, there is the revolt against authoritarianism, dogmatism, and totalitarianism. This revolt can be traced back to the protests of Roger Bacon and William of Ockham against the excesses of Scholasticism. Indeed there are even signs of revolt

30. For an interesting sketch of the development of the medieval system, see Mulhern, A History of Education, pp. 247-93.

in the teachings of Peter Abelard (1079-1142), the boldest as well as one of the most brilliant spirits of the Middle Ages. Later, of course, it found a voice in the Renaissance, in the Protestant Reformation, in the scientific movement, and in various other movements. At any rate, in terms of the stress placed on individualism, on experimentation, on freedom, and on creativity,[31] this spirit remains one of the dominant characteristics of the contemporary scene. Nowhere, in fact, is it more evident than in the system of John Dewey and in the Progressive Movement. Although by no means an unmixed blessing, when taken as a whole, this revolt constitutes something of an advance in terms of liberating the human spirit.

Closely related to the above is what has been called naturalism or realism. The emphasis here is on education for life by bringing the learner directly in touch with the problems and processes of life and with things—the world of nature. Whereas the older schoolmen stressed concepts and abstractions, here a radical nominalism is in the saddle: the particulars of experience are given primary consideration.

In his enthusiasm for the place and function of the senses in the art of teaching and learning, John Amos Comenius (1592-1670) accepted the old theory: *Nihil est in intellectu quod non prius fuerit in sensu* (nothing is in the intellect which was not first in the sense). Naturalism in this sense is even more evident in Jean Jacques Rousseau who has been called "the Copernicus of modern civilization." [32] Rebelling against the artificiality of French aristocratic society, this great educational reformer—under the spell of the recapitulation theory of human development—insisted that the child should learn directly from experience those things which will prove most useful to him at each stage of his life.

31. For the new interest in creativity which has developed during the last dozen years, see Jacob W. Getzels & Philip W. Jackson, *Creativity and Intelligence* (New York: John Wiley & Sons, 1962), p. 279, n. 16. Later we shall deal with creativity at length.

32. By Eby in *The Development of Modern Education*, Ch. 13, p. 319 ff. Rousseau, Comenius, Pestalozzi, and Froebel, however, were not *metaphysical naturalists*.

Similarly Johann Heinrich Pestalozzi stressed the use of real objects as a means of invoking the child's interest and understanding. In this connection mention must likewise be made of Friedrich Froebel's classic, *The Education of Man*, of John Dewey, and of all the modern pragmatists, experimentalists, and progressives.[33]

The third aspect of modern educational advance is akin to the second and may be designated as the humanization of education: it constitutes a vigorous protest against arid formalism, mere rote, mechanical drill, and the harsh, rigid discipline which usually accompanied them. Like so many things modern, this movement found its source of inspiration in the Renaissance. Yet, after such promising beginnings, the new learning itself became formal, rigid, pedantic, and severe. The Latin classics, especially Cicero, became virtual fetishes. It was *Ciceronianism* which provoked the just rebuke of the great humanist, Desiderius Erasmus. Moreover, it was the brutal corporal punishment together with other inhuman practices which brought the creative responses of men such as Comenius, Pestalozzi, and Froebel—whose concern for children has been surpassed only by Jesus of Nazareth. Their concern is aptly expressed in Froebel's well-known words: "Let us live with our children." Modern education is definitely child-centered; and while the extreme progressives have invited a justly deserved criticism, yet, when seen in the lurid light of the old, rigid, pedantic disciplinary system, this modern attempt at humanization constitutes a real landmark.

Though idealism is still taboo in some educational circles, and even though naturalism and realism and scientism are still in the saddle, it cannot be denied that idealism, especially in terms of personalism, exerts considerable influence. At any rate, at the beginning of the twentieth century, idealism, while being vigor-

---

33. See especially Dewey's *Democracy and Education* (New York: The Macmillan Co., 1916, paperback reprint, 1961); and for a lucid exposition of the views of the chief builders of modern education, see Meyer, *The Development of Education in the Twentieth Century*, pp. 1-162. Peterson, *A Hundred Years of Education*, pp. 107-43 is also very illuminating. For the religious educational aspects, see Butler, *Religious Education*, pp. 68-112.

ously challenged by thinkers from many quarters, was still the predominant influence in American education. In fact, William Torrey Harris (1835-1909), the first United States commissioner of education, was an idealist. Idealism, as over against all forms of metaphysical naturalism, emphasizes the primacy of mind not only as both the center and interpreter of experience, but also as both that which is educated and that which educates. Along with this idealists are known for their stress on wholeness and synopsis and on the objectivity of values. Moreover, the new idealism, as over against the older forms, builds on the sciences, especially on the new physics. Here again then we have a movement which may be regarded as a landmark; for, in spite of its present eclipse by the various forms of naturalism, pragmatism, and positivism, it still stands on guard in an hour when there is great danger that the higher life of man may be disregarded and even destroyed by the fascinations of the cult of mechanism.[34]

A fifth tendency, which, in some ways at least, constitutes a real advance, is the scientific and empirical. In its modern form it has its roots in Copernicus and Galileo. For a long time, in spite of the growing influence of science, education remained predominately classical. The break came with the publication of Thomas Huxley's *Science and Education*. Today the scientific spirit is decidedly dominant. Indeed, with the advent of the Nuclear Age, governments have spurred technological research by means of vast subsidies; a tendency which, since so much of the research goes for more efficient weapons, must be viewed with increasing alarm. That the effect of science on both educational theory and practice has been immeasurably great is evident not only in the interest in psychological measurement, but also in the effect of pragmatism and experimentalism and in the influence exerted by the analytical philosophies. Later we shall attempt to

---

34. On the rise and significance of idealism, see Eby, *The Development of Modern Education*, pp. 411-30. In the next section we shall give further consideration to idealism.

deal more thoroughly with the dangers as well as the creative possibilities inherent in science.

Mention must also be made of the influence of democracy not only in terms of educational theory through the influence of philosophers such as John Dewey, but also in terms of two contemporary movements. The first of these is the mass education movement which, though it had its beginnings largely in this country, today, especially with the emergence of so many new nations, is really world wide. Although it has its dangers, it also, if not allowed to get out of hand, has a vast potential. After all, democracy by its very nature implies that every child, regardless of class or race, must be given adequate opportunity for self-development. More than this, since the pupil is also the potential voter, the fate not only of democracy itself but also of the entire human race is dependent upon the success of mass education and mass enlightenment. While there are real dangers in mass education—chief among which is the tendency toward mediocrity—whatever the reactionaries may say, the same is not true of the second movement, namely, desegregation. In fact, the most hopeful sign on the American horizon today is the progress that has been made in this direction; but, though desegregation itself is inherently good as democracy in action, there is danger of violence from extremists in both camps.

So far as the contemporary scene is concerned, another hopeful sign is education's attempt at revaluation in the light of recent criticisms. Although there were many criticisms both destructive and constructive before, since Sputnik these have become legion.[35] In due time we shall ourselves attempt to offer certain criticisms and evaluations. Among other things, special attention must be given to the charge that, in its neglect of the humanities in general and of philosophy and religion in particular, education has lost sight

35. In this connection, see especially James D. Koerner, *The Miseducation of American Teachers* (Boston: Houghton Mifflin Co., 1963). Although this book is a bit drastic and one-sided in certain respects, yet, since it calls attention to certain real defects and abuses, it merits serious attention.

of an all-embracing goal great and worthy enough to provoke our youth to the highest creative excellence.

While, as we shall see later, perhaps most American educators lack vision and tend to be conformists, yet, in response to the world crisis there is another new note in modern education: namely, internationalism or universalism with its vast potential. Although citizenship will always remain an aspect of the total aim of education, today, as never before, we are beginning to see that it must also—in some vital sense—mean world citizenship.[36] Failure to realize this fact means failure everywhere, final and total failure—ultimately a planet in ruins. Be that as it may, the presence of danger should be no reason for despair. Its very presence and on such a scale may, in fact, provoke mankind to unparalleled creativity.

One striking evidence of this new universal outlook in contemporary education is the new interest in history, in the philosophy of history, and in other cultures. It is also evident in the increasing number of educational exchange programs. Along with all this, there is likewise the presence of the United Nations and the United Nations Educational, Scientific, and Cultural Organization (UNESCO). The aim of the latter is nothing less than the building of a solid intellectual and cultural basis for international cooperation. UNESCO has helped over 42,000,000 children.

Although existentialism has not developed a philosophy of education in any specific and explicit sense, there are three reasons why it must be mentioned here and why we must consider it again later: it is very influential as a philosophical tendency; it has profound educational implications; and George F. Kneller, in his book, *Existentialism and Education*,[37] has set forth these implications in a graphic manner. Later we shall have more to say about this book.

36. See Stringfellow Barr, *Citizens of the World* (Garden City: Doubleday & Co., 1952). Though written over a dozen years ago, this book is still basically relevant.
37. (New York: Philosophical Library, 1958.)

Finally, aroused by the scandal of the many conflicting educational philosophies, a wholesome tendency toward synthesis and synopsis has come into being. It is this tendency which we particularly want to enhance. Consequently, in the section which follows, an attempt shall be made to approach this all-important problem of synthesis from the broadest possible perspective. After dealing with the nature of philosophy and the philosophy of education, special attention shall be given to the chief points of view. This in turn shall be followed by a process of criticism and evaluation in order to set forth the differences and the likenesses in bold relief. The section shall conclude with a chapter on the perplexing problem of goals or aims.

Part II

Perspectives for Synthesis

III

Education and Philosophy

Among other things, it became clear as the result of our survey in Chapter II that the relations of education and philosophy have been very intimate in the past. The great philosophers themselves —from Socrates and Plato to Thomas Aquinas and from Thomas to Kant and Hegel and Dewey and Whitehead—were primarily teachers. Similarly many of the leading modern educational pioneers were profoundly interested in philosophy. Besides John Dewey, who was really as much an educationist as he was a philosopher, the names of Friedrich Froebel,[1] J. F. Herbart, and William Torrey Harris come readily to mind.

For the last thirty years or so, of course, we have been witnessing a reaction against philosophy in educational circles; but this is undoubtedly a manifestation of the *Zeitgeist* (the spirit of the time) in terms of the prevalent irrationalism, and will soon pass.[2] After all, the basic problems out of which philosophy developed are perennial, and further investigation can no more be stopped than tomorrow's sunrise. Moreover, as Eby points out, the protests against a narrow, naturalistic educational program,

1. For the philosophical foundations of Froebel's educational scheme, see *The Education of Man*, trans. W. N. Hailmann (London: Sidney Appleton, 1907), p. 1 ff.
2. On intellectual trends, see James Mulhern, *A History of Education*, pp. 656-60; and Frederick Eby, *The Development of Modern Education*, pp. 628-34.

43

devoid of the larger perspectives of philosophy, are becoming increasingly more vocal.[3] Therefore, in spite of the fact that we shall fail for the most part, no apology is necessary for what follows. In this difficult field even a slight advance constitutes a substantial gain.

1. The Nature of Philosophy

As every student of philosophy knows, today there is dispute, as there always has been, not only about solutions to such basic problems as the nature of reality, the relations of mind and body, free will, etc., but even about the nature of this great discipline. Consequently, one can find books which approach the basic problems involved primarily from the standpoint of the nature of philosophy itself.[4] The two extremes are undoubtedly those of the analysts, on the one hand, who would reduce philosophy to little more than linguistic analysis, and the apriorists, on the other, who take an approach that is essentially rationalistic, speculative, and— at times—even dogmatic. Since our own approach is synoptic, instead of tarrying here, we shall attack the problem from the broadest possible perspective.

The term philosophy itself comes from a combination of two Greek words, *Philein* (to love) and *Sophia* (wisdom).[5] Hence, from the etymological standpoint, philosophy, simply means the love of wisdom, and, therefore, the philosopher himself, traditionally speaking, is a lover of wisdom. Yet, while this sheds some light, since philosophy at its best has always tried to speak to life and its perplexing problems, it is hardly sufficient for our purposes. In other words, since philosophy—besides illuminating living issues— also aims to be a serious intellectual discipline and has developed

3. *Ibid.*, p. 628.

4. See, for example, Samuel M. Thompson, *The Nature of Philosophy* (New York: Holt, Rinehart & Winston, 1961), and Elmer Sprague, *What Is Philosophy?* (New York: Oxford University Press, 1961).

5. What follows in this chapter is largely an expansion of a part of my article— "Educational Philosophy for Today"—which appeared in *The Philosophical Quarterly* (India), XXXIV (July, 1961), 95-101. Used by permission.

as such across some 2,500 years, decidedly more precision is needed.

We shall begin our task by isolating the basic element in philosophy. This basic element is undoubtedly *reason*. As practiced by the greatest philosophers, both ancient and modern, both Eastern and Western, and in spite of some irrationalists, in the final analysis, there has always been the appeal to reason in the very highest sense of the word. Moreover, in terms of this appeal to reason, philosophy has three basic aspects.

The first is the *empirical*. By this we mean the appeal to experience in the broadest possible perspective. The trouble with most empiricists is that they have defined experience altogether too narrowly, that is, merely in terms of sensation. While sensation most certainly constitutes a vital aspect of experience which mystics and apriorists among the philosophers have neglected to their peril, it is but one province of the vast empire of experience. By experience as used here, we mean nothing less than all that man has achieved and all that he has been aware of at all times. Thus conceived it constitutes many realms, chief among which are the realms of science, history, religion, art, and ethics. Furthermore, since experience in this broad perspective is limitless, it opens up vast horizons and thus constitutes, in terms of philosophic vision, an unending task and a perpetual challenge to human creativity. At any rate, for reason to operate at all it must try to master experience in its totality.

The second aspect is the *analytical*. This means a critical examination and evaluation of experience; for the philosopher, more than all others, is suspicious of naïve experience. In his search for reality, rather than accepting things merely as they appear, he tests everything. In this respect philosophy resembles science upon which, of course, it is decidedly dependent for some of its most significant data. Unlike science, however, in its analytical processes, philosophy cuts much deeper; for in its *Gedankenexperimente* (thought experiments), it tries, as Aristotle pointed out long ago, to get down to basic categories or first principles.[6] In this search all the presuppositions of science, and, in fact, the basic categories of all thinking, are exposed to the most rigid scrutiny. It is this, in particular, which makes philosophy so strangely forbidding to some laymen.

This brings us to the third and most characteristic aspect of philosophy, namely, the *synoptic*. Synopsis simply means the attempt at *wholeness, totality, adequacy*. As the *scientia scientiarum* (science of the sciences), philosophy seeks to embrace all experience in the totality of its vision with the purpose of fathoming its deeper meaning. Indeed philosophy's final aim is nothing less than the attempt to grasp the ultimate meaning of the universe as a whole, that is, in terms of a world view *(Weltanschauung)*. Thus Plato conceived the philosopher as the synoptic man who seeks, "the whole truth" and contemplates "all time and all existence." [7] In short, the search for *wholeness, integration, totality, adequacy* constitutes the high aim of philosophy. That this is difficult, virtually impossible, and even rash, no philosopher in his right mind will deny.

At the same time, however, two important facts offer some encouragement: on the one hand, the fact that man is driven by the very highest reaches of his nature to philosophize, so that even the avowed foes of philosophy turn out to be philosophers of a sort;[8] and, on the other hand, the further fact that, in spite of its limitations, the human mind—by means of universals—is able to transcend the narrow limitations of the senses which bind brutes to mere particulars. Hence, even though finality is impossible, it seems safe to conclude that no sincere search for truth is likely to be doomed to absolute failure.

Philosophy includes the following six fields: methodology (logic); epistemology (theory of knowledge); metaphysics (theory

6. See his *Metaphysics,* Book IV, 1003*a*, 18-31.
7. See the *Republic,* VI, 485.
8. Moreover, anti-metaphysical philosophers, such as the logical positivists, inevitably end up as metaphysicians; see Gustav Bergmann, *The Metaphysics of Logical Positivism* (New York: Longmans, Green & Co., 1954).

of reality); axiology (theory of value which embraces ethics and aesthetics); history of philosophy; and specialized topics (philosophy of science, philosophy of history, philosophy of education etc.).[9] After this brief consideration of the nature of philosophy as a whole, we are now ready to deal with that speciality which constitutes our chief concern in this book, namely, philosophy of education.

2. The Significance of Philosophy of Education

Many educators as well as philosophers look askance at the philosophy of education. One current authority on education, though he is willing to allow it a place in the college curriculum (that is, if it is taught by professional philosophers), half seriously wonders "if such a thing exists." [10] Others, especially those with an analytical bent, would limit its scope to little more than an analysis of concepts.

What then is the philosophy of education? We have already seen that, along with such disciplines as philosophy of science and philosophy of history, it constitutes one of the special fields contained in general philosophy. It is really that division of philosophy which concerns itself with the educational aspects of experience. In other words, it is the difference in subject matter rather than fundamental method of approach which differentiates the philosophy of education from the various other specialities. Basically it is philosophy itself as applied to the education of man.

Consequently the philosophy of education has the same fundamental functions as philosophy in general. Like the latter it must be *empirical*, that is, in the sense of taking all human experience, and particularly all of man's educational experience, seriously. It cannot operate in an ivory tower nor in some pleasant corner.

9. Here I have followed Edgar Sheffield Brightman, *An Introduction to Philosophy* (revised edition; New York: Henry Holt & Co., 1951), pp. 8-10.

10. James D. Koerner, *The Miseducation of American Teachers*, p. 275. For an excellent discussion of the philosophy of education by four thinkers, see "Discussion" in *Harvard Educational Review*, XXXIII (Spring, 1963), 219-236. The subject is Robert Ulich's *Philosophy of Education* (New York: American Book Co., 1961).

Likewise it must be *analytical*. It must deal with experience in general, and with educational experience in particular, *critically*. This means that it must especially subject the various educational theories to drastic criticisms; and this also means taking into account both their presuppositions and their consequences in terms of the broadest possible perspective. Similarly it must be ready to subject scientific theories to criticism: that is, insofar as they are unproved in terms of involving presuppositions which are shaky.

Finally, and most significant of all, it must be *synoptic*. The philosophy of education is profoundly intercultural and universal in its total outreach. Nor is it interested only in contemporary education. For it seeks to grasp and encompass the process in its totality, as it has appeared and developed down the ages. Thus the philosophy of education is closely related at this point to the history of education, and this fully justifies what we tried to do in Chapter II. Besides this, it is decidedly integrative, seeking to relate not only the various aspects of education itself, but likewise the entire educational process to life and its needs and its pressing problems.

Moreover, as a vital aspect of its synoptic outreach, philosophy of education is concerned with values, norms, goals. While science furnishes us with means, we must look to the philosophy of education for light on the all-important question of direction. Indeed the problem of aims and goals is so important that we shall devote an entire chapter to this question. No matter how efficient our means, if we are going in the wrong direction, the final consequences are bound to be tragic.

From this perspective then, one can see why philosophy of education is important. It is important, first of all, because, like philosophy in general, it raises questions which are perennial and irrepressible. Since we are human beings endowed with reflective self-consciousness, we cannot avoid raising them. Again, like philosophy in general, philosophy of education, especially in terms of its critical analysis of educational experience and its synoptic outlook, is in a position to obtain insights and in the light of these insights to make constructive, farsighted proposals. This is particularly true of the crucial question of a goal or goals. Third, as at least one outstanding thinker has pointed out, since some of the "most important contributions to philosophy" have come from thinkers who "wrestled" with the problems arising in other fields, philosophy of education may, if given proper encouragement, serve to stimulate philosophical creativity as a whole.[11] At any rate, educational experience, which is the special concern of philosophy of education, is probably capable of suggesting something of importance not only about man but also about this mysterious universe in which man arises with all his creative capacities—not least among which is his capacity for learning far surpassing that of any beast.

In preparation for the difficult task ahead—the task of philosophic synthesis—two things have been attempted in this chapter: an understanding of the nature of philosophy of education together with an understanding of its significance for these times. The time has now come to take a look at the various prevalent philosophies of education. This is the aim and purpose of the next chapter.

If the student expects to find a detailed account of the various contemporary philosophies, he shall be disappointed. For these more detailed expositions, he must go to the various sources as indicated in the footnotes. In keeping with our attempt at perspective, the essence of these systems shall be presented in bold relief. This will greatly facilitate what we especially have in mind, namely, the process of evaluation and synthesis in the chapters which follow.

11. Charles Frankel in *Harvard Educational Review*, XXXIII, 224-25. For other outstanding discussions by many thinkers representing many points of view, see also *Harvard Educational Review*, Vol. XXVI (Spring, 1956). This "Symposium" constitutes a rich mine of information concerning current trends and tendencies in the philosophy of education.

IV

The Strife of Systems

Although, for the sake of background, in the last section of Chapter II, we presented a bird's-eye view of the modern and contemporary scene, we did not attempt to deal adequately with any of the various schools or systems. In short, the aim of this present chapter is to deal as adequately as possible with the various leading contemporary points of view in philosophy of education.

Today, as never before, everything seems to be fluid, dynamic, changing, and headed no one knows where. So far as philosophies of education are concerned, the situation is decidedly pluralistic; and it can best be described in terms of the strife of systems. Indeed, one is tempted to think in terms of *tendencies* rather than systems. Yet, amid these tendencies, one can still discern what may still be called schools or systems.[1]

Furthermore, most of these tend to fall, more or less naturally, under the following four general headings: pragmatism and experimentalism, progressivism, essentialism, and authoritarianism. To accommodate the three which do not fit this scheme so well, we add a fifth general heading: other types.[2]

1. The above was suggested by a very stimulating paper—"Tendencies in Contemporary Philosophy of Education"—which Dr. William K. Frankena of the University of Michigan presented at Albion College on May 12, 1964.
2. For perspective on what follows, see: John S. Brubacher (ed.), *Modern Philosophies of Education* (second edition; New York: McGraw-Hill Book Co., 1950); John

1. Pragmatism and Experimentalism

While pragmatism as a movement is largely American, yet it was from Immanuel Kant (1724-1804) that Charles Peirce (1839-1914) got the term itself. Peirce influenced William James (1842-1910), and both of these thinkers influenced John Dewey (1859-1952). As developed by Dewey, pragmatism came more directly under the spell of the sciences, particularly biology to which Darwin had imparted a new dynamic. Since Dewey and his disciples have tried to carry the scientific method over into philosophy and the philosophy of education, their school is also known as experimentalism.

Although Dewey started his philosophical career as a Hegelian, and even though to the very end traces remained—especially in his doctrine of experience—yet, as time went on, he moved further and further away from Hegel. Metaphysically speaking, he came to view the universe largely in terms of flux. Everything is in process, and man, as an aspect of this flux, finds himself in a precarious situation. His only hope of salvation lies in the application of intelligence to phenomena in terms of scientific control. This brings increasing security through the mastery of nature.

In keeping with his pragmatism, experimentalism, and instrumentalism, Dewey tried to banish all changeless truths together with all absolutes. The bane of philosophy has been its tendency to depreciate action, while searching for an immutable realm beyond the flux of phenomena. Dewey had an aversion for contemplation and for what he called "the spectator" theory of knowledge. He dethroned mind to the level of an instrument, conceiving it largely in biological terms as a means of adjustment. Similarly truth is regarded as that which works; acts which bring favorable

---

P. Wynne, *Philosophies of Education* (New York: Prentice-Hall, 1947); J. Donald Butler: *Four Philosophies: And Their Practice in Education and Religion* (revised edition; New York: Harper & Row, 1957); Theodore Brameld, *Patterns of Educational Philosophy* (Yonkers: World Book Co., 1950); Adolph E. Meyer, *The Development of Education in the Twentieth Century*, and William F. Cunningham, *The Pivotal Problems of Education* (New York: The Macmillan Co., 1940).

consequences are true; and that which works can be determined by experimentation.[3]

While there were strong relativistic elements and behavioristic tendencies in Dewey, he was neither a thoroughgoing relativist nor a thoroughgoing mechanist. Unlike some of his anarchistic disciples, whom he rebuked upon occasion, he did believe in the necessity of discipline—the discipline afforded by intelligence.[4] He was also profoundly interested in values, especially the meaning of democracy as a way of life as well as a political theory. Nor did his rejection of theism mean that he was opposed to all religion. Confusing as his theology most certainly is (since this was a field which he never explored sufficiently), yet, theologically speaking, his creed seems to have been a kind of humanistic naturalism.[5] In short, his general philosophical position is best described in terms of a pragmatic, experimental, and humanistic expression of metaphysical naturalism.

Vast as Dewey's influence has been on contemporary educational thought and practice, he himself would have been the last to claim complete originality. He was decidedly influenced by Rousseau, Pestalozzi, Froebel, and Herbart.[6] The source of his theory of interest is found in Rousseau. The influence of Pestalozzi is most evident in his stress on activity, projects, and learning by doing. Even though he rejected Froebel's philosophical idealism, he accepted his ideal of growth—but gave it a pragmatic twist. Finally, while he subjected Herbart to criticism, he agreed with him in no less than three ways: in his stress on interest, in recognizing the

3. For Dewey's general outlook, see *The Quest for Certainty* (New York: Minton, Balch & Co., 1929). For able criticisms of Dewey's philosophy, see Paul Arthur Schilpp (ed.), *The Philosophy of John Dewey*, in *The Library of Living Philosophers*, Vol. I (Evanston: Northwestern University, 1939). For the student, this volume is especially important.

4. See particularly his *Experience and Education* (New York: The Macmillan Co., 1938), pp. 8, 58-59, 84.

5. On his theology, see *A Common Faith* (New Haven: Yale University Press, 1934).

6. On his relation to the great educational pioneers, see Meyer, *The Development of Education in the Twentieth Century*, pp. 46-49. He is, of course, much more pragmatic than any of them.

importance of individual differences, and in his conviction that one must attempt to understand the child before trying to teach him.

Coming now more directly to Dewey's educational philosophy, it is important to remember that he was a spirit in revolt against the *status quo*. He strongly opposed traditionalism, rigidity, and formalism in philosophy. Like Pestalozzi, Dewey was opposed to what someone has called teaching "the unknown by means of the incomprehensible." Yet, iconoclast that he was, the positive aspects of his philosophy of education are even more significant. More concerned with the new age that was dawning than with the old one that was in its death throes, he was particularly sensitive to the demands of democracy, science, technology, and industrialism.[7]

In spite of the utilitarian tone of much of Dewey's educational theory, it must not be thought that he was a thoroughgoing utilitarian or an out-and-out vocationalist in the narrow sense of the word. In some respects at least, education is for him as wide as life itself—nothing less than "that reconstruction or reorganization of experience which adds to the meaning of experience."[8] This implies that the aim is not only to change and modify present experience, but also to enrich it and direct it in such a manner as to produce a continual process of further enrichment.

In keeping with his concept of education as continual "reconstruction," Dewey conceived the basic aim or goal in terms of "growth." By growth, however, he did not mean advance to some static or fixed and immutable ideal. In his dynamic conception of the universe, there are no absolutes. Growth leads to nothing beyond itself; for all growth has the potential for "more growth."[9] Thus the total educational process is conceived as an unending movement involving continuous growth. Moreover, while some place is given to the necessity of preparing the child for the re-

7. See especially the Preface to his famous *Democracy and Education: An Introduction to the Philosophy of Education* (paperback; New York: The Macmillan Co., 1961), p. iii.

8. *Ibid.*, p. 76.

9. *Ibid.*, p. 51.

sponsibilities of adult life, the chief concern is not for the future or for the past but for the present. "Present experience" must be made "as rich and significant as possible." [10] Along with all this, of course, there is the emphasis on interest and activity. As everyone knows, Dewey and his followers practiced the doctrine of learning by doing. This was the basic idea behind the famous Laboratory School which was organized in 1896.

At the same time, Dewey's profound regard for democracy was evident. The school itself was conceived as nothing less than a miniature society based upon democratic principles; and a real effort was made to carry out these principles in the actual conduct of the group involved. Dewey was particularly interested in overcoming conflicts between groups arising from the class struggle. He hoped that through schools such as this, which emphasize cooperation rather than competition, differences could be overcome and children could actually learn to live democratically.

A word is also in order regarding Dewey's conception of the relation of philosophy to education.[11] While the former must avoid metaphysics, there are two necessary tasks which it can perform relative to the latter. The first is critical and analytical. With true scientific objectivity, it must criticize the educational process, carefully distinguishing between that which is obsolete and which must be abandoned and that which can be reconstructed to meet present needs. The second is experimental and constructive. Philosophy is called upon to project "generous hypotheses," serving not as delineations of reality, but rather as "plans of action" capable of giving "intelligent direction" to those who seek to make the world a better home for man. Dewey thus, as William James before him, was a meliorist: through the proper application of man's creativity the possibilities for improvement are virtually limitless.

We have dealt with John Dewey somewhat at length because,

10. *Ibid.*, p. 56.
11. See especially his Introduction to his *Philosophy of Education* (Ames, Iowa: Littlefield, Adams & Co., 1956), pp. 3-20. Originally published as *Problems of Men.*

even though his influence has waned somewhat (especially since his death), he is still a power to be reckoned with. Among other things, he has left behind a group of loyal disciples. Chief among these is Sidney Hook. In the latter, as in Dewey, we find the same emphasis on the pragmatic method and attitude and on values and social problems.[12]

2. Progressivism

Closely related to John Dewey's pragmatic and experimental approach to the philosophy of education is the progressive movement. While largely a twentieth-century phenomenon, many of its basic ideas reach far back into the past. Interestingly enough, in ancient Athens Plato insisted that "compulsion" should be avoided and that "children's lessons" should take "the form of play" as an expression of their natural bent.[13] Likewise progressivism's concern for the child as a person can be traced back to the Hebrew-Christian tradition.

The movement is also greatly indebted to the earlier humanistic aspects of the Renaissance. The pioneers of modern education, including the saintly John Amos Comenius, have similarly left their mark. Finally, many Americans—such as Horace Mann, Henry Barnard, Francis Parker, Felix Adler, Junius L. Meriam, Marietta Johnson, William H. Kilpatrick, and John Dewey—have made important contributions.[14]

12. For an excellent epitome of Hook's philosophy of education see his article—"The Scope of Philosophy of Education"—in *Harvard Educational Review*, XXVI (Spring, 1956), 145-48. For a more thorough account of Hook's view, see his *Education For Modern Man: A New Perspective* (New York: Alfred A. Knopf, 1963).

13. See *The Republic of Plato* edited and translated by Francis Macdonald Cornford (New York: Oxford University Press, 1941), p. 252 (VII, 536).

14. On the general background of the movement, see Brameld, *Patterns of Educational Philosophy*, pp. 132-37; Meyer, *The Development of Education in the Twentieth Century*, pp. 64-68; and Butler, *Four Philosophies*, pp. 105-12. For added insight into the beginnings and the chief sources of the movement, see also George F. Kneller, *Existentialism and Education* (New York: Philosophical Library, 1958), especially p. 39. Kneller thinks the movement has three "segments": the first "begins with Rousseau and proceeds through Froebel"; the second "prefers" Pestalozzi; while the third ("romantic progressivism") draws its inspiration from Rousseau and Madame Naumberg (see Meyer, pp. 66-67).

On its negative side, progressivism is even more radical in its revolt against formalism, pedantry, and rigid discipline than Dewey and his followers. Some progressives, in fact, seem to have such a morbid fear of imposing their ideas on their children that they give them little direction. Education is conceived largely as an informal, natural process for the purpose of awakening the creative impulse. In accordance with this ideal, there is a minimum stress on discipline. Closely related to all this is the fear that the child may develop a complex—which some moderns dread more than the ancients dreaded devil possession.

Coming now to the positive principles, there is, first of all, the emphasis on the learner rather than the subject matter.[15] One still occasionally hears the remark: "I teach children rather than subjects." In a similar vein and in keeping with the spirit of Rousseau, there is also the stress on the pupil's interests, his natural development, and the direct expression of his ideas and desires. Thus, for fear of *forcing* interest, one teacher tells us that she employs no classroom method to encourage creative work beyond reading certain choice bits of literature to her pupils.[16] In other words, the progressivist insists that interest must come naturally and spontaneously.

The movement is likewise known for its strong reliance upon sense experience. Progressives take the old dictum seriously: *Nihil est in intellectu quod non prius fuerit in sensu* (nothing is in the intellect which was not first in the sense). Thus a contemporary progressive speaks of "sharpening" the five senses.[17] In fact, this tendency to stress sensation rather than thought leads toward anti-intellectualism. Closely related to this is also the marked concern

15. For the chief principles as formulated by the Progressive Educational Association, see Meyer, *The Development of Education in the Twentieth Century*, pp. 71-72.

16. See Gertrude Hartman & Ann Shumaker (eds.), *Creative Expression* (second edition; Milwaukee: E. M. Hale & Co., 1939), pp. 183-84. See also Carl R. Rogers, "Learning to Be Free," in Seymour M. Farber & Roger H. L. Wilson (eds.), *Man and Civilization: Conflict and Creativity;* a Symposium (New York: McGraw-Hill, 1963), pp. 279-87. Rogers deals with the college level.

17. Hartman & Shumaker (eds.), *Creative Expression*, pp. 182-83.

for the present as over against the past or the future. Progressives never tire of warning against the dangers of assuming that children are miniature adults.

Not unlike the pragmatists, they practice the doctrine of learning by doing. As in Dewey's scheme, the school is conceived as a kind of laboratory under the general direction of the teacher as source of information. In the desire not to be guilty of an arch sin against her view of democracy, the conscientious progressive teacher, nevertheless, takes far more precaution not to impose her ideas on her pupils. The child must be left free to develop his creative capacities according to the demands of his own nature, genius, and normal inclinations. Some have even voiced the opinion that far more is actually learned through free, spontaneous play than through formal instruction.[18]

So far as the underlying philosophy is concerned, progressivism constitutes a strange mixture of idealism and pragmatic naturalism. While its idealistic elements consist largely of its emphasis on the value of personality and the importance of human creativity together with its stress on freedom and democracy, the pragmatic and naturalistic are evident in its preoccupation with sensation, behavior, and concrete objects. As over against Dewey's system, however, it tends toward sentimentalism and a laxity which finally led to Dewey's break with the movement.[19] Today, although still present as an influence, largely due to its excesses, it is in retreat.

3. Essentialism

What is known as essentialism constitutes a many-sided tendency. Its roots go far back in the past. Both Plato and Aristotle were basically essentialists. At the same time, it is also modern: not only were most of the modern classical philosophers in some sense essentialists, but it is still with us today. There has even been

18. *Ibid.*, p. 319.
19. For Dewey's break with Progressivism and his reasons for it, see Frederick Eby, *The Development of Modern Education*, p. 630.

something of a revival of essentialism within the last twenty years. Perhaps the best indication of this is the famous Harvard Report, *General Education in a Free Society.*

Before considering the two chief aspects of essentialism, namely, idealism and realism, it is probably best to look at some of the things which essentialists have in common. To begin with, in striking contrast with the two schools previously discussed, these thinkers tend to lay more emphasis on the permanent rather than the changing. While fully aware of the dynamic nature of the universe, they also point to the fact that underlying these processes there are certain unchanging factors which must not be neglected. They are horrified at the insistence of the pragmatists that everything, including truth itself, is in flux—that it is basically utility and can even be made. The facts of history and the fundamental principles of mathematics, for example, are true forever. In short, in contrast to the pragmatists, both the idealists and the realists insist that truth or reality basically constitutes an order amid the flux which is not made but rather *discovered.*[20]

Moreover, essentialists are much more interested in man's cultural heritage. Thus Bagley speaks of "the significance of a community of culture," [21] while Breed drastically criticizes the progressives for their disregard of our heritage from the Greeks.[22] Similarly, Hocking holds that education has two primary tasks: teaching the young the best that their own particular group has to offer, but, at the same time, leading them to look beyond their

20. The two best statements from the standpoint of idealism are still Herman Harrell Horne's *The Philosophy of Education* (revised edition; New York: The Macmillan Co., 1927)—see especially p. 303; and his *Democratic Philosophy of Education* (New York: The Macmillan Co., 1932)—see especially pp. 420-21. For realism's view, see Frederick S. Breed, *Education and the New Realism* (New York: The Macmillan Co., 1939)—especially p. 51. For an essentialist view of truth by an author who tends to fuse idealism and realism, see Marie Collins Swabey, *Logic and Nature* (second revised edition; New York: New York University Press, 1955).

21. William C. Bagley, *Education and Emergent Man* (New York: Thomas Nelson & Sons, 1934), p. 139.

22. Breed, *Education and the New Realism,* p. ix.

own culture to the total experience of mankind through the centuries.[23]

In accordance with all this, essentialists, though recognizing the importance of the learner, have a healthy concern for the importance of subject matter. While the progressives stress an activity curriculum, the former are much more interested in "a common core curriculum" based on a "common culture." Thus, in an attack on progressivism at the convention of the National Educational Association at Atlantic City in 1938, the essentialists insisted that young Americans could best be prepared for "adult responsibility" through the mastery of subjects such as reading, writing, arithmetic, history, and English.[24]

This emphasis on subject matter also involves the concept of intellectual discipline. Essentialists have no faith in the appeal to mere interest, pointing out that required effort and systematic training often arouse an interest. Hence Bagley was bitter in his criticism of the American tendency to reject "mental discipline as an ideal." [25] Similarly, Koerner in a recent book makes a biting attack on the current "anti-intellectualism" and pleads for "clear standards of subject-matter mastery in teaching." [26] At any rate, the groups of thinkers comprising this movement have nothing but scorn for the "soft pedagogy" which produces pampered misfits and neurotics rather than men and women capable of taking their places in a democratic society as responsible citizens. For they contend that real freedom can only be achieved through real discipline.

Although essentialism sometimes leads to conservatism, this is hardly true of most essentialists. Among the great classical idealists

23. William Ernest Hocking, *Human Nature and Its Remaking* (New Haven: Yale University Press, 1929), pp. 253-61. For a volume which has profound educational implications for our times, see also his more recent book, *The Coming World Civilization* (New York: Harper & Row, 1956).

24. Meyer, *The Development of Education in the Twentieth Century*, p. 149.

25. William C. Bagley, *Education, Crime, and Social Progress* (New York: The Macmillan Co., 1931), pp. vii-viii.

26. James D. Koerner, *The Miseducation of American Teachers*, pp. 17-18, 261.

who possessed genuine social concern, there are such names as George Berkeley, Wilhelm Leibniz, Immanuel Kant (whose little book, *Eternal Peace,* foreshadowed the United Nations), and Josiah Royce. Among our contemporaries William Ernest Hocking and Edgar Sheffield Brightman come readily to mind. Moreover, no one less than Dr. Martin Luther King, Jr., studied with Brightman, and anyone who has heard him speak knows that Brightman made a lasting impression.[27] Speaking for the realists, Breed insists that, with their regard both for values and facts rather than visionary schemes, they are more likely to lead mankind aright in the long run.[28] Be that as it may, among those who have called themselves realists in one sense or another are such socially minded philosophers as Bertrand Russell and Roy Wood Sellars.

The chief differences between essentialists, as we shall see, stem primarily from their differences in metaphysics. We begin with a brief exposition of the basic principles of idealism together with brief statements concerning its various types and its general background.

For all idealists, mind rather than things constitutes the primary concept, the clue to reality. Everything that exists is, in some sense, of the nature of mind or mindlike. Idealists are also known for their opposition to relativism and behaviorism. Truth, beauty, and goodness, as aspects of the Universal Mind, are universal and absolute rather than merely relative. Moreover, man has dignity and worth, freedom and creativity by virtue of possessing a spiritual nature capable of striving toward these absolutes and realizing them in an increasing measure.

Although there are not less than five types of idealism, the two most important are absolute idealism and personalism.[29] The former differs from the latter in two significant respects: while, on the

27. For King's acknowledgement of his debt to Brightman, see Peter A. Bertocci, "Brightman—Ten Years Later," in *The Philosophical Forum,* XX (1962-1963), 10.
28. Breed, *Education and the New Realism,* pp. 225-26.
29. See Edgar Sheffield Brightman, *An Introduction to Philosophy,* pp. 289-93. Robert N. Beck in his 1963 revision of Brightman's book adds a sixth form; see pp. 309, 312-13.

one hand, it is much more monistic than the latter, on the other hand, in its more extreme forms, it also tends toward pantheism and an impersonal view of God as over against the theistic and personalistic view of the latter. In other words, while absolute idealists often think of God as the All or as some kind of impersonal Principle, personalists think of the Deity in terms of self-conscious, purposive cosmic Mind and Will.

Two other things must be made clear. The first is the fact that, although probably most absolute idealists have believed in human freedom and creativity, the personalists, since they tend to conceive the universe as more pluralistic and therefore as less tightly knit, have much better grounds for these elements. The second is that within the camp of personalism itself, there are certain important differences: for, though virtually all personalists are social and theological liberals, there is a right wing as well as a left wing theologically speaking. The chief difference between the two lies in the conception of God: that is, the latter, following the lead of Brightman, rejects the more orthodox conception of an omnipotent or all-powerful Creator. With Plato, William James, John Stuart Mill, Henri Bergson, Alfred North Whitehead, and many others, this left wing holds that God is in some ways limited by an irrational factor or factors not of his own making.[30] This movement within idealism and personalism shows that the system is not nearly so rigid as some of its opponents have at times supposed. It must also be added that many personalists, along with some less extreme absolute idealists, are making strenuous efforts to keep abreast of science.[31]

The roots of idealism, at least in the West, go deep into both the Greek and the Hebrew-Christian traditions. Plato is, in reality, the founder of Western idealism. Moreover, Christianity and

---

30. On Brightman's view, see his *Philosophy of Religion* (New York: Prentice-Hall, 1940), pp. 240-341. For a defense of a similar point of view, see my *History and God* (New York: The Ronald Press Co., 1952), especially pp. 197-242.

31. One of the best recent books by an idealist with something of a Hegelian point of view is Errol E. Harris' *Nature, Mind and Modern Science*. As among the less extreme absolute idealists, Harris is theistic and personalistic.

Judaism have played an important role in determining the strong theistic and personalistic elements. The system is also greatly indebted to Descartes, Berkeley, Leibniz, Kant, Fichte, Hegel, Royce, and other modern classical philosophers.[32]

Among modern American idealists with a distinct interest in education are to be found such names as Bronson Alcott, William Torrey Harris (United States Commissioner of Education, 1889-1906), Herman Harrell Horne (a student of Royce), William Ernest Hocking, Ralph Tyler Flewelling, and Edgar Sheffield Brightman.[33] Although during the last twenty years idealism has been somewhat overshadowed by other philosophies, there are signs that this state of affairs is in process of change.[34]

Having seen the main characteristics of idealism, we now look briefly at realism, the other chief representative of essentialism. Since the term realism has meant so many different things philosophically and otherwise, it is difficult to describe the system that goes by this name—if indeed it can be called a system. Perhaps it can be best understood by contrasting it with idealism. Whereas idealists stress the thinking self or subject, realists stress the object of thought. They never tire of reminding us that things exist independent of thought. Consequently, they boast of being seriously objective, of fearlessly taking things as they are—not as we might wish them to be.

Furthermore, from a strictly metaphysical standpoint, in direct contrast to all idealists, realists are firm in their conviction that something nonmental exists. They differ decidedly, however, concerning the precise nature of this nonmental reality: that is,

---

32. On the nature and general background of idealism, see Butler, *Four Philosophies*, pp. 131-220.

33. While Brightman really wrote little on education as such, he was famous for his seminar on teaching philosophy which he gave for the benefit of his graduate students.

34. See my article, "The Coming Philosophic Revolution," in *The Personalist*, XLII (Winter, 1961), 5-13.

whether it is to be called matter, energy, neutral entities, abstract universals, or some unknown and unknowable stuff. The truth of the matter is that there are many types. Brightman, as in the case of idealism, lists five general types.[35]

For our purposes, nevertheless, it is sufficient to make the distinction between what may be called *thoroughgoing* and *halfway* realism. The former holds that everything is basically nonmental, and what we call mental (minds or self-conscious, reflective processes within organisms) is derived from what is nonmental or physical. Thus, for the most part at least, those realists who may be described as *thoroughgoing* have been naturalistic in the *metaphysical* sense.[36] This means that they have taken nature rather than God (in terms of self-conscious Mind and Will) as the ultimate reality. At the same time, however, many of these naturalistic realists have also been humanists, and by means of the principle of emergence they have tried to provide a metaphysical basis for values.

A case in point is William C. Bagley's *Education and Emergent Man*. Basically John Dewey himself fits into this category: that is, in terms of his naturalistic metaphysics and his humanistic ethics. Yet this is not true in other respects, particularly so far as Dewey's theory of truth is concerned: for all essentialists, as we have already pointed out, are suspicious of the pragmatic theory of truth.

As over against the *thoroughgoing* realists, the *halfway* realists are actually dualists. Since they not only uphold the objectivity of ideals in the absolute sense, but also insist that mind exists as something different and superior to matter, they really exhibit a mixture of idealism and realism. Most of them, in fact, are theists, and, therefore, are as critical of naturalism as are the idealists.

35. In his *Introduction to Philosophy*, pp. 273-80.

36. The fact that they are *metaphysical* realists distinguishes them from the simple realism and naturalism of educationists such as Rousseau and Comenius; see p. 34 n. 32.

Among the dualists, besides Thomas Aquinas, one finds such thinkers as Descartes, J. B. Pratt, and John Wild.[37]

Realism, as a philosophical tendency, like so many other things, can be traced back to the Greeks, and especially to Aristotle. Realism in the dualistic sense was also present in the system of Thomas Aquinas during the Middle Ages, since he held that the universe is composed of both form and matter. Much later John Locke (1632-1714) developed what has been called representative realism, while during the eighteenth century Thomas Reid established what is known as the Scottish School of realism—which eventually found its way to America.

So far as the philosophy of education itself is concerned, modern science has, since the days of Francis Bacon (1561-1626) and even more after Thomas Huxley (1825-1895), exercised a very strong realistic influence. Metaphysically speaking, Comenius, Rousseau, and Pestalozzi must, of course, never be regarded as naturalists. At the same time, however, they exerted a realistic influence by virtue of their stress on sense objects as means of instruction.

The rise of neorealism and the acrimonious debate which it occasioned belong more to the realm of technical philosophy and need not concern us here.[38] It is true, nevertheless, that outstanding realistic educationists of the caliber of William C. Bagley and Frederick C. Breed, together with realistic sociological thinkers such as Ross L. Finney and educational psychologists like Edward L. Thorndike, have exercised a profound influence upon both contemporary educational theory and practice.[39]

37. For a rather thoroughgoing examination of realism, see Butler, *Four Philosophies*, pp. 289-413; and for a brief survey for the beginner, see Harold H. Titus, *Living Issues in Philosophy* (fourth edition; New York: American Book Co., 1964), pp. 244-47.

38. On these controversies, see W. H. Werkmeister, *A History of Philosophical Ideas in America* (New York: The Ronald Press Co., 1949), pp. 369-518; and William P. Montague, "The Story of American Realism," in Dagobert D. Runes (ed.), *Twentieth Century Philosophy* (New York: Philosophical Library, 1947), pp. 419-48.

39. On contemporary realists, see Brameld, *Patterns of Educational Philosophy*, pp. 245, 249-50.

In view of the many differences between the two types of essentialism, it may be well to summarize their very important likenesses. It has become clear that they have at least the following in common: an objective view of truth together with a certain stress on the permanent rather than the changing; a profound interest in man's cultural heritage; emphasis on the subject matter as well as on the learner; and, finally, a deep respect for intellectual discipline and scholarly excellence.

4. Authoritarianism

Although there are many forms of educational philosophy which may be classified as authoritarian, all of these naturally tend to fall into two general classes: the religious and the secular. These in turn may be further divided. While the various types of authoritarianism are very different in many ways, they do have the following significant similarities: they all possess rather well-defined, rigid systems of doctrines; they all tend to exalt the principle of authority in one way or another; and they stress discipline and indoctrination.

a) RELIGIOUS TYPES

In spite of the fact that its long history shows clearly that religion need not be authoritarian, that, as the masses become enlightened, liberalism is as natural as it is inevitable, yet in the past, for the most part at least, authoritarianism—as in politics—has been the rule. Worse still, even today, due largely to the confused state of the world, authoritarianism—both religious and secular—is growing in some quarters.

There have been and are many kinds of religious authoritarianism. The truth of the matter is that all the great religious systems have their orthodoxies and their heterodoxies, their fundamentalists and their liberals. Nor is the general pattern so different: for it usually involves the infallible institution with its infallible leader, or the infallible book—even at times, in fact, all three of these together in the same package. Since, however, it is beyond our

scope to be all-inclusive in this particular respect, we shall confine
our attention to the two forms most prevalent in the West, namely,
Roman Catholicism and Protestant fundamentalism.

(1) Roman Catholicism

In certain respects the Roman Catholic structure is stately and
magnificent. That is the reason why it still attracts men of ability.
For its ideal Catholicism still looks to the Middle Ages, particularly to the twelfth and thirteenth centuries which are regarded
as the Golden Age of the church. That there is something impressive about this particular period of human history is un-
questionable. The threefold division of society, together with the
theocracy under the jurisdiction of the Pope as king of kings,
finds its prototype—in certain interesting respects at least—in
the Platonic social ideal as found in the *Republic* and the *Laws*.
Moreover, the church with its Pope was decidedly cosmopolitan,
as over against the many petty kings and feudal lords. It even
represented something both of the Christian and the Stoic dream
of a kingdom of God upon earth.

Nor must it be forgotten that Thomas Aquinas (1225?-74),
"the Angelic Doctor," chief architect of Roman Catholic philosophy, and one of the half-dozen greatest thinkers of all times,
flourished during the thirteenth century, making the Golden Age
even more resplendent. Among other things, he succeeded in in-
corporating Aristotle into his system. Yet, in spite of this, it is
still predominately Roman Catholic. Thus, while Aquinas insists
that the existence of God can be proved by the natural light of
reason, the deeper mysteries of the faith can be known only by
revelation as made manifest by the Scriptures and as interpreted
by the theologians and the infallible church under its "Sovereign
Pontiff." [40]

At any rate, Roman Catholic philosophy, both general and edu-

40. For St. Thomas' view, see *The Summa Theologica* in Anton C. Pegis (ed.), *The
Basic Writings of Saint Thomas Aquinas* (New York: Random House, 1945), I, 5-24.
91-111; II, 1055-73.

cational, can still be best understood in terms of the system of Aquinas. To begin with, it is strongly theistic and supernaturalistic. This explains Cunningham's sharp distinction between Roman Catholic "Supernaturalism" as a philosophy of education and "Materialism," "Humanism," and even "Idealism." [41] In short, all Roman Catholic thinking about education is decidedly theocratic with strong otherworldly tendencies.

Surprisingly enough, the system as a whole embraces two somewhat contradictory aspects. Stemming from what "the Angelic Doctor" said about God's concern for his creatures, especially man, there is a profound humanistic and democratic tendency. This is very strong in philosophers such as Jacques Maritain.[42] In keeping with this ideal, there is the tendency to state the goal of education in personalistic terms.[43] In accordance with this ideal or goal, the church has taken a strong stand against war and against racialism. This was especially true of Pope John XXIII, who may go down in history as one of the greatest of all times. Be that as it may, it is this aspect of Catholicism which gives some point to one writer's insistence that the church is "the Mother of all true democracy." [44] Indeed, if this were the only aspect, we would have found it necessary to classify Roman Catholic educational philosophy as thoroughly essentialistic.

Unfortunately, over against this profoundly humanistic, liberal, and democratic aspect, there stands what we must call the dogmatic and authoritarian element. That Catholicism has in the past, whatever may be true in the future, exhibited autocratic rather than democratic religion is evident from the stress placed on the infallibility of the Pope.[45] Nor does this fact fail to color and deter-

---

41. Cunningham, *The Pivotal Problems of Education*, p. 49.

42. See Jacques Maritain, "The Humanism of St. Thomas Aquinas," in Runes (ed.), *Twentieth Century Philosophy*, pp. 295-311.

43. See Jacques Maritain, *Education at the Crossroads* (New Haven: Yale University Press, 1943), pp. 7-11, 34-43.

44. Franz DeHovre, in John S. Brubacher (ed.), *Eclectic Philosophy of Education* (New York: Prentice-Hall, 1951), p. 216.

45. See the statement by Pius XI in Brubacher, *Eclectic Philosophy of Education*,

mine the philosophy of education. Since the church is the ark to which has been entrusted the faith once delivered to the saints, indoctrination becomes natural and unashamed.[46] Worse still, in lands where the power of the church has been undisputed, it has often exercised a repressive influence. In spite of some indications of a coming change, there is also its opposition to birth control.

Nevertheless, Roman Catholic education possesses certain positive characteristics which may be summarized as follows.[47] First of all, it is actuated by a lofty purpose. This, in the words of Pope Pius XI, is nothing less than "to form the true and perfect Christian." Closely related to this is its emphasis on religion as a vital aspect of the curriculum on all levels. The chief reason for maintaining parochial schools is the fear that the secular schools will neglect this important realm of human experience. As an element of their essentialism, Catholics also stress intellectual discipline and subject matter as well as the learner. Moreover, in contrast with extreme pragmatists, they manifest a genuine respect for the values inherent in tradition. There is likewise, due to the strong Aristotelian influence, a real attempt to develop the whole man. Finally, today one senses a strange restlessness among Catholic educationists. This is especially evident in a number of articles which appeared a few years ago in the very important nonsectarian journal, *Religious Education*.[48] In short, the spirit of creative change is present in Roman Catholic education today as never before.

(2) Protestant Fundamentalism

Brief consideration must now be given to the movement within Protestantism known as fundamentalism. To begin with, it must

---

pp. 295-96; also Roy J. Defferrari (ed.), *The Philosophy of Catholic Higher Education* (Washington: Catholic University of America Press, 1947), pp. 47-48, 193.

46. *Ibid.*, p. 60.

47. See also Butler, *Religious Education*, pp. 346-47, 373, 393-407.

48. See the following especially in the journal, *Religious Education*: C. J. Neusse, "Education for Living in a Changing World: Some Premises of a Catholic View," May-June, 1961, pp. 185-91; Vincent J. Giese, "New Trends in Catholic Catechesis," July-August, 1961, pp. 252-56; and Benedict M. Ashley, O.P., "A New Curriculum of Christian Doctrine for Catholic Schools," *ibid.*, pp. 271-78.

be made clear that it by no means represents the thinking of most thoughtful Protestants. While some Protestant educationists lean in the direction of pragmatism and others toward progressivism, the majority are probably essentialists in some form or fashion.

Within the last forty years there has arisen within Protestantism, largely due to the influence of Karl Barth, an important movement known as neoorthodoxy or the theology of crisis. While it is sometimes confused with fundamentalism, in spite of certain dogmatic tendencies, it really has more in common with theological liberalism; for it accepts the canons of modern biblical criticism. Furthermore, as Butler has pointed out, most neoorthodox thinkers are probably educational realists in some sense of the word.[49] Later, in dealing with religion, we shall have more to say about this movement.

The roots of fundamentalism go back to the Protestant Reformation, that is, particularly to those followers of Luther and Calvin who became rigid literalists. As a distinct, self-conscious movement, however, fundamentalism developed after the First World War—largely as a response to the challenges of the Higher Biblical Criticism and the theological storm aroused by the theory of evolution.

The central concept of fundamentalism is the doctrine of the infallible Bible as the final authority. Some fundamentalists, of course, insist that only the original manuscripts—which have perished—were inerrant, the errors having crept in due to the carelessness of copyists. Along with the belief in the infallible Bible, fundamentalism stresses such doctrines as the virgin birth, the bodily resurrection of Jesus, and the blood atonement. Decidedly otherworldly, unlike Roman Catholicism, it tends to look to the future rather than to the past. Profoundly pessimistic as far as human efforts to eliminate social evils and to promote progress are concerned, fundamentalists are apocalyptic—looking for Christ's Second Coming as the only real ground of human hope.

49. Butler, *Religious Education*, pp. 382-83, 386-89, 391-92.

This system resembles Catholicism, however, in its emphasis on *belief*—coupled with a rigidity which makes the reception of new truth extremely difficult.

Given such a dogmatic system held with such rigidity, it is only natural that the resulting philosophy of education should be dogmatic and authoritarian. Fortunately this philosophy has been set forth recently by an able writer.[50] Suffice it to say that, while there are some signs of a coming change,[51] basically the system is still dogmatic, anti-scientific, and archaic.

b) SECULAR TYPES

While there was a time when the greatest threat to freedom came from autocratic religion, this is no longer true today. So far as the twentieth century is concerned, the chief danger stems from secular sources. Totalitarian systems have arisen which have demanded a faith and a devotion equaled only by religion. In view of the significance of these movements, especially in terms of the dangers which they represent, some attention must now be given to them. We shall begin with those of the extreme right.

(1) *Fascistic Forms*

The term "fascism" is derived from the Latin *fasces*, indicating the rods fastened to an ax which was borne before Roman magistrates as a symbol of authority. While it was first used by Mussolini as the name for his particular political system, today it applies to all similar systems. In what follows we shall employ it in this broader sense.

Although there are certain suggestions in Plato and even in Aristotle, though neither was basically fascistic, modern fascism

---

50. See Frank E. Gaebelein, *Christian Education in a Democracy* (New York: Oxford University Press, 1951). One of the best recent brief accounts of fundamentalism is found in William Hordern's little book, *A Layman's Guide to Protestant Theology* (New York: The Macmillan Co., 1955), pp. 56-76. It also contains a list of three important books written by leaders in the movement, see p. 216.

51. The leading and most progressive thinker among contemporary fundamentalists is undoubtedly E. J. Carnell—see Hordern, *A Layman's Guide to Protestant Theology,* pp. 74-75, 216.

finds its prototype in ancient Sparta—a nation which was wholly regimented educationally and otherwise. Again, while modern thinkers such as Niccolò Machiavelli (1469-1527), Thomas Hobbes (1588-1679), and Friedrich Nietzsche (1844-1900) contributed something to it, fascism found its primary source in the modern nationalistic state. The best examples, of course, are Italy, Germany, and Japan—as they were before the Second World War brought their systems to an end.[52]

The central concept of all such systems is the totalitarian state with its deified leader. The state, in a real sense, takes the place of God: it is absolute, ultimate, and all-inclusive. Hand in hand with all this, there is, of course, the emphasis on national culture, land, and race—often mingled with a blind hatred and abuse of some minority group which serves conveniently as a scapegoat.

Anti-intellectualism also runs rampant; reason is repudiated along with freedom. Thus, in Hitler's educational scheme, physical training came first and the intellectual last. Dictators fear intellectuals—they ask too many questions. In short, reason is dethroned by the will to power, and might makes right. In his glorification of the cult of power, Mussolini even went so far as to declare that war "puts the stamp of nobility upon the peoples who have the courage to meet it."

When such thinking is in the saddle, education becomes the tool of tyrants. In Mussolini's Italy Giovanni Gentile, the philosopher, even went so far as to pronounce the school an aspect of the state —that aspect whose chief function is to indoctrinate, to condition the young to throw themselves willingly and gladly before the juggernaut. How complete this subjection can become is illustrated even better by Nazi Germany where most classes—from the kindergarten to the university—began with the shout: "Heil Hitler"

---

52. In this and what follows, these sources have proved valuable: on Hitler and Mussolini, Albert R. Chandler, *The Clash of Political Ideals* (revised edition; New York: Appleton-Century-Crofts, 1949), pp. 206-24; and on the educational systems, Meyer, *The Development of Education in the Twentieth Century*, pp. 260-307; Brubacher, *Modern Philosophies of Education*, pp. 225-32; and Frederick Lilge, *The Abuse of Learning* (New York: The Macmillan Co., 1948).

Most absurd of all, for grace before meals little children were taught a special prayer addressed to Adolf Hitler as "Savior." [53] Never in all history did any great nation prostrate its schools so utterly before irrational power.

While the particular forms of tyranny described above have fallen, their spirit is still with us. The threat is present even in countries with strong democratic traditions such as our own. If world conditions should suddenly take a turn for the worst or if the worst elements in both camps should suddenly threaten violence on an unparalleled scale in the racial struggle, in an evil moment a frightened people might sell their birthright for a mess of pottage. This is especially true in a time such as this when reactionism is making a desperate effort to capture the seat of power. If it does not succeed this time, it may the next.

Be that as it may, the truth of the matter is simply this: when both security and freedom hang in the balance and a choice must be made between them, the people are more likely to choose the former. Hence the pragmatist's stress on education for democracy and all that this implies is imperative.

(2) Marxian Communism

Like so many things modern, Marxian communism or dialectical materialism has its roots in certain aspects of Plato's Republic, on the one hand,[54] and, strange as it may seem, in certain aspects of the great Hebrew-Christian tradition, on the other. Though rejecting the basic theism of the latter and its belief in the power of love and nonviolence, communism has borrowed no less than three important elements from the latter, namely, its moral indignation, its concept of the classless society, and its belief that the world can and must be changed.[55]

53. See Meyer, The Development of Education in the Twentieth Century, pp. 271-72.

54. For these Platonic roots of Soviet education, see George S. Counts and Nucia Lodge, The Challenge of Soviet Education (New York: McGraw-Hill, 1957), p. 10.

55. On this point see also my History and God, pp. 29-32. It is very doubtful that Marxianism could have developed in a completely non-Christian environment.

So far as modern thinkers are concerned, the communistic scheme owes much to G. W. F. Hegel (1770-1831). Although Hegel was an idealist and would have been shocked had he been living, the truth of the matter is that Marxianism consists of a fusion of the Hegelian dialectic with materialism. The father of modern communism or dialectical materialism is, of course, Karl Marx (1818-83); and whatever may have been true of Stalin, there can be no doubt that Friedrich Engels (1820-1895), and V. I. Lenin (1870-1924) also made outstanding contributions.

Although in certain respects Marxianism looks like a faith after the manner of the religions, it is also a philosophy. For, among other things, it has an ontology or theory of being. Since it regards matter or nature as ultimate, it is a form of materialism or naturalism—and as such constitutes a type of realism. Yet, while dialectical materialism stresses the primacy of material forces both in the historic process and in nature, it is not—as many suppose—a crass form of materialism wholly devoid of any sense of values or of the significance of man's higher nature. Along with the primary law, the law of strife and unity of opposites which keeps the process moving in accordance with the dialectical pattern of thesis, antithesis, synthesis, there is also a secondary law which transforms brute quantity into quality. This is how values emerge from the cosmic process. At this point the system really becomes a form of evolutionary naturalism in some respects reminiscent of the systems of such non-Marxian philosophers as Samuel Alexander and Roy Wood Sellars.[56]

Like most forms of authoritarianism, Marxianism involves a number of contradictions. Thus, from the standpoint of meta-

56. On Marxianism, the following primary sources are helpful: Lewis S. Feuer (ed.), *Marx & Engels: Basic Writings on Politics & Philosophy* (Garden City: Doubleday & Co., 1959); and V. I. Lenin, *The Teachings of Karl Marx* (New York: International Publishers, 1930). The following secondary sources are also helpful: John Somerville, *Soviet Philosophy* (New York: Philosophical Library, 1946); John Somerville, "Dialectical Materialism," in Runes (ed.), *Twentieth Century Philosophy*, pp. 469-509; H. B. Mayo, *Democracy and Marxism* (New York: Oxford University Press, 1955); and I. M. Bochenski, *Contemporary European Philosophy*, translated by D. Nicholl and K. Aschembrenner (Berkeley: University of California Press, 1961), pp. 61-71.

physics, it has never resolved the contradictions between freedom and determinism. While, on the one hand, the Marxist sees all history as determined by economic and social forces and, as such leading inevitably to the triumph of the communist ideal, on the other hand, it stresses the place of the human agent and his creativity. A case in point is that, even though in *The Communist Manifesto* and in his prefaces to *Das Kapital*, Marx is emphatic that the economic forces determine human thought and behavior, in his famous "Theses on Feuerbach" he insists that "it is men that change circumstances."

Coming now more directly to the communist philosophy of education, like the Roman Catholic, it has both humanistic and rigid, authoritarian aspects. We begin with a brief account of the first, and shall then deal similarly with the second.

As part of its heritage from Judaism and Christianity, it must be granted that, in certain respects at least, communism manifests a real concern for social justice. Thus, in *Das Kapital* Marx, when condemning the injustices of the capitalistic system in England during the earlier phases of the Industrial Revolution, occasionally sounds like a Hebrew prophet. Often, in fact, Marx's followers seem to show more social concern than the followers of Jesus Christ. It is this aspect of Marxianism which makes such an appeal to the underprivileged throughout the world.

Moreover, from the standpoint of education, experts agree that there has been a vast improvement as compared with the conditions prevailing under the Czars. The Revolution, in fact, had scarcely been over when plans were made for completely overhauling the entire educational system with the hope of abolishing illiteracy. It is also interesting to note that from 1921 to 1931 Soviet education smacked so much of American progressivism that George Counts called it "the romantic period." [57] After 1931, however, there came a decided reaction against these tendencies as

---

57. Counts, *The Challenge of Soviet Education*, p. 60. For an enthusiastic Russian account, see Albert P. Pinkevitch, *The New Education in the Soviet Republic* (New York: John Day Co., 1929).

Stalin became much more firmly established in the seat of power.

At any rate, in spite of its efficiency and in spite of certain hopeful tendencies at present of which more must be said later, Russian education has been and still is basically dogmatic and authoritarian. Even during the "romantic period" there were evidences of authoritarianism. Albert Pinkevitch himself, who wrote during the twenties, cannot help letting the cat out of the bag occasionally. In other words, he had to admit that, in the final analysis, the entire program was still organized around the Soviet concept of the nature of the state—and it is the nature of the state to indoctrinate.[58] Still, regardless of the authoritarian aspects of these ultimate aims, it must be said that the system in its actual operation during this period was quite liberal; in some respects even to the point of license.

As the night of Stalinism descended, however, all traces of liberalism vanished. More and more the whole educational process became subject to the whim and fancy of one man. Even the natural scientists had to make sure that their theories did in no way conflict with communist dogma.[59] This is totalitarianism with a vengeance!

How then shall we characterize present Soviet education both in terms of its debit and its credit sides? These factors most certainly belong to the debit side: the underlying authoritarianism in terms of the large doses of indoctrination and too much control from the top; the heavy concentration on technology and the practical at the expense of the humanities; and the general stifling of creativity through an overstress on discipline and curriculum uniformity. On the credit side, however, there are the following: the determined effort to stamp out illiteracy; a real concern for the children and youth; the dedication of many Russian teachers in terms of their efforts for the common good and for the welfare

58. *Ibid.*, pp. 29-30, 390-92.
59. On education under Stalin, see George S. Counts & Nucia Lodge, *The Country of the Blind* (Boston: Houghton Mifflin Co., 1949).

of their pupils; in spite of the stress on mass education and uniformity, the beginnings of a real interest in the gifted—including
those talented in the humanities; and, perhaps most important
of all (something which the American public in general and
American politicians in particular might well take to heart) that
in Russia a college education is absolutely free for anyone who
meets the qualifications.[60]

To the credit side something else must be added. Lately there
has come to my attention a very remarkable collection of articles
written by leading Russian educationists for some of the leading
Russian journals.[61] In reading these articles three things impress
the fair-minded reader: a new concern for the education of the
whole man; a new stress on the importance of the humanities; and
genuine signs of a new interest in creativity.

At any rate, the future depends largely on the political climate.[62]
What is needed—on both sides of the Iron Curtain—is a more able
and more imaginative statesmanship capable of entertaining and
executing policies which will bring the cold war and the arms race
to an end. Only then, when the full resources of mankind are set
free to be used creatively, will the future be safe.

5. Other Types

Besides the types or systems or tendencies which fall more or
less naturally under the four general headings with their sub-
divisions, there are three other types to which we must now give
some consideration. We begin with existentialism.

60. The above analysis is largely based on the following: George Z. F. Bereday, *et al*
(eds.), *The Changing Soviet School* (Boston: Houghton Mifflin Co., 1960)—published
for the Comparative Education Society; Alexander G. Korol, *Soviet Education for
Science and Technology* (New York: John Wiley & Sons, 1957); and Deana Levin,
Soviet Education Today (New York: John DeGraff, 1959).

61. Fred Ablin (ed.), *Education in the USSR: A Collection of Readings from Soviet
Journals* (New York: International Arts & Sciences Press, 1963), Vol. I.

62. Although the new leaders of Russia have given some indications that they favor
"coexistence," yet, with the fall of Khrushchev, at this moment at least, the picture still
remains confused.

a) EXISTENTIALISM

In many respects (though some attempts have been made to combine them) existentialism is the direct opposite of the analytical philosophies which are still strong in this country and in England— and which we must consider later. For one thing, existentialism is much more difficult to define. Walter Kaufmann, in fact, has gone so far as to insist that, instead of being a philosophy, it is nothing more than "a label for several widely different revolts against traditional philosophy." He also reminds us of the strange fact that most of the contemporary thinkers who are usually regarded as existentialists "have repudiated this label." [63] It is also well to remember that the movement is composed of two rather diverse wings: a right wing which stems primarily from Kierkegaard and which is theistic (to which Karl Barth and the other neoorthodox theologians belong along with some who are chiefly philosophers), and a left wing which stems largely from Nietzsche and which is decidedly atheistic (of which Sartre is the best living example).

Yet, in spite of differences, those philosophers who are generally regarded as existentialists—Martin Heidegger, Jean-Paul Sartre, Karl Jaspers, Gabriel Marcel, etc.—have a number of things in common. First and foremost among these is their concern with man and his predicament, especially as he faces tragedy and death. Moreover, like the personalists, they protest against philosophical abstractions and anything that dehumanizes and depersonalizes man—particularly the excesses of modern science and technology. They are unlike the personalists, however, in certain significant ways: they are much more subjective; they have far less regard

63. See Walter Kaufmann (ed.), *Existentialism from Dostoevsky to Sartre* (New York: Meridan Books, 1956), p. 11. For the understanding of the movement the following are also suggested: John Wild, *The Challenge of Existentialism* (Bloomington: Indiana University Press, 1959); and F. H. Heinemann, *Existentialism and the Modern Predicament* (New York: Harper & Row, 1958). For further investigation the following are important: Martin Heidegger, *Being and Time*, translated by J. Macquarrie and E. Robinson (New York: Harper & Row, 1962); Karl Jaspers, *Reason and Existenz* (New York: Noonday Press, 1955); Karl Jaspers, *The Future of Mankind* (Chicago: University of Chicago Press, 1958); and J. P. Sartre, *Being and Nothingness* (New York: Philosophical Library, 1956).

for reason and for science; and some of them (especially Heidegger and Sartre) tend to stress the tragic and the irrational aspects of experience. Finally, one other thing must be mentioned: like the personalists and progressives, existentialists emphasize freedom and creativity.[64]

As we pointed out in Chapter II, while existentialism has not developed a full-fledged educational philosophy, it not only has profound educational implications, but not so many years ago George Kneller tried to set forth these implications in his interesting little book.[65] In the light of this perspective, we shall now attempt the difficult task of briefly summarizing the most significant educational implications of existentialism.

To begin with, Kneller makes it clear that existentialism is relevant to education because the problems with which it is concerned—the great basic problems of human existence—*inevitably* become problems of education.[66] Again, existentialism favors that kind of education which is interested chiefly in man's uniqueness as an individual and in his creative capacities. Consequently, the *humanities* rather than the sciences must be *central*.[67] Like the pragmatist, the existentialist is opposed to formalism. Education must really be related to life and it must minister to life; but the existentialist never views the matter in a narrow pragmatic way. Rather the highest goal of education must always and everywhere be kept in mind, namely, "man's search for himself." [68] He also recognizes the importance of the emotions as sources of creativity. In fact, he regards them as more important than the intellect.[69] Mention must also be made of the fact that existentialists insist

64. Among all the philosophers who are usually regarded as existentialists, Karl Jaspers is the most socially minded and the most constructive, and therefore the most important for educationists.

65. *Existentialism and Education.*

66. *Ibid.*, p. 42.

67. *Ibid.*, pp. 124-25. As Kneller points out all existentialists are deeply interested in "literary and artistic creations."

68. *Ibid.*, pp. 66-69, 117. Existentialists are really much more humanistic than Dewey—at least in certain respects.

69. *Ibid.*, p. 158.

that education must help the individual to look honestly at the tragic and the destructive aspects of life.[70] Finally, the existentialistic theologians especially insist on the need of commitment. In short, education must prepare men to be participants in life's drama rather than mere spectators only.

b) THE ANALYTICAL PHILOSOPHIES

We now come to types of philosophy which are quite different from existentialism. Moreover, while existentialism is prevalent in certain countries of Europe, these other philosophies, while showing signs of decline, are still very much in evidence in England and in this country. These are the analytical philosophies. Among the leaders are A. J. Ayer, Bertrand Russell, Ludwig Wittgenstein, G. E. Moore, and the individuals who gathered around Moritz Schlick—who came to be known as the Vienna Circle.[71]

Although there are many differences between analysts, like the existentialists, they have certain things in common. As the name indicates, they all stress the analytical method. In fact, as Bertrand Russell points out, they "make logical analysis the main business of philosophy." [72] For them the central problem of philosophy is the problem of meaning. Consequently, many of them are chiefly interested in linguistic analysis. Along with this, there is also their emphasis on clarity and precision. Finally, though some of them are beginning to change,[73] most of the analysts are indifferent and even hostile to metaphysics.

70. *Ibid.*, pp. 105-13.
71. For an illuminating account of the rise and development of the analytical philosophies, see the editor's Introduction to A. J. Ayer (ed.), *Logical Positivism* (The Free Press of Glencoe, 1959), pp. 3-28. The book as a whole contains selections from outstanding leaders in the movement such as Rudolf Carnap, Moritz Schlick, etc. Another similar book is Herbert Feigl & Wilfred Sellars, *Readings in Philosophical Analysis* (New York: Appleton-Century-Crofts, 1949). For general background Morton White, *The Age of Analysis* (paperback; New York: New American Library, 1955), pp. 189-236 is also important. The student should also read A. J. Ayer's *Language, Truth And Logic* (second revised edition; London: Victor Gollancz, Ltd, 1946).
72. In his *History of Western Philosophy* (New York: Simon & Schuster, 1945), p. 835.
73. See especially Gustav Bergmann's book, *The Metaphysics of Logical Positivism.*

Although Bertrand Russell wrote a book back in 1926 in which he stressed a few analytical principles such as the principle of "exactness" (but which is not otherwise analytical), and an article which is more definitely analytical in its emphasis on science and scientific objectivity,[74] analysts, since their first love is elsewhere, have not written much on the subject of education. Fortunately, however, not so many years ago, a leading analyst wrote an article in which he discussed the chief educational implications of the analytical philosophies.[75] As in the case of Kneller's book, we shall attempt to formulate a brief summary of the most important aspects of Pap's article.

First of all, he attacked the concept of " 'integration' in higher education" by means of "survey courses." Instead, he suggested that integration could be best attained by "prescribing" certain courses in philosophy for every student.[76] Since, however, philosophy itself has gone through "a silent revolution" in becoming more analytical, this raises the question whether it is still capable of performing this task. Pap believes that it can by applying "the new precision tools" of logic and the "semantic analysis of language" to the "old problems"—and thus banishing those that prove insoluble while concentrating on the ones which can in some real sense be verified.[77] Pap also stresses "the habit of precise, critical thinking" which the application of the principles of the analytical philosophy would produce in students.[78] Moreover, he would apply these principles to all areas of human life. Finally, he insists that the very fact that analytic philosophy was suppressed in both Nazi Germany and Soviet Russia shows that it can be a power for freedom. In other words, any citizen who is equipped with the weapons

---

74. See his Nobel Prize Winner, *Education and the Good Life;* and his article "The Place of Science in a Liberal Education," in his *Mysticism and Logic* (Garden City, N.Y.: Doubleday, 1917), pp. 32-43.

75. Arthur Pap, "The Role of Analytic Philosophy in College Education," *Harvard Educational Review*, XXVI (Spring, 1956), 114-18.

76. *Ibid.*, p. 114.

77. *Ibid.*, p. 115.

78. *Ibid.*, p. 116.

of critical analysis is not as likely to be "misled by oratory and slogans." [79]

c) RECONSTRUCTIONISM

This brings us to Theodore Brameld's reconstructionism. It is unique due to the fact that it is chiefly the work of one man. In its general approach it is social, cultural, anthropological, and even political. Again, from the standpoint of metaphysics, it is naturalistic, humanistic, and this-worldly.[80]

Even though Brameld is critical of pragmatism, especially since it tends to overstress intelligence while underestimating the irrational forces, yet in terms of his basic approach to education, he is fundamentally pragmatic. Along with this, there is an intense interest in values—including his particular brand of nontheistic, humanistic religion. He also ties religion in with the "overarching value" of his system, that is, with what he calls "social-self-realization." [81]

While reconstructionism is in some respects like progressivism, socially speaking the former is much more radical. In other words, as the term itself implies, it aims at the reconstruction of society. Though Brameld believes that progressivism is well suited to meet the demands of a stable society, he thinks that it cannot meet the pressing problems of our dynamic, unstable, highly explosive world. Present conditions, arising from the wars—both hot and cold—and the unparalleled dangers of the Nuclear Age, demand large-scale reconstruction. Brameld is, in fact, at his best when he deals with the social responsibilities of education. He is critical of all forms of authoritarianism both of the right and of the left. Thus it is obvious that the kind of social reconstruction which he envisages, like that of Dewey, falls within the general framework

79. *Ibid.*, p. 118.
80. Brameld's three chief books are: *Patterns of Educational Philosophy; Toward a Reconstructed Philosophy of Education* (New York: Dryden Press, 1956); and *Education for the Emerging Age* (New York: Harper & Row, 1961).
81. See his article, "The Place of Religion in Educational Theory: A Reconsideration," in *The Philosophical Forum*, XX (1962-1963), 77.

of a liberal and responsible democracy. He is looking for a new society capable of realizing the very highest and best that is in man.

Whereas progressivism emphasizes the present and other systems idealize the past, reconstructionism looks hopefully to the future. Thus, like Dewey, Brameld is a meliorist: although things look bad and man may actually destroy himself, the hope of a better future still beckons—and whether this hope shall ever be realized depends on us. At any rate, it is much better to go down trying than to give up. Unlike the great utopians of the past, even though he is by no means an anti-intellectualist, he does not put his faith primarily in reason. Goals, he insists, are not mediated by reason but rather surge up out of the rich resources of life itself. Hence they are capable of tapping and releasing vast powers which may be used to attain them.

Unlike some educationists, Brameld has a high regard for philosophy. More than this, he insists that all future teachers should be required to study educational philosophy with as much time devoted to it as to psychology of education; that those who are sufficiently interested should be given the opportunity for more intensive study; and that throughout, not only should the "cultural setting" of educational philosophy be stressed, but it should also be used to integrate and unify all the other realms of knowledge. Thus he conceives the educational philosopher as " 'liaison officer' " or "interdisciplinarian." [82]

6. Conclusion

As this chapter shows, there is today considerable diversity and confusion in the field of educational philosophy. Still, in view of the fact that there are certain distinguishable types, and that these types have many things in common, the diversity and confusion is far from being total or absolute. The great need, however, especially since our world is so chaotic, is to bring the essentials of the various tendencies or types into some kind of unity. In the chapters which follow, we hope to contribute something to this end.

82. See his *Education for the Emerging Age*, pp. 204-14.

V

From Diversity Toward Unity

1. Purpose and Method

A professor of philosophy tells of his experience as an undergraduate in his first course in the history of philosophy. So many thinkers and systems were thrown at him with little attempt at evaluation and synthesis that he became confused and discouraged. In the light of experiences such as this, it is clear that our task was only half done in the last chapter. It is not enough merely to describe tendencies, types, and systems. Something must also be done to compare and to evaluate them, and if possible, to find a basis of unity. This is nothing short of imperative in this age in which we are living—which Susanne K. Langer has rightly described as "this story age of transition." [1] This quest for synthesis and unity is the difficult task which awaits us in this chapter.

In pursuit of this aim a number of methods come to mind. We might make a procrustean bed of some dogma or principle and cut off everything which does not fit, but this would expose us to all the weaknesses of the authoritarian systems—which we shall criticize later in this chapter. Nor, in view of the fact that they open the floodgates of irrationalism, is it wise merely to follow our intuitions and "hunches." Again, while analysis and experimentation

1. See her stimulating article, "On the Relations Between Philosophy and Education," in the *Harvard Educational Review*, XXVI (Spring, 1956), 141.

are aspects of sound method, since they can neither deal adequately with the all-important problem of the intangibles such as minds, ideals, and ultimate goals, nor lead toward any prospects of synthesis, unity, and wholeness, they are obviously too narrow and limited for our task.

If, then, we are to do full justice to what Whitehead has called the "togetherness" of things,[2] it is clear that we must use a method which, while embracing both analysis and experimentation, at the same time transcends them in its total outreach and in its inclusiveness. This—the *synoptic* method, which is really as old as Plato— basically is nothing but the appeal to reason in the very highest meaning of the word. In this sense, besides making use of the results of analysis and experimentation, it aims at inclusiveness both as to *facts* and *methods,* and, in terms of its comprehensiveness, there is a real concern for *wholes* and for the broadest possible *perspective.* It is this method which underlies what we shall attempt in this chapter. Suffice it to say that its very *inclusiveness* and *comprehensiveness* constitutes its best possible defense.

2. Weaknesses and Contributions

a) PRAGMATISM AND EXPERIMENTALISM

Dewey is dead, and his influence is not as great as it was, yet, since he left a powerful wake and still has many disciples, we must again deal with him somewhat at length. Moreover, in trying to evaluate his philosophy of education and that of his followers, some consideration must be given to his general philosophy. To begin with, it must be remembered that, while he began his career as a Hegelian idealist, he soon left Hegelianism, and for a time he seemed to be drifting in the direction of a dogmatic positivism. The tone of his *Quest for Certainty* is, in truth, decidedly antimetaphysical. In a manner reminiscent of Auguste Comte, he insisted that it is better to find whatever security is within reach

2. See his *Process and Reality* (New York: Harper & Row, 1929), pp. 29, 32, 48, 86, 147, 288-89.

through the application of science to nature rather than contemplating the Infinite in quest of an illusory security beyond time. A careful analysis of the book reveals the fact that Dewey really had a metaphysics: that is, a badly mixed and even contradictory metaphysics composed of naturalistic, neorealistic, and even idealistic tendencies and assumptions.

Even though in his *Experience and Nature*, Dewey did attempt (but without succeeding very well) to do justice to the facts of unity, order, and structure,[3] he conceived the universe, as a disciple of the ancient Heraclitus, chiefly in terms of flux. Unlike Heraclitus, however, he gave altogether too little attention to the Logos—the principle of order underlying change. Hence, like many of our contemporary philosophers as well as artists, he is open to the charge of being dominated altogether too much—at least in his metaphysics—by the chaos so dominant in our badly confused world.

As Dewey became older, he moved increasingly away from his positivistic tendencies and closer to what may be called a naturalistic metaphysics.[4] This explains his tendencies in the direction of behaviorism and epiphenomenalism.[5] His theory of mind, not unlike his metaphysics in general, is rather badly mixed up. While on the one hand, he reduced mind to little more than a biological process serving as an instrument of adjustment (his instrumentalism), on the other hand, he seems to have taken it for granted that the human mind is endowed with wonderful creative capacities increasingly capable of mastering, directing, and transforming nature's flux in accordance with its own purposes. If mind is merely an instrument of adjustment, whence these remarkable powers to understand and control nature increasingly? Moreover,

3. (La Salle, Ill.; Open Court Publishing Co., 1958); see especially Ch. II, pp. 37-66.
4. See particularly his "Experience, Knowledge and Value: A Rejoinder," in Paul Arthur Schilpp (ed.), *The Philosophy of John Dewey*, p. 604; and George Santayana's "Dewey's Naturalistic Metaphysics," in *ibid.*, pp. 245-61.
5. See his *Experience and Nature*, especially p. 251. Here he seems to take a *deterministic* view of consciousness; it has no efficacy.

no naturalist has yet given a good answer to Thomas Hill Green's question: "Can the knowledge of nature be itself a part or product of nature?" Later, in the section on creativity, we shall come back to these questions.

Like most modern naturalists, Dewey took naturalism altogether too much for granted. For, while naturalism—this modern David —with its supreme confidence in science seems to have little difficulty with the Goliath of the older supernaturalism, it has never really come to grips with the new theism and personalism which, instead of opposing science, really draw support from the revelations of scientific investigation. Later in this chapter we shall return to this attempt at a criticism of naturalism. It is enough to say here that, as the sciences mature (physics is the best example), there is a marked tendency to turn back not only to metaphysics, but also to theism and personalism.[6]

Similarly the pragmatic theory of truth is open to serious criticisms. As Herman Harrell Horne points out in his criticisms of Dewey, there are really two views of truth. The first is the pragmatic view that truth is merely utility: ideas are not true because they interpret reality correctly, but simply because they serve as tools or processes enabling the organism to adjust itself to its environment. The second or nonpragmatic view holds that an idea is not true just when it works, but only when it discloses reality as it actually is. This view, as Horne points out, is held by both idealists and realists. Interestingly enough, the pragmatic theory leads to the question whether, in terms of its own conception of truth, pragmatism itself is true; for, while it seems to work for pragmatists, it does not work for nonpragmatists. Thus the end

6. On this point see my chapter, "Personalistic Religion and Science," in Edwin P. Booth (ed.), *Religion Ponders Science* (New York: Appleton-Century, 1964), pp. 160-79; and also the following: Werner Heisenberg, *The Physicist's Concept of Nature* (New York: Harcourt, Brace & Co., 1958); Max Planck, *The Philosophy of Physics* (New York: W. W. Norton & Co., 1936); Lecomte du Noüy, *Human Destiny* (New York: Longmans, Green & Co., 1947); and L. W. Friedrich (ed.), *The Nature of Physical Knowledge* (Bloomington: Indiana University Press & Milwaukee: Marquette University Press, 1960).

result can only be a ruinous individualism which destroys all objectivity.[7]

Finally, by means of an illustration, Horne shows very graphically how really contradictory the pragmatic conception of truth can become in certain instances. He asks us to imagine a "clever thief" stealing the original painting by an old master and replacing it with a substitute. If the owner does not know the difference, would his belief be true since it works for him? When finally detected, was the illusion really true while it lasted? [8]

Dewey's general philosophy is vitally related to his philosophy of education. His naturalistic metaphysics affects his educational theory at the point of ruling out the great intangibles. On the one hand, he ruled out theism without giving it the serious consideration which it rightfully deserves, while on the other, as we have already seen, since mind does not fit in well with his narrow scheme, he tried to make it fit by trying to reduce it to the level of a biological process. His behaviorism, however, was not fully developed until he began writing his *Experience and Nature;* and, as Albert William Levi has pointed out, it shows the influence of George Herbert Mead.[9] Dewey's basic trouble is that he "subordinates the conceptual order to the perceptual." [10]

Closely related to all this is Dewey's theory of the self as a social process and product. The individual is swallowed up in society. Consequently, by trying to imprison it within the limitations of the tangible and the temporal, the great pragmatists restricted the human spirit altogether too much. While some of our theologians seem to forget the finite in their concern for the infinite, Dewey was so preoccupied with the former that he ignored the claims of the latter. There is truth in Whitehead's contention

7. See Herman Harrell Horne, *The Democratic Philosophy of Education,* pp. 500-501.
8. *Ibid.,* p. 502.
9. Albert William Levi, *Philosophy and the Modern World* (Bloomington: Indiana University Press, 1959), n. 37, p. 561.
10. See Horne, *The Democratic Philosophy of Education,* p. 502. Plato would have said that Dewey exalted the lower world of sense experience—the world of shadows—above the real world of the mind. See his famous "Allegory of the Cave."

that in his unconcern for "ultimacies" and in his concern for "security," Dewey narrowed the scope of philosophy to matters of fact.[11]

There are those, of course, who tend to belittle the relationship between metaphysics and educational theory and practice.[12] Although philosophy of education neither springs full grown from metaphysics, nor can be deduced from certain basic metaphysical propositions as some have supposed, two things still remain true: that philosophy of education always involves assumptions about the ultimate meaning of man and of the world; and that, whatever may be true in the short run, in the long run metaphysics does seem to have effects in terms of the character of the students, their basic attitudes, and, finally, their behavior.

That Dewey and his followers, in spite of their disdain for "ultimacies," do have a metaphysics has already become evident. It is also certain that this metaphysics is directly related to their educational philosophy, for it affects and colors it. The same is also true of their educational practice. A case in point is their behavioristic view of the self. This most certainly has had and is still having a depersonalizing effect both inside the classroom and outside. After all, what a man thinks and does is determined to a large extent by what he thinks of himself—of his ultimate role as a man. Here the existentialists are quite right.

Another case in point is the pragmatic theory of truth, which is a metaphysical theory. As stated by John Dewey in his *Reconstruction in Philosophy*,[13] it is most *confusing*. While, on the one hand, he tried to find some objective basis, on the other—blinded by his polemic against the rigidities of dogma and dogmatism—he sounds like a thoroughgoing relativist and thus lays himself open to all the strictures which, as we have seen, Horne pronounced

11. See Lucien Price, *Dialogues of Alfred North Whitehead* (New York: New American Library, 1956), pp. 145, 206, 271.

12. See, for example, Sidney Hook's article—"The Scope of Philosophy of Education" —in *Harvard Educational Review*, XXVI (Spring, 1956), 146.

13. (Paperback; New York: New American Library, 1950), pp. 128-34.

against his theory. This is especially true when he speaks of "truth as utility" and refers to it as "adverbial." With such a mixed-up, confused view of truth, instead of the clarity which he promised, Dewey has added to the general confusion—a confusion that may lead to the chaos that would destroy us. Metaphysics does—in the long run—have practical effects.

Another very important thing must be made clear before we go further. In spite of his interest in creativity, Dewey's behaviorism, his scientism and factualism, and his rejection of the transcendental, together with his conception of truth have served to stifle the creative impulse. Pragmatism confronts man with no "infinite goal." Doomed to be sense bound, he hears no higher Voice challenging him to strain at the bit of his finiteness. Instead of realizing his highest potentiality by attempting to storm the heights of heaven, he sinks deeper and deeper into the bog of utilitarianism and materialism.

In his exaggerated emphasis on the present at the expense of the past, Dewey is also subject to criticism.[14] While he was never as extreme as some of his disciples, when one reads his *Quest for Certainty* or his *Reconstruction in Philosophy,* and after one has made due allowances for his services as an iconoclast, the haunting suspicion remains that he has failed to do justice to the mighty thinkers of the past. Perhaps he was more in the thralls of the American *Zeitgeist* (the spirit of the time) than he himself realized. In keeping with this mention must also be made of his almost unlimited faith in science. Important as science undoubtedly is, it also (as we shall see later) has obvious limitations. In short, Dewey and his followers have virtually made a religion out of science—the cult of scientism.

Finally, so far as goals are concerned, Dewey seemed to be content with the simple concept of "growth"—a term taken from biology. Since growth is relative to nothing beyond itself, education

14. See also Levi's interesting comments on Santayana's insistence that Dewey stressed the "foreground" or the immediate altogether too much. See *Philosophy and the Modern World,* pp. 295-96.

is reduced to nothing but a continuous process of becoming. Besides, as Horne reminds us, growth processes of all kinds exist—pernicious and abnormal as well as healthy and normal.[15] Thus education as growth leaves unanswered the larger question: Growth in what direction? Dewey's concept does not help us to distinguish between true and false goals. The truth of the whole matter then seems to be that growth can only have meaning in terms of something toward which one should grow.[16]

Yet, even after the critic has done his worst, the great pragmatist's contributions still remain vast. Although he went too far in stressing the tangible and the finite, he did philosophy a service in bringing it down to earth. Above all else, it was important to link it up with science and with our pressing social problems. Here he served as a wholesome corrective to the dogmatic, smug, unempirical idealists of the nineteenth century, who scorned science and declared war upon it.

Again, few will question most of Dewey's criticisms of the old formalistic education. The latter was certainly guilty of emphasizing subject matter and discipline to the neglect of the learner and his desires and interests. Why should education be inhuman or uninteresting? The uninteresting has no virtue in itself. Nor can there be any question concerning the importance of activity in the education of children. Plato recognized this long ago.

Similarly the experimental method has proved valuable in education. The only way light can be shed on some problems is by means of new, bold experiments. Thus Dewey shed new light on education, and particularly democratic education, through his

15. Horne, *The Democratic Philosophy of Education*, pp. 52-53.
16. In an interesting address—"An Interpretation of John Dewey's Basic Ideas and Their Influence on Classroom Practices"—Dean Harold G. Shane of the School of Education at Indiana University tried to defend Dewey's concept of growth as the chief educational aim; but in so doing he virtually reduced it to Brameld's "social-self-realization" (see Ch. IV, p. 81 on Brameld). The real trouble with Dewey's concept of growth is that it is *ambiguous*. He should have used a better word. For Dean Shane's address, see *Kent State University Bulletin*, May, 1960, pp. 7-17, especially p. 15.

Laboratory School. In certain respects, then, he must be considered as a great contemporary educational pioneer.

In spite of its ambiguities and its inadequacies as a total goal, the concept of growth must also be given an honored place. It ties the educational process in with life and represents it as an unending process of development. This concept of education is especially necessary to meet the demands of the dynamic situation which twentieth-century man faces.

This leads us to Dewey's passion for democracy. In his *Democracy and Education*, he states specifically that he seeks to link up "the growth of democracy" with the developments in the various sciences and also with the "industrial reorganization" which has taken place. He feared (and rightly so) that democracy has not kept pace with these developments; and, above all, he was interested in seeing what "changes" both in "subject matter" and in educational "method" are necessary to meet the demands of the situation.[17] More than this, in his concern for democracy, he took an active part in the stirring social issues of his day. Upon occasion he even took off his philosophical robes and appeared in the guise of a reformer.

As a matter of fact, his most important contribution may be his social philosophy, that is, his meliorism: for the faith—that bad as things are, they can be made better—is sorely needed today. As long as man was enthralled by fatalism, religious or otherwise, little could be done to deliver him from bondage. Here science came as liberator, making man realize as never before that—within limits at least—he is the master of his fate. The great need is that wedding of the religious and the scientific spirit which could result in a new earth and a new and better day for mankind. At any rate, in spite of his excesses in the direction of secularism and utilitarianism, John Dewey will continue to stand as a sentinel against those pessimists, who, having lost their faith in man's God-given creativity, would lead us back to do obeisance before an in-

17. P. iii.

scrutable Absolute to whose command our only response can be a blind, unthinking submission.[18]

b) PROGRESSIVISM

The chief fault of progressivism is its tendency to go too far. While there have been and are moderate progressives, the school as a whole was not known for its moderation. Breed tells the story of the visitor who arrived early one day to observe a progressive teacher in action. Upon inquiring about the program for the day, the teacher assured him that such matters had to wait until the children arrived and could be consulted.[19] Similarly Dewey himself, who greatly influenced the movement and for a time was directly associated with it, tells—with strong disapproval—of hearing about teachers who surrounded their pupils with objects and materials, but then allowed them to follow their own fancies.[20] Dewey's disciple, John P. Wynne, after carefully distinguishing between experimentalism and progressivism, even goes so far as to call the latter "educational *laissez faire*" or "the drifting theory." [21] Even such a staunch supporter of the more moderate aspects of the system as Boyd H. Bode vigorously criticized it for its general aimlessness. Like Horne in criticism of Dewey, he asked the crucial question: "Growth whither?" [22]

Another type of criticism comes from Brameld. He accuses the progressives of a lack of social realism. Our critical times demand a much more serious attempt to grapple with the pressing social, economic, and political problems.[23] In a more recent volume, besides insisting that the progressives did not seem to know where they were going, he also charges them with a loss of the pioneering

---

18. For further evaluation of Dewey, see my article, "John Dewey in Retrospect," in *The Christian Century*, Sept. 30, 1959, pp. 113-14.
19. Frederick S. Breed, *Education and the New Realism*, p. 25.
20. See his *Experience and Education*, p. 84.
21. See his *Philosophies of Education*, pp. 7-11, 408.
22. Boyd H. Bode, *Progressive Education at the Crossroads*, pp. 83 ff.
23. For an extensive criticism, see his *Patterns of Educational Philosophy*, pp. 167-208.

spirit. In fact, he thinks that this is the chief reason why the Progressive Educational Association folded up during the fifties.[24]

It is also true that, in exaggerating the place of interest, the progressives forgot two facts. First, if the pupils serve as the chief directing power, the result will be a preoccupation with the immediate, the trivial, and the easy at the expense of the basic, the more exacting, and the more difficult. Even on the college level the general tendency is to take courses taught by instructors who practice "soft pedagogy." Second, students often discover their more profound and abiding interests under a measure of discipline and even compulsion. Many an exacting teacher has lived to see the day when he was thanked profusely by many of his students who finished graduate school. "Soft pedagogy," whether in the lower grades or in high school or in college, far from being merciful, may ultimately be the most cruel. For, in the bitter end, it only serves to swell the casualties on the undergraduate and graduate levels.

Likewise the doctrine of learning by doing, in spite of its merits, entails certain dangers. If overstressed, it inevitably leads to "busy work." After all, there are also many other ways of learning. Not least among these is learning by thinking—including wrestling with difficult books. One of our greatest shortcomings is the deplorable habit of replacing profound and sustained thinking with superficial doing. This is one reason why we do not produce more great theoretical scientists, more first-rate philosophers and theologians, and more foresighted and creative statesmen.

In its reaction against formalism, progressivism also did not fully appreciate the place and function of memory. In order to solve problems in the sciences as well as elsewhere, a good memory is indispensable. At least certain facts, formulae, ideas, hyptheses have to be available from this vast reservoir. The creative reason cannot work in a mind that is empty. More than this, for the enrichment of life itself, nothing is more valuable than a richly endowed

24. *Education for the Emerging Age,* pp. 26, 31.

memory. Many a modern mind is so barren that seven devils enter and make it their dwelling. This is at the root of much of modern man's discontent. The unconscious, after all, consists largely of what one puts there. Later, in dealing with creativity, we shall return to this matter.

Finally, progressives are also guilty of fostering the false antithesis of child-centered versus subject-centered education. In reality, both factors are important. If either is lacking, something may be going on, but it can hardly be called education. If the significance of the learner is not stressed, the process degenerates into mere training, and thus becomes inhuman and brutal. If there is carelessness concerning subject matter—the besetting sin of extreme progressives—the result is an exchange of ignorance, a waste of time, and empty heads.

In spite of all its failures and weaknesses, the progressive movement has enriched modern education. Its concern for the child is drawn from the deepest wells that have fed Western culture. This means not only the great modern pioneers such as Comenius, Pestalozzi, Rousseau, and Froebel, but also, in the final analysis, the great Hebrew-Christian tradition.

As we shall see later, the final, overall goal of education, if there is such, must embrace this personal element which the progressives have stressed. Without this all-important factor, it would remain abstract, lifeless, and inhuman. Therefore it is not too much to say that, while progressivism's head has not always been right, there can be no doubt about its heart. As a matter of fact, this movement, perhaps more than any other, has served to humanize education. Children are happier because of it.

Closely related to all this is its significance as a liberating influence. The progressive protest against arid formalism, trivial pedantry, heartless rigidity, and stern discipline has greatly enhanced the freedom of the human spirit. When compared with the old formalism, it strikes us like a fresh sea breeze.

Finally, there is its concern for creativity and spontaneity. Many a progressive teacher has been an inspiration to her pupils. Nor must progressivism's commitment to democracy be forgotten. It was these things which caused Bode, back in 1938, in spite of his drastic criticisms of extremists, to call it "the strongest and most evangelistic movement" on the American scene.[25] In an hour when the tides of reactionism are threatening us at home and communism is threatening us abroad, there is great danger that we jump from the frying pan into the fire by encouraging a Prussian type of education at the expense of the humanities. Consequently, the truth which lies at the heart of progressivism is more important than ever before.

c) ESSENTIALISM

In the last chapter it became clear that there are two basic types of essentialism—idealism and realism. Idealism is always subject to two great dangers. First of all, it always faces the temptation of becoming unempirical, unscientific, vague, and, like progressivism at its worst, even sentimental.

Lilge tells the sad story of how science had to struggle in the German universities with what was known as *Naturphilosophie*.[26] Firmly convinced that the only valid approach to nature is the speculative, the followers of Hegel and Schelling—ridiculous as it seems to contemporary idealists—refused to make use of the results of scientific observation and experimentation. They even regarded the vast system of knowledge built up by Newton and others with "contempt." No wonder that a critic accused Schelling of trying to produce the universe itself "as from an empty shell." The results were tragic: the thin, unempirical pronouncements of the philosophers led the scientists to declare open war against philosophy itself, causing a breach which is only now beginning to heal. Even today, in spite of the change of attitude on the part of idealists generally, the very term "idealism" is sufficient to arouse the suspicions of scientists.

25. Bode, *Progressive Education at the Crossroads*, p. 9.
26. Frederic Lilge, *The Abuse of Learning*, pp. 57-63.

Idealists are also prone to be dogmatic and authoritarian at times. This fault has plagued idealism ever since the days of Plato. We find with dismay in his *Laws* (the product of his old age) the scheme which served as a prototype for the Spanish Inquisition.[27] Many centuries later, as we have seen, it was the pontifical spirit of the German idealists which led to the disastrous war with science. The tendency toward authoritarianism and political absolutism is particularly characteristic of certain kinds of absolute idealism. It found supreme expression in the fascist, Giovanni Gentile. Among other things, he was responsible for that monstrosity, the theory of the ethnic State.

It was examples such as the above which gave idealism a bad name. The truth of the matter is, however, that idealism, by its very nature, is the opposite of anything that smacks of totalitarianism whether of the right or of the left. This is certainly true of personalism with its basic theism, its stress on values, on human creativity, and on human freedom.

Opponents of idealism, besides pointing to the dangers which idealism involves, usually make use of two arguments aimed at its basic epistemological and metaphysical principles. The first is that it is absurd to insist that everything is of the nature of mind or mindlike. Some would even go so far as to accuse idealists of solipsism. The second and most telling argument is based upon the fact of evil. In the light of evolution (the vast suffering involved, the appearance of monstrosities, the brutal struggles, and the slow progress), this argument appears much more cogent than ever; and it is doubtful that the traditional forms of idealism are capable of giving an answer that can really satisfy the modern mind. This is why many idealists have given up the idea of a God or the Absolute conceived in the traditional sense as omnipotent. As we noticed in the last chapter, this is particularly true of those left wing personalists who follow in the wake of Edgar Sheffield Brightman.

Perhaps the greatest weakness of realism lies in the metaphysics

27. See the *Laws*, Book X, 909.

of the dominant tendency: for, while some realists have been dualists (that, is basically theistic and even, in certain respects idealistic), most realists are naturalistic and, in some instances, even behavioristic.[28] In fairness to certain naturalistic realists who must be distinguished from thoroughgoing materialists and mechanists, it must be said that they are doing everything possible within the limitations of their scheme to safeguard values. Bagley even hoped that by means of the concept of "emergent evolution" he could link "idealism and naturalism." [29]

The trouble with courageous attempts such as that of Bagley is that, since there is no place for the transcendent and for God as conscious Cosmic Mind and Will, in the final analysis, all values are at the mercy of blind, impersonal forces. At all times, of course, we must attempt to be objective, that is, in the larger sense of also trying to give due consideration to *all* the facts of experience—not just the facts derived from scientific investigation; and, if the ultimate truth about the universe is that it is impersonal and indifferent to values, we have to grit our teeth and make the most of it; but the fact still remains that, if it is unphilosophical to give way to our hopes too easily, it is even more unphilosophical, especially from a pragmatic standpoint, to give way to despair too easily.

At any rate, naturalism has really no adequate explanation of certain massive converging strands of facts: on the one hand, such outstanding characteristics of nature as order, unity, organization, vital capacity, beauty, and grandeur—which look like aspects of Cosmic Mind and Will furnishing idealists with grounds for their conviction that nature is mindlike; and, on the other hand, the appearance of such great intangibles as selves (with such capacities as self-consciousness, reflective thought, and creativity—including

28. On this naturalistic tendency in realism, see John S. Brubacher (ed.), *Modern Philosophies of Education*, pp. 314-16. Besides the naturalists and the dualistic realists, there are also the neorealists, but, with a few exceptions, they have been more concerned with the more technical aspects of epistemology than with the philosophy of education.

29. William C. Bagley, *Education and Emergent Man*, p. 64.

an ever increasing ability to control natural processes), values, ideals, moral and religious experience—involving a widespread report of an awareness of God.

Furthermore, the naturalist's attempt to explain these facts in terms of "emergent evolution" fails at the point of *adequacy*. For rather than offering a reasonable explanation of *why* these things occur, "emergent evolution" merely *describes how* they occur. The naturalist, in truth, has a difficult time offering a reasonable explanation of evolution itself: that is, the appearance of fit organisms plus a fit environment plus the remarkable upward push, proceeding as it does from level to level as though in the fulfillment of a purpose. Thus the universe of the naturalist, especially since the physicist has reduced matter to energy (something very intangible), becomes a scene where perpetual miracles occur without rime or reason—they just happen. This forces him to appeal to certain blind, innate tendencies in nature and, ultimately, to chance—a most inadequate principle.[30]

Mention must also be made of the strong naturalistic tendency toward reductionism, behaviorism, and determinism. Even those naturalists who stress creativity find it virtually impossible to avoid this inclination. The best illustration, as we have already seen, is the system of John Dewey which rests on a naturalistic metaphysics. In my discussions with prominent naturalists at philosophical meetings, I have noticed this characteristic many times.

Since later, in the section on creativity, we shall subject reductionism, behaviorism, and determinism to drastic criticisms, two observations must suffice at this time. The first is that some things, especially selves when viewed in terms of all their highest capacities, do not fit the naturalistic scheme very well. Self-consciousness

30. This writer has a book on metaphysics in process in which he tries to explore these problems much more thoroughly and adequately. Obviously, here we have to be brief. On the inadequacies of naturalism, see Edgar Sheffield Brightman, *Nature and Values* (New York and Nashville: Abingdon-Cokesbury Press, 1945); and on the inadequacies of chance see du Noüy, *Human Destiny*, pp. 26-39. The trouble with many naturalists is that they do not take time to read the writings of idealists and personalists.

offers a constant source of embarrassment to them. The second observation is simply this: that it seems rather arbitrary to attempt to reduce something higher to something lower chiefly to meet the demands of a system. It smacks of dogmatism.

Concerning the weaknesses of essentialism as a whole, its critics would sum them up in such words as "conservative" and "reactionary." Thus Brameld speaks of "the obsolescence of essentialism," and of "essentialism as cultural lag." [31] What truth is there in these charges? First of all, as we have already noticed, some essentialists have not only been staunch guardians of the *status quo* but even arch-reactionaries. Second, any movement seriously concerned with man's cultural heritage always faces the peril of the backward look. In other words, while pragmatism and progressivism often become too preoccupied with the present, essentialism must beware of becoming absorbed and enthralled by the past.

Since, however, essentialism is strong where pragmatism and progressivism are weak, it has much to offer—especially in an age of confusion. Chief among these is its view of truth: for, instead of regarding truth merely as something that works, it conceives truth in terms of correspondence to reality. Here, in an age that has stumbled so close to the precipice of nihilism, is a means of direction. While it is necessary to recognize the fact of change (as one must in a dynamic universe such as ours), it is also important to see the changeless which underlies these dynamic processes. As Heraclitus himself, the father of all process philosophies recognized long ago: deeper than change itself lies the law of change *(Logos)* which is universal and changeless. If this were not true, neither philosophy nor science would be possible. In fact, faced with such an unending process of meaningless becoming, we would all go stark mad. Even though the new physics has badly shaken the old mechanistic view of nature and even though the laws of nature may be to a certain extent statistical, this has in no

---

31. Brameld, *Patterns of Educational Philosophy*, pp. 277-78; and *Toward a Reconstructed Philosophy of Education*, especially p. 10.

sense disturbed the basic orderliness of nature; an orderliness which underlies all the specific instances of natural law.

Similarly there is essentialism's emphasis on the value of our human heritage. Current American thinking is dominated altogether too much by a shortsighted contemporaneousness. Being told by their teachers that they know much more than Plato and Thucydides and even than such architects of modern science as Newton and Darwin, our youth soon develop a disdain for the great classics in all fields, and with this disdain a certain mental flabbiness together with a lack of perspective. If some of our scientists, especially in such relatively young sciences as psychology and sociology, knew more about the history of science, they would be less dogmatic.

Essentialism serves to deliver us from the prison of contemporaneousness. Not only does it stir the imagination by opening a great door so that modern man can enter vicariously into the life of other ages, but this larger perspective also sheds light on the present in at least two important ways: it gives us insight into the nature of man himself, while, at the same time, it also provides us with an understanding of those very significant structures called civilizations. Toynbee is right in his insistence that, unless we are willing to learn from history, the fate of our civilization may be even more tragic than the Greco-Roman—which failed largely because it did not respond to the challenge of the world crisis with a creativity that might have replaced the international anarchy by some kind of an effective international law and order.[32]

Closely related to this emphasis on cultural heritage is essentialism's synthesis of the dichotomy of the learner and the subject matter. If it has at times stressed the latter a bit too much, even this is something of a *felix culpa* (happy fault) serving as a corrective to the excesses of pragmatism and progressivism. Heads filled with ignorance and "half-baked" ideas are as much to be abhorred as that brutal formalism which subjects the learner to

32. Arnold J. Toynbee, *Civilization on Trial*, pp. 47-62.

regimentation. What monstrous shapes have arisen from the fetid swamps of ignorance to plague mankind!

Along with this healthy regard for man's cultural heritage and for subject matter, there is essentialism's respect for discipline. If many generations of young Americans are allowed to follow their inclinations by a soft, spineless pedagogy, the collapse of our culture is certain. After all, there is no greater tyranny than the tyranny of impulse, which, after promising a glad freedom, unchains ten devils, each going in a different direction, till absolute chaos brings irretrievable ruin. Thus essentialism, in view of the mounting juvenile delinquency, on the one hand, and the lack of intellectual discipline and excellence, on the other, constitutes a warning against an evil which is eating at the heart and brain of American society like a treacherous cancer.[33]

Nor is it necessarily true that essentialists need be conservative and reactionary. Although mention has already been made of this fact, yet, since they have been so often accused of these things,[34] and since some of them have really been guilty, it behooves us to give fuller consideration to this matter at this juncture. First, as far as contemporary realists are concerned, their aim is to find the mean between a radicalism which is apt to be visionary and thus lead to disillusionment, and a conservatism which seeks to freeze the *status quo*. Hence, while criticizing many of the schemes of pragmatism, progressivism, reconstructionism, and idealism, they believe that their own critical approach will eventually result in more real and lasting progress.[35]

Contemporary idealists, especially the personalists, are willing

33. On discipline from the standpoint of idealism, see William Ernest Hocking, *Human Nature and Its Remaking,* pp. 22-39; and from the standpoint of realism, William C. Bagley, *Education, Crime, and Progress,* pp. vii ff., 41-65. Even Sigmund Freud realized the need of some discipline; see *Civilization and Its Discontents,* translated by Joan Riviere (New York: R. O. Ballou, 1930), p. 93. It is also interesting to note in this connection that James Bryant Conant found that in most of our high schools the best students are "not working hard enough." See his book, *The American High School Today* (New York: McGraw-Hill Book Co., 1959), p. 23.

34. Among recent critics, as we have already noticed, is Brameld.

35. See Breed, *Education and the New Realism,* especially pp. 221-26.

to go much further than the realists. To begin with, the personalists go beyond other groups in their stress on the uniqueness, the dignity, and the significance of personality. Moreover, they support their social concern with a profound metaphysics. In other words, for them, personality, in terms of the self-conscious mind and will, constitutes the fundamental principle of metaphysical explanation, the clue to the riddle of existence. They reason that, since mind is not only a product of the universe but also—as far as we know—its highest product, it is more likely to be, basically and ultimately, like this—its highest product—than like its lowest. In presenting their case, they also make use of all the other teleological facts, something after the manner in which we tried to state them on pages 97-98, in presenting our criticisms of naturalism. It has also become evident that some modern personalists, in view of the fact of evil, have accepted the idea of a struggling rather than an omnipotent God. Moreover, unlike the older idealists who despised science, personalists, along with other contemporary idealists, draw a considerable amount of their support for their point of view from the findings of the various sciences. In short, for most idealists and for personalists in particular, the universe itself, with its signs of law and order, purpose and value is regarded as an expression of the Cosmic Mind.[36]

For most idealists subject matter itself is not regarded as something dead and impersonal, but rather as an aspect of the living truth. Instead of being composed merely of isolated facts, truth forms a system which has its source in the Supreme Mind. Hence, truth must be respected as something sacred. Again, since truth has no meaning apart from minds, but degenerates into a meaningless

36. On personalism, see Edgar Sheffield Brightman, *Nature and Values;* and his article, "Personalism," in Vergilius Ferm (ed.), *A History of Philosophical Systems* (New York: Philosophical Library, 1950), pp. 340-52; also Ralph T. Flewelling, "Personalism," In Dagobert D. Runes (ed.), *Twentieth Century Philosophy* (New York: Philosophical Library, 1947), pp. 323-41. For personalistic philosophies of education, besides Horne, *Philosophy of Education*, see Peter A. Bertocci, "Unless Educators Be Philosophers, and Philosophers Be Educators," *Harvard Educational Review*, XXVI (Spring, 1956), 158-61.

abstraction, and since minds starve without truth, it is obvious that the two belong together as aspects of the universe. More than this, it is the task of the teacher to join truth and the learner together into an indissoluble union. Thus, idealism, more than any other system, succeeds in transcending the false antithesis of the learner versus the subject matter. Both are of great value and dignity and must be respected as such.

Idealism then, by virtue of this and many other things, has much to offer in terms of a philosophy of education for these perilous times. This is even more true so far as the very important question of goals is concerned, to which due consideration must be given in the next chapter. Moreover, essentialism as a whole, with its stress on objectivity, on our rich cultural heritage, and on discipline, provides a source of stability as well as aspiration for our "time of troubles."

d) AUTHORITARIANISM

(1) Religious Types

The basic weaknesses of the two chief types of religious authoritarianism are so evident that we can afford to be brief. Roman Catholicism's belief in the infallible church with its infallible Pope is as fallacious as Protestant fundamentalism's faith in the infallible Book—its "paper pope"; and with the collapse of these primary dogmas, many secondary dogmas also meet their Waterloos.[37] It is surprising that such beliefs—vestiges from other ages—can so long survive.

Yet, in the final analysis, as in the case of the other systems, one cannot but find a vast amount of good in both. Within limits, the principle of authority itself has a place and function: that is, insofar as it implies the necessity of expert counsel and guidance in life as a whole as well as in religious matters. When one goes to

37. For criticisms of Catholic dogma, see Auguste Sabatier, *Religions of Authority* (New York: George H. Doran Co., 1904), pp. 55-144; and for criticisms of dogmatic Protantism, see *ibid.*, pp. 165-234; also Arthur W. Munk, *Perplexing Problems of Religion* (St. Louis: Bethany Press, 1954), pp. 83-86.

his physician or his lawyer for advice, he recognizes the validity of this principle. Nothing, in fact, brought more reproach on progressivism than the faith of its extremists in the ability of immature children to direct the educational process.

Besides their stress on discipline, there is also their sincere concern for ultimates. Even idealism, in spite of its metaphysics, along with pragmatism and progressivism, may at times become little more than a mirror reflecting the changing scenes and the vacillating moods of the *Zeitgeist*. Here the stubborn refusal of the religious authoritarians—in obedience to a higher law—to conform to the passing fads may serve as a genuine corrective. Their emphasis on the importance of religion is likewise greatly needed in a time when secularism has run riot.

Finally, it became clear in the last chapter that, in spite of its authoritarian nature, Roman Catholicism is making many outstanding contributions to democracy and to world peace. The great hope lies with the liberals within the system. Chief among these are the late Pope John XXIII and his followers. Mention must also be made again of the liberal democratic spirit of great Roman Catholic educational philosophers. The most outstanding among these, of course, is Jacques Maritain.[38] No one has made a greater effort to apply Thomistic principles to modern problems. Suffice it to say that leaders and thinkers such as these represent the best in a great tradition.

(2) Secular Types

The excesses of fascism are so glaring and have cost the world so much in "sweat, blood, and tears" that we can promptly dismiss it with the comment that it is the attempt to turn the race back to a monstrous modern form of tribalism. It has taught us one important thing, however, namely: that this is the way that the human race must not go. With its doctrine of the totalitarian state, it can lead to nothing but racial suicide.

Marxian communism or dialectical materialism also has many

38. For his educational philosophy, see particularly his *Education at the Crossroads*.

weaknesses, as we noticed in our descriptive analysis in the last chapter. Metaphysically, it is, of course, materialistic and naturalistic—with all the weaknesses which this kind of philosophy implies. It became clear in Chapter IV that it really involves a number of contradictions which have never been fully resolved. Among these are its stress on freedom versus its stress on economic determinism; its humanistic spirit versus its authoritarianism; and its opposition to religion versus the fact that it is itself on the verge of becoming a kind of religious faith. To these one other contradiction must be added, that is, its relativism versus its absolutism. While, on the one hand, it holds that everything is relative to the economic forces, on the other, it insists that its own basic doctrines are absolute.

There are also its dogmatic self-righteousness and its violence in times past. During the Stalin regime Russian education reached its nadir. The creative spirit was crushed as distinguished scholars were either silenced or forced to conform to the pattern set by communist politicians. Thus education on all levels became the lackey of the state.[39]

Yet, in spite of what some politicians and commentators may say, there is another side to the picture. To begin with, we have something important to learn from the Marxian philosophy. After all, Marx himself was one of the half dozen or so greatest philosophers of history of all times. His genius consists, above all else, in the fact that he recognized the significance of the economic forces. Although he exaggerated their role in the historic process, yet since his time—more than ever before—thinkers have realized their importance.

Again, in spite of his overemphasis, he put his finger on something important when he stressed the class struggle. This famous passage from the *Communist Manifesto* contains more than a grain of truth: "The history of all hitherto existing society is the history of class struggles." Marx has also called our attention to the

39. See also previous discussion, Ch. IV, p. 75 and n. 59.

estrangement of vast masses of human beings due to the advancement of technology. Uprooted from the soil and forced to labor for giant corporations at dehumanizing tasks, vast masses in his day were in a sore plight; and, in view of the progress of automation and the fact that many countries are just beginning to experience the dislocation due to the inevitable advance of industrialization, the problem, instead of being solved, may still be in its very beginnings. Nor can there be any doubt as to its explosive possibilities if left unsolved. The most discouraging aspect of the problem so far as this country is concerned is the fact that our politicians—for the most part at least—are so ignorant as to its real nature that they try to solve it by using Hitler's fallacious method: that is, by drafting the young men and putting the rest to work in factories producing the instruments of universal death and destruction.[40] One of the tasks of education is to acquaint the public with the real nature of the vast problem that we are facing; for, if something is not done soon, an *explosion* is *inevitable*.

In spite of his deterministic inclinations, Marx recognized the dynamic nature of the universe in general and of the historic process in particular. Consequently, he stressed the possibilities of human creativity in the realms of economics and politics. In accordance with this idea he wrote in his "Theses on Feuerbach": "The philosophers have only *interpreted* the world, in various ways; the point, however, is to *change* it." This concept of Marx is the secret of communism's success in our dynamic, rapidly changing modern world. If the democracies refuse to see the handwriting on the wall but continue to look back wistfully to the nineteenth century (the age of Western white supremacy) and refuse to respond creatively to the world crisis, they will disappear—and the whole human race may disappear with them.

One of the most hopeful signs in today's world is the fact that

---

40. There is hope, however, that the draft will soon be abolished: that is, unless we get into a disastrous war in Asia. The President's program for "war on poverty" also offers hope; but it will fail if something is not done in terms of birth control among the poverty-stricken masses.

Russion communism seems to be in the process of creative change. Among other things, for the first time in Russia's history a large-scale attack has been made on ignorance. Moreover, in spite of what our reactionaries are telling us, there is hope for the future both educationally and otherwise. Given the opportunity, much good may come out of Moscow. We must not despair of a people that produced a Leo Tolstoy and a Feodor Dostoevski. It was this conviction which led a group of philosophers within the American Philosophical Association to form an organization for the study of Marxianism.

e) THE THREE OTHER TYPES

This brings us to the three philosophies which in the last chapter we placed under the general heading: Other Types. As before, we begin with existentialism.

The weaknesses of existentialism are manifest. To begin with, it became clear in the last chapter that it is in no sense a well-defined movement. The term itself, in truth, has been used in so many ways that it has become virtually meaningless. Worst of all is the irrationalism which characterizes the movement: that is, its subjectivity, its hostility to science, and the tendency of some existentialists (especially Sartre) to dwell upon the morbid and the abnormal aspects of life. Besides all these negative aspects, it is also true—as Kneller points out—that it seems to be most at home in a sick society.[41]

Nevertheless, it became certain in the last chapter that, since it has profound educational implications, it can make important contributions.[42] First of all, it can help keep education from becoming trivial by reminding it of the great problems of human existence which are really inescapable. Closely related to all this is its emphasis on man himself: that is, on his uniqueness as an individual, on his basic human need for knowing himself and his

41. George F. Kneller, *Existentialism and Education*, pp. 152-53. For all his major criticisms, see pp. 152-55.
42. For a more thorough discussion of the contributions than is possible here, see *Ibid.*, pp. 156-62.

role, and on his creativity. There is also the emphasis which existentialists place on the primacy of the humanities. This is especially important in a time when the stress is on the sciences and technology and when the great danger is the dehumanization and the depersonalization of man. Mention must likewise be made of existentialism's concern for the education of the emotions. Finally, there is its insistence that every person must be taught to face the tragic aspects of existence heroically and creatively.[43]

The basic weaknesses of the analytical philosophies are quite different from those of existentialism. The first and most fundamental is, of course, the tendency to overemphasize analysis. Although, as we saw in Chapter III, analysis is a very important aspect of philosophy, it also became evident that it is neither the only nor the *most* important aspect. By following analysis alone, the analyst is apt to miss one of the most significant characteristics of the universe, namely, the unity or "the togetherness" of things. Worse still, mere analysis leads him to impersonal abstractions and even to triviality. There is also the danger—a very real danger in this country today—that philosophy may become so highly technical as to be nothing short of esoteric. Likewise, there is the hostility to metaphysics on the part of most analysts. This hostility is unwarranted in the light of two considerations: it means the attempt to stifle one of man's highest creative capacities as a human being, which is unreasonable; and, since even the anti-metaphysicians have a metaphysics, their attempt to destroy metaphysics is futile.

Like existentialism, however, the analytical philosophies have something to offer to education. This became clear in the last chapter, that is, in our summary of Arthur Pap's article.[44] Chief among these are the importance of *analysis*, of *exactness*, and of *precision*. Furthermore, since the student who has formed the habit of critical

---

43. For the importance of education concerning death, see Randolph Crump Miller, *The Clue to Christian Education* (New York: Charles Scribner's Sons, 1950), pp. 191-200.

44. See previous discussion, Ch. IV, pp. 80-81 and nn. 75-79.

analysis and is equipped with its tools is less likely to be misled by demagogues, analytical philosophy may also become a weapon in the arsenal of democracy and freedom.

Finally, there is Brameld's reconstructionism. Its chief weakness is that, even though it possesses lofty ideals and an amazing social vision, like other naturalistic, pragmatic, and humanistic systems, it does not provide an adequate metaphysical foundation for values. Again, while recognizing the dangers inherent in myths, Brameld, in a recent article, calls for a new "religious myth" centered upon the concept of "world civilization." [45] Since we must beware of myths, even if they have a certain value for a time, it would have been better for Brameld to have used the words *world view*. For, if there is anything that modern man needs, it is a world view which not only makes for wholeness, but which also makes sense. Our big job is finding an adequate world hypothesis which may serve as the basis of a world civilization.

In spite of its metaphysical deficiencies, reconstructionism has much in its favor. Many American educators are altogether too smug and complacent. Perhaps the chief mission of reconstructism is to function as a goad. If today, while there is still the opportunity for creative thought and action, educators are content to sit in their ivory towers, tomorrow there may be neither ivory towers nor educators.

3. Conclusion: Contrasts and Similarities

In conclusion, perhaps it is well to bring the various types or tendencies before us again in epitomized form. This will prove helpful not only in recognizing the differences and the similarities, but it will also serve as a means toward the synthesis which we hope to sketch in broad outline in the final chapter.

Pragmatism is naturalistic, and it stresses change, experimentation, utility, activity, growth as the aim or goal and democracy as the social ideal. Similarly progressivism is humanistic, stressing

45. "The Place of Religion in Educational Theory: A Reconsideration," in *The Philosophical Forum*, XX (1962-1963), 80.

the centrality of the learner with his interests, desires, and creativity. In contrast with the two mentioned above, essentialism emphasizes the permanence which underlies change, the objectivity of truth, the importance of the subject matter as well as the learner, *disciplined* freedom, and the conservation of values. Metaphysically speaking, essentialism, of course, has two chief aspects, the realistic (which is largely naturalistic) and the idealistic; and, while both the naturalistic realists and the idealists of all types have sought metaphysical adequacy as a basis for human freedom and creativity, the personalists have probably been the most successful.

Although authoritarianism as a whole is known especially for its stress on discipline and order, in its Roman Catholic form (which is definitely theistic) and to an increasing extent in the Russian form of the Marxian (which is atheistic), there are elements of *ethical humanism*. While existentialism stresses man as an individual as he faces the great facts of life and of death, the analytical philosophies concern themselves chiefly with the need of logical analysis, exactness, and precision. Finally, reconstructionism, which has much in common not only with pragmatism and with progressivism but even with certain aspects of essentialism and Marxianism, serves, above all else, as an impetus to creative social change.

Seen in this perspective, it is clear that the sharpest contrasts are obtained between the two secular forms of authoritarianism as over against the other philosophies. This is even more true of fascism than of Marxianism, since the former really represents a turning back to certain aspects of primitive tribalism. It is man in despair looking back toward his old gods—gods that can only bring the final ruin, the Götterdämmerung. Moreover, from a *metaphysical* and a *theological* standpoint, while personalism, dualistic realism, the two forms of religious authoritarianism, and certain types of existentialism are basically theistic, pragmatism, progressivism (in part at least), Marxianism, the analytical types (for the most part), and some existentialists (e.g. Sartre and probably Heidegger) are basically atheistic and impersonalistic.

Amid these contrasts and similarities, these differences and likenesses, is there no common principle lying at the basis of them all in some meaningful sense—a principle which may serve as the foundation upon which may be built in time a vast superstructural unity? It seems evident that the principle of *ethical humanism* constitutes such a basis. Fundamentally, as over against literary humanism or theological humanism, it simply means belief in the worth and dignity of man and that, since he possesses worth and dignity and a vast creativity, he should be given every opportunity for the development of his capacities. In this broad sense both theists and theological humanists can also be *ethical* humanists. With the exception of the Fascists, nearly all, if not all, thinkers would accept *ethical humanism*. In spite of the Marxian stress on the mass man, as we noticed both in this chapter and in Chapter IV, important traces of this ideal remain. Furthermore, regardless of the fact that their philosophy as such has few traces of *ethical humanism*, most analysts, as part of their personal conviction, accept this principle. Indeed many of them opposed Hitler.

Certainly the great need of our time is unity, wholeness. Moreover, important as metaphysics is in this vital matter of developing something of a common world view, yet *ethics*, as Kant recognized in terms of the principle of *human dignity*, is *primary*. It represents the first big step in the direction of a world view. Interestingly enough, this principle is found in India and China (especially in Confucius, Mencius, and Mo-tzu) as well as in the great Hebrew-Christian-Greek tradition; and, since the Universal Declaration of Human Rights, as adopted by the United Nations, is based upon this principle, the building of the superstructure has already begun.

In this chapter then, at least some progress has been made toward synthesis. In accordance with the synoptic method, the various philosophic systems and tendencies have been evaluated, their likenesses and differences have been made manifest, and a common principle has been found. We must now turn our attention to this all-important question of goals.

VI

The Question of Goals

While, in an instinctive and unreflective sense, there is a striving for ends even on life's lowest levels, in man this goal seeking becomes reflective as well as dominant; for in him alone consciousness, which lies dormant in the vegetable and fitfully dreams in the animal, becomes fully awake. He is, in the words of William James, "a *fighter for ends*"; with him "*real* ends appear for the first time . . . upon the world's stage." [1] As a matter of fact, the more reflective man becomes, the larger his goals. They stretch even into the far future: man hopes to storm the very gates of death. Hence, since education involves man as learner, it cannot avoid this all-important question of goals.

1. Why the Concern for Goals?

Unlike the animal, whose behavior is so largely determined by its natural equipment, Homo sapiens is subject to moral and spiritual tensions. Not only does he have to think in terms of goals, but

1. See his *Principles of Psychology* (New York: Henry Holt & Co., 1890), Vol. I, p. 141. On man as goal seeker, see also Gordon W. Allport, *Personality: A Psychological Interpretation* (New York: Henry Holt & Co., 1937), pp. 112-14. For a stimulating discussion from the standpoint of educational philosophy, see Theodore Brameld, *Toward a Reconstructed Philosophy of Education*, pp. 78-80. Most of this chapter on goals is really an expansion of a part of my article—"Educational Philosophy for Today"—which appeared in *The Philosophical Quarterly* (India), XXXIV (July, 1961), 95-101. Used by permission.

he is also often forced to choose between various goals. The old dilemma of "Hercules at the crossroads" is still with us. In some situations, in fact, the matter is crucial. When statesmen or educators choose the wrong road, unspeakable tragedy may follow. Thus, paradoxical as it may seem, the source of man's greatest creativity—freedom of choice—is also often a source of danger.

2. The Current Aimlessness

It has become clear that the question of goals is crucial. Both man's nature as a goal seeker and the total human situation in which he is involved bear witness to this fact. As Susanne K. Langer has reminded educators, this question of goals or "aims" probably constitutes "the most urgent philosophical problem in the whole pedagogical field today." [2]

In view of the general confusion, it is not surprising that modern education is conspicuous for its lack of any central aim or goal. Both Dewey and Maritain expressed concern about this matter. While the former insisted that "at the present time education has no great directive aim," [3] the latter charged that our educators are so fascinated by methods and the latest teaching techniques that the ultimate aim is "forgotten or discarded." [4]

The chief trouble is not so much that there are no aims or goals, but rather that there are too many which, in the absence of any *basic* unifying aim, make for confusion, drift, chaos. In short, the great need is unity in terms of some comprehensive goal which will give a sense of direction to the educational process as a whole.

The present condition cannot continue forever. John Wild has warned that "civilization cannot endure in chaos." Sooner or later, if "reason fails," the appeal will be made to force, which can only serve to stifle "freedom and creative endeavor." [5]

2. In her article, "On the Relations Between Philosophy and Education," in the *Harvard Educational Review*, XXVI (Spring, 1956), 141.

3. John Dewey, "Some Aspects of Modern Education," in John S. Brubacher (ed.), *Eclectic Philosophy of Education*, p. 178

4. Jacques Maritain, *Education at the Crossroads*, p. 3.

5. John Wild, "Philosophy of Education in the West: A Desperate Need," *Harvard*

In this dilemma what must be done? Obviously, the time has come for educators to cease congratulating themselves merely on their ability to raise questions without making a real effort to find reasonable answers. Answers must be found in terms of a sense of direction. Amid our welter of techniques and methods and petty aims, we must set our sights according to some great overarching idea comprehensive enough to embrace all the lesser ends.

Undoubtedly this is difficult. In the final analysis, it will even mean facing those ultimate metaphysical and religious problems which many contemporary educators and philosophers have tried to dodge. All educational problems, if carried far enough, always and everywhere lead to ultimates; and the failure to face them implies both a false sense of modesty and a lack of courage. John Wild has truly said that the chief task before philosophers is the formulation of a world view which may serve as a "guiding purpose" to our "disintegrated culture." [6]

Of course, the primary purpose of this present venture is philosophy of education rather than metaphysics as such. Still, the philosophy of education, in the final analysis, cannot avoid metaphysics, particularly when it tries to deal with the nature of mind, the question of freedom, and this matter of goals. We shall at least, then, as we have already done, point in the general direction where we believe the truth may lie.

3. In Search of a Criterion

The existence of so many competing and conflicting aims makes it exceedingly difficult to single out an overarching goal—if there is such. How then shall we proceed? Our first task is to find an adequate criterion—if such is available. Of course, since all things human are fallible, we cannot expect absolute accuracy or infallibility. This insistence that they possess something infallible—whether in terms of a leader, a party, a book, or an institution—

Educational Review, XXVI (Spring, 1956), 181. This issue of the Review is very important to the problem in hand.

6. Ibid., p. 183.

is the mistake which the authoritarians make. In other words, our search is not for an infallible criterion, but rather for the most adequate possible under our human conditions and circumstances.

Now it became clear in Chapter V that the most illuminating approach to philosophy of education is by way of the synoptic method which commends itself by its appeal to *reason* and by its very inclusiveness. This likewise suggests the most adequate criterion available, namely, reason itself in the very highest sense of the word.[7] Consequently, our criterion includes at least the following basic aspects: (1) *critical analysis* (no aim or goal must be accepted at face value, since appearances often lie, but must be taken apart and carefully scrutinized); (2) *consistency* (any goal deemed worthy of being final or ultimate must be consistent both with all the significant and relevant facts and also with all lesser goals and principles—insofar as they have proved themselves); (3) *inclusiveness* (besides passing the tests of critical analysis and logical consistency, the general or comprehensive goal must be capable of embracing all the relevant and significant facts in the total situation and establish meaningful relationships among them, as well as embracing all that is valid in all the lesser or partial goals); and (4) *fruitfulness* (instead of leading from more to less, it must lead from less to more, that is, awaken human creativity by its suggestiveness).

This fourth aspect—fruitfulness—requires further comment. That it is in harmony with scientific method is clear. Among other things, what the creative scientist, who is not afraid to venture beyond the frontiers of the known, requires of a good hypothesis is that it be fruitful in terms of stimulating further inquiry. Thus Newton's theory, Einstein's theory, and Darwin's theory proved profoundly stimulating.

One other thing needs to be clarified. Although ignorance of certain facts may involve failure at any time (that is, until these

7. Reason, as used here, is similar to what Edgar Sheffield Brightman calls "coherence"; see his *Introduction to Philosophy*, pp. 68-74. In this age of anti-intellectualism and irrationalism, the great need is the application of reason to educational problems.

facts are available), the appeal to reason, as here defined, is inevitable—it really constitutes a kind of supreme court. Along with other things, unlike dogmatic authority or mere intuition, it has the means both of going forward in search of the missing facts and, after having found them, of going back and correcting its own mistakes. Nor can there be any doubt that reason underlies all that is known as scientific method. In what lies ahead, then, an effort shall be made to apply our criterion as far as it is possible. Thus, while the end product will fall far short of being, in any sense, an absolute solution, it will at least point in that general direction.

4. A Critique of Ten Important Goals

Fortunately, in this vital matter, we need not start from scratch. At the same time, however, it is in no sense necessary to begin with some rigid metaphysical scheme. Perhaps, then, it is best to begin, in the light of our criterion, with a scrutiny of certain aims or goals which have been widely held and which still have defenders. Even though it is really impossible to render full justice within the limits of this venture, we shall at least attempt the best possible under the circumstances.

a) TRANSMISSION OF THE CULTURAL HERITAGE

This is certainly the very oldest goal. While in primitive societies it involves little more than the transmission of skills, beliefs, and traditions based on a very limited circumscribed experience and outlook, today it may mean nothing less than the transmission of the richest and most significant elements of man's total heritage. Thus in Chapter I we gave it due recognition as an outstanding aspect of the educational process itself. Similarly in Chapter V it was emphasized as constituting one of the outstanding contributions of essentialism. This transmission of the wisdom of the ages is also the chief motive behind the Great Books program as developed by Robert Maynard Hutchins and his followers.

Although this aim or goal is in accord with our criterion in some respects, yet critical analysis reveals its weaknesses. Since it is not inclusive enough, when it is pursued as the one and only goal, it is not fruitful in the highest sense of the word. Whenever transmission of the cultural heritage is central, due justice is not given to creativity, spontaneity, and novelty. Thus education tends to become mechanical, fossilized, and sterile, and intellectual freedom is in danger of being stifled by the dead weight of the past. No wonder that pragmatists, progressives, existentialists, and even many essentialists, especially the personalists, have protested vigorously. All analysts who have any concern for educational problems whatsoever would also be critical. While transmission of the cultural heritage must always remain a vital phase of any comprehensive goal, it is obvious that it can never be that goal.

b) CITIZENSHIP

This goal is also far from new, since it was the ideal of Greek and Roman education. So far as thinkers are concerned, Aristotle stressed it in the ancient world and Thomas Aquinas during the Middle Ages. Among Protestants, Luther was one of the strongest advocates of the "citizen ideal" and even Comenius favored it to a certain extent.[8] Today, with the rise of nationalism in much of the world, this ideal is still altogether too dominant.

That it still has considerable value, especially when construed in terms of democracy at its best, there can be no doubt. After all, along with the family, the church, and the school, the state constitutes one of man's basic institutions—without which chaos would reign. Besides, citizenship—particularly when free from nationalism in the narrow sense of the word—lifts the individual out of his natural self-centeredness and makes possible those habits of cooperation upon which the public welfare rests.

Nevertheless, in the light of our criterion, citizenship has many weaknesses, limitations, and is easily subject to abuse. It has often degenerated into blind nationalism, chauvinism, and militarism.

8. On the development of the ideal of citizenship, see James Mulhern, A History of Education, pp. 371-72.

Under the guise of this ideal, the most ruthless dictators have fastened themselves upon the immature, stealing their loyalty for their own unscrupulous purposes.

So far as the present scene is concerned, nothing is more obvious than the fact that "patriotism is not enough." If the chief aim of education is the making of "good" citizens, that is, jealous devotees of the many petty, rival nations which constitute the modern pantheon, then mankind is doomed. In a world that needs unity as badly as ours, in spite of its value as a limited objective embraced within a larger whole, citizenship must be transcended. If mankind is to survive during this very crucial period of the Nuclear Age, a global consciousness must be created. Time is running out.

c) DISCIPLINE

Education for discipline is likewise ancient and venerable. Educationally speaking, however, the word has meant not less than four things. First of all, it has meant discipline in terms of punishment for some infraction of the rules. Often this has included corporal punishment. Second, there is what is known as moral discipline: teaching the young to exercise self-control in terms of moral principles. Third, it has implied the disciplined mind, that is, the ability to master subject matter and to think systematically and logically. Finally, it has meant discipline in the narrow, formal sense. This latter demands further explanation since it has had such an interesting history.

Discipline in this sense goes back to the old faculty psychology: the theory that the mind is composed of a number of more or less independent faculties or abilities, each of which may be perfected through certain types of training. This led to the belief that geometry is very useful in training the reason, history the memory, drawing the ability to observe, etc. Underlying this old theory is, of course, the idea that, once a certain faculty is trained, the general habit acquired in the process is available everywhere and under all circumstances. In short, the ability to reason acquired in the study of geometry is applicable to politics or theology or to any other field of discourse.

While the ghost of the old theory still lingers in some quarters, the old faculty psychology, as everyone knows, has been generally discredited. Whatever else may be true of the human mind, it is not composed of a number of different departments functioning somewhat separately. Instead it seems to constitute a dynamic unity ever striving toward greater integration and harmony.

Yet, in their reactions to the excesses of the old theory of learning, some of our experimental psychologists such as Thorndike, seem to have gone to the opposite extreme. They have even gone so far as to insist that no "transfer of learning" takes place in any general way. Since, however, today a more moderate view seems to have possession of the field, this controversy need not occupy our attention any further.[9]

In terms of our criterion, as far as discipline as an aim is concerned, two things are evident. First, as one goal among many and as a significant aspect of a more inclusive goal, it still has an honored place. The havoc wrought by the excesses of progressivism is ample proof of this. Unless parents and teachers begin stressing discipline, the young barbarians of which we already have too many will take over and wreck our social order. All that is needed is some leader like Hitler to arise. They would make splendid storm troopers.

Second, in spite of its necessity, there are three good reasons why it should never be regarded as the chief goal. To begin with, it is not inclusive enough. Closely related is the fact that it constitutes primarily a means toward an end, not an end in itself. As legs are disciplined to win races, so minds are disciplined to think effectively and profoundly. Finally, if it were regarded as the chief end, the chances are that it would be abused: that is, there

9. On the doctrine of formal discipline and on the debate over "transfer of learning," see the following: Allport, *Personality: A Psychological Interpretation*, pp. 259-85; William C. Bagley, *Education, Crime, and Social Progress*, pp. 126 ff.; Frederick Eby, *The Development of Modern Education*, p. 303; and Adolph E. Meyer, *The Development of Education in the Twentieth Century*, pp. 479-80.

might even be a return not only to a stress on formalism, but even to the inhuman treatment of the learner.

d) RELIGION

Religion constituted the chief goal in ancient Israel, in ancient India, and in medieval Europe. While it is still considered important today, it is far from central—having lost its central place in Western education with the passing of the medieval Christian world view. Consequently, the West has no "great overarching structure of ideas." [10]

In certain ways, religion as the goal is more comprehensive and adequate than any of the others discussed thus far. This is especially true since the idea of God, at least in the monotheistic sense, is one of the most universal ideas which man has conceived. Again, the great civilizations have gotten most of their chief structural ideas from the great religions. No one has stressed the role of religion more than Toynbee;[11] and Hocking has even gone so far as to insist that religion is "the *mother of the Arts*." [12] At any rate, in Chapter II it became evident that Western civilization is greatly indebted to the Hebrew-Christian tradition in general and to the church in particular.

When we examine religion, however, in terms of our criterion, insurmountable difficulties begin to appear. In spite of the attractiveness and the advantages of the religious ideal as an all-inclusive goal in certain respects, and whatever may be true in the future when mankind may have achieved far greater religious unity than we have attained, today it presents obstacles which cannot be overcome any time soon. In view of the many different religions, sects, and cults, there is, first of all, the question as to which one should be selected out of this welter. There is also the danger of dogmatism if certain authoritarian groups should ever

10. On this point, see John Wild, "Philosophy of Education in the West," in *Harvard Educational Review*, XXVI, 181.

11. See particularly Arnold J. Toynbee, *Reconsiderations*, pp. 68-102.

12. William Ernest Hocking, *The Meaning of God in Human Experience*, p. 14.

become powerful enough to dominate the situation. The truth of the matter is that religion as it is usually found, that is, in the rather narrow, sectarian sense, is not comprehensive enough to serve as the all-embracing goal. There is also the problem of the nonreligious and the anti-religious groups who constitute a rather large section of our population. They would certainly oppose any attempt to establish and to implement any such goal. In the light of these difficulties, it is clear that religion as such cannot function as the all-inclusive goal.

This does not mean that religion is to be omitted from the final end or all-inclusive goal. It must, indeed, occupy a *very important place* as an aspect of any educational scheme worthy of the name. This will become clearer in the chapter on creativity in religion.

e) SECULARISM

Over against religion with its transcendental claims stands secularism. As a matter of fact, it is dominant in the West today —as well as in the Soviet Union. In its milder forms, however, it is not necessarily hostile to religion as such, but rather finds expression through certain lesser goals, some of which may be judged good, others neutral, and a few pernicious. Amid this vast array, we find such things as health, devotion to science (especially in terms of technology), vocationalism, athleticism, and, finally, the gaining of wealth, prestige, and power for their own sakes.

Undoubtedly, a sane secularism has often operated as a corrective to a morbid otherworldliness; and, for all that we may know, it may do so again. Moreover, this milder form of secularism can even claim a certain amount of support from the great Hebrew-Christian tradition; for neither Judaism nor Christianity is basically ascetic: that is, in the extreme sense of a certain contempt for the flesh and the world. Indeed, in the Scriptures God himself is represented as taking delight in all his works, including the material, and pronouncing them "very good" (Gen. 1:31). It must also be said in favor of the milder secularism that such aims as health, science for the purpose of conquering nature and thus enhancing human life, and vocationalism in the larger sense of self-realization and the efficient discharge of social responsibilities are so important that they must have a place in any comprehensive goal worthy of the name.

Yet, in the light of our criterion, secularism is inadequate on two counts: it is not inclusive enough, and, since it may dry up the springs of creativity through its emphasis on the tangible, it may lead to unfruitfulness in the end. Since it tends to neglect the transcendental, its horizons are altogether too limited; it offers man no infinite ideal. Worse still, it easily degenerates into vulgar forms of materialism and mechanism. Finally, while the unphilosophical forms are inclined to be very shallow and superficial, the more philosophical tend to become just as dogmatic and rigid as any authoritarian religious system has ever been. Fascism and Marxianism (at its worst) are the two best examples.

f) CULTURE FOR ITS OWN SAKE

This view of the educational goal is closely related to what has been called a liberal education. In addition, it serves as a standing protest against a narrow, utilitarian pragmatism which threatens to reduce education to the bread and butter level. It also remains true, even in a pragmatic culture like ours, that disinterestedness must always find a place in education as well as in life. A refined taste has an intrinsic value all of its own. Acquaintance with the world's greatest literature, art, music, and drama is priceless. Yet many Americans, in spite of having passed through college, prefer jazz to Beethoven and a cheap movie to Shakespeare.

Important as culture for its own sake is, nevertheless, as the only goal, it is insufficient.[13] Education based primarily on this ideal is always in danger of becoming purely ornamental, and, therefore, unfruitful. It may also produce an ivory tower attitude toward life and its pressing problems. Worst of all, it might lead to the establishment of a snobbish intellectual aristocracy reveling in aesthetic

13. For the values as well as the dangers of the above, see John S. Brubacher, *Modern Philosophies of Education*, pp. 173-76.

delights while, at the same time, despising the masses of workers who have to sweat and toil, and without whose work the scornful intellectual could not exist. After all, if anything resembling democracy and the good life is to be realized for all that desire it, there must be a union of head and hand. Let us remember that the greatest weakness of European education in the past, like that of ancient Greece, has been its snobbishness with all the attendant evils.

g) KNOWLEDGE FOR ITS OWN SAKE

Knowledge for its own sake is closely akin to culture for its own sake. Among other things, it is also directly related to the idea of a liberal education. Like so many important matters in education and otherwise, this emphasis had its beginning with the Greeks. Aristotle, interestingly enough, regarded reason as the highest human capacity, and the contemplation of truth as the ultimate and final aim of human life—as did his great teacher, Plato, before him. Since God himself spends eternity "thinking on thinking," in contemplation man is really imitating Deity and thus realizing his own highest potentiality.[14]

Many centuries later medieval thinkers took this idea from Aristotle, so that it became an aspect of the monastic ideal. This is especially true of the more philosophically inclined. Thus, while Thomas Aquinas taught that the Christian must not neglect human affairs when "necessity" is involved, yet, like Augustine before him, he certainly held that the contemplative life is superior to the active.[15] In modern times this view found supreme expression in John Cardinal Newman's classic, *The Idea of a University*. Indeed, he went so far as to say that "Liberal Education" itself consists in "the cultivation of the intellect" with "intellectual excellence" as its ultimate aim.[16]

Even though closely related to culture for its own sake, this aim, since it stands in contrast not only to crass materialism and

14. *Metaphysics*, Book XII, 1074*b*, 9-1075*a*, 10.
15. See *The Summa Theologica* in Anton C. Pegis (ed.), *The Basic Writings of Saint Thomas Aquinas*, II, 474.
16. See John S. Brubacher (ed.), *Eclectic Philosophy of Education*, p. 181.

utilitarianism, but also to all forms of hedonism including the most refined, has even more to commend it. Furthermore, it stands as a corrective to behaviorism and all other psychologies based largely upon the study of animal behavior and reductive philosophies which debase man by leveling him down to fit their schemes; for, unlike these, it stresses reason as the highest and most truly human quality.

Besides all this, as in the case of aesthetic appreciation to which it is akin, there is a real joy in knowledge for its own sake. More than this, it serves to satisfy a kind of divine curiosity and craving within man which lies at the basis of much of his creativity. So far as science itself is concerned, it is this kind of disinterestedness that really constitutes the inner secret of its greatest discoveries. Before the more pragmatical-minded technologist can play his part, he must be willing to sit at the feet of his more theoretically and philosophically minded colleague. A good case in point is Einstein himself, whose contributions in theoretical physics helped to open up the vast nuclear field. Later, in the section on creativity, we shall return to this important matter.

Yet, when subjected to critical analysis, it becomes clear at once that knowledge for its own sake suffers from certain serious defects and inadequacies. Chief among these is the fact that, like Aristotle's God, it may cause the thinker to retreat from the world. When the human situation becomes desperate, the insidious temptation appears to use this as a means of escape.

There is cause to believe that many of our contemporary philosophers who bury themselves in the trivialities of logical analysis and semantics, and, likewise, many of our theologians who revel in the transcendent and are often hopelessly obscure, are making use of this device. The decisive answer today—always and everywhere—is that retirement to ivory towers now may mean that tomorrow no ivory towers will be left standing; nor are there likely to be any philosophers or theologians.[17]

17. For an interesting criticism of knowledge for its own sake, see the section from Clarence Irving Lewis in Brubacher, *Eclectic Philosophy of Education*, pp. 181-82.

Closely related to all this is also the fact that the pursuance of knowledge for its own sake may actually have a decidedly dehumanizing effect. This was certainly true of some of the medieval monks. It is likewise true of many scientists. Darwin himself lamented the fact that his zeal for science had transformed his mind into a kind of machine "for grinding out scientific laws," so that he had practically lost his sense of aesthetic appreciation.

At any rate, like most of the other goals which we have considered, this one limits the scope of the total educational enterprise altogether too much. Besides knowledge for its own sake, there are many other aspects which must be given a place. Among these, as we have observed before, bodily health is most certainly important. Many an earnest student has broken down simply because he was careless of his health. I once saw a pitiful case in a mental institution, and I was informed that the man was a priest who combined excessive fasting with long hours of strenuous intellectual activity. As the supreme goal then, this ideal fails both in terms of practical effectiveness and inclusiveness. Knowledge, after all, must also be for humanity's sake, not just for its own sake.

h) GROWTH

In the last chapter it became clear that both the pragmatists and the progressives tend to look upon growth as the goal of the educational process; but, since an attempt was made to evaluate it there, we need not dwell on it here.[18]

i) METAPHYSICS

Appalled by the materialism, the triviality, the irrationality, and the general aimlessness of contemporary American education, Robert Maynard Hutchins has proposed metaphysics as the ultimate unifying aim. Following in the footsteps of Aristotle, he reasons that, since "the aim of the higher education is wisdom" and since metaphysics is really "the highest wisdom" (because it deals

18. See Ch. V, pp. 89-90 and n. 16.

with first principles), this field affords our best basis for unity.[19] In terms of higher education, this would mean that all students, regardless of their vocational interests, would receive exactly the same philosophical grounding. In anticipation of criticism he insists, however, that he is not contending for any "specific" metaphysical system, but rather that students would receive the same thorough grounding in metaphysics as such.[20]

Here Hutchins undoubtedly has his finger on certain basic weaknesses of American education, especially its lack of unity and its brazen unconcern for ultimates. That there must be a greater interest in metaphysics in our colleges and universities, we would be the last to deny. Indeed, one of our chief criticisms of John Dewey included his apparent contempt for metaphysics and his desire to banish it. Moreover, we have contended that one of modern man's greatest needs is an adequate world view—which would certainly involve metaphysics.

Still, while fully recognizing the role of metaphysics in higher education and the necessity for an adequate world view, there is some doubt about making it the final all-embracing goal. To begin with, there is the danger of trying to impose a specific system. As a matter of fact, Hutchins' critics have not been slow in pointing out that, in spite of his insistence otherwise, he does seem to have a specific type in mind, namely, a synthesis of the systems of Plato, Aristotle, and Thomas Aquinas. Moreover, it has been contended that, in spite of the importance of these thinkers, undue concentration on them would of necessity produce something of a backward look. This is, in fact, well illustrated by the Great Books program as launched by Hutchins and his colleagues. An analysis has shown that not less than three fourths of the material was written before 1800, and two thirds before 1700.[21]

19. Robert Maynard Hutchins, *The Higher Learning in America* (New Haven: Yale University Press, 1936), p. 98 ff.
20. *Ibid.*, p. 105.
21. See Meyer, *The Development of Education in the Twentieth Century*, p. 61, n. 23.

In the light of these facts, there is real point to the criticisms of the realists that Hutchins and his fellow neoscholastics are unwilling to look at the real world. Similarly idealists are not altogether wrong in their insistence that the claims of the full personality are neglected. Perhaps most telling of all, however, are the criticisms of the pragmatists and of the reconstructionist, Brameld, who charge Hutchins and his disciples with marked reactionary tendencies.[22] In short, Hutchins' view lacks inclusiveness, in the light of critical analysis, and it is not likely to be fruitful in the highest sense of the word.

j) SELF-REALIZATION

Among what may be called the classic goals, self-realization is in many respects the most significant. As usually understood, it means the harmonious development of all of man's essential powers and capacities—physical, social, esthetic, intellectual, moral, and spiritual. Thus, it aims to be synoptic.

All man's numerous capacities, however, are not given equal consideration. The distinction, ever since the days of Plato and Aristotle, has been made between the higher and most truly human and the lower—those which man tends to share with the brute. In other words, the former are given the place of honor as worthy of ruling over the latter. Personality is conceived as something of a hierarchy, that is, as a rational system or cosmos. In terms of education, then, while some attention would be given to all important aspects of man's nature, including the physical, special efforts would be made to perfect the higher capacities. Hence self-realization is also known as perfectionism.

At any rate, this ideal has had a long and honored history. The emphasis on reason and the subordination of the lower aspects of man to the higher, although developed by Plato and Aristotle, was also adopted by the Stoics. It was the latter, in fact, who insisted that man must live according to nature; but, instead of meaning a

22. *Ibid.*, p. 62. For Brameld's criticisms, see his *Education for the Emerging Age*, pp. 43-46.

return to something primitive as Rousseau did many centuries later, this meant that, as God, the rational Soul of the universe, governs nature (which constitutes his body) by reason, so man likewise must govern his own nature by reason—the divine spark within him.[23]

It is interesting to note that the stress of perfectionism on harmony and moderation can be found in the teachings of Confucius as well as in the systems of the great teachers of Greece. In its modern forms, in the West at least, it is, of course, greatly indebted to the Hebrew-Christian tradition, especially so far as the principle of the dignity and worth of personality is concerned; though this element is also present in the Platonic and Stoic traditions. Suffice it to say that perfectionism, in certain respects at least, seems to represent a fusion of the best that Greece and Palestine had to offer.[24]

Here, then, in many respects, we seem to have found the goal that we have been seeking. Self-realization or perfectionism is not only deeply rooted, in one form or another, in all the great traditions, but, at the same time, it is also still widely held today—particularly by idealists. Moreover, it has much in common with ethical humanism (which must not be confused with theological humanism since it does not necessarily deny God's existence), that common bond which seems to link and relate, in one way or another, all the leading contemporary philosophies of education.

Besides all this, unlike some current philosophies, it sees the deeper implications of ethical humanism. This simply means that

23. In spite of this strong self-realizationist element, the Stoics were primarily formalists in ethics—Kantians before Kant.

24. On self-realization, the following are important: Arthur C. Fleshman, in Brubacher, *Eclectic Philosophy of Education*, p. 182; Charles H. Patterson *Moral Standards* (second edition; New York: The Ronald Press Co., 1957), pp. 242-304—this constitutes one of the best recent accounts; James Bissett Pratt, *Reason in the Art of Living* (New York: The Macmillan Co., 1950), pp. 85-99; J. C. Friedrich von Schiller, *Letters upon the Aesthetic Education of Man*, in Charles Eliot (ed.), *The Harvard Classics* (New York: P. F. Collier & Son Co., 1910), XXXII, 209-95; and Radoslav A. Tsanoff, *Ethics* (revised edition; New York: Harper & Brothers, 1955), pp. 119-40. As all philosophers know, perfectionism is especially significant in ethics, since it represents one of the great historic schools which is still very much alive today.

perfectionism includes a profound understanding of the higher reaches of personality. Thus it tends more in the direction of idealism and even theism rather than naturalism. It also has much in common with the stress which existentialists like Marcel and Jaspers place on the dignity of personality. Moreover, it aims to be synoptic and inclusive.

Yet it is by no means free from faults. Brubacher speaks of certain "ambiguities," among which are its inability to state what potentialities are to be developed fully, and its failure to designate precisely the nature of the self to be realized.[25] Even more significant is Pratt's criticism that the term self-realization not only seems to suggest egoism and hedonism, but that it also seems to rule out self-sacrifice. In fact, he does not think that it gives us much light concerning the "fundamental moral principle" involved in ethical thought and activity.[26] To this the perfectionists may make the reply that this is an area in which precision is impossible, but that, under the circumstances, self-realization does seem to offer the best clues. Furthermore, they may insist that, when they speak of the self, the larger universal self, finding expression through the higher reaches of reason and love, is envisaged.

To overcome some of the difficulties involved in the term *self-realization*, Brameld coined the combination "social-self-realization." [27] The only real difference is that he tends to stress the social aspects of the self more than the perfectionists. Indeed, like Dewey, he seems to be influenced so much by the *Zeitgeist* that, at times at least, he overstresses the social at the expense of the personal.[28]

25. See his *Modern Philosophies of Education*, pp. 106-108.

26. Pratt, *Reason in the Art of Living*, p. 91. While Pratt's criticisms are not as devastating as they look at first blush, they do have a point which must be taken seriously.

27. See *Education for the Emerging Age*, pp. 118 ff., 168-210; also his *Patterns of Educational Philosophy*, pp. 480 ff.

28. In justice to Brameld, it must be pointed out that there are times when he does attempt to do full justice to the personal aspects of the self as over against the social; see his *Patterns of Educational Philosophy*, p. 122. He is not a behaviorist.

In other words, he does not emphasize that solitariness which is so essential in enabling the thinker to forge those ideas destined to become a power in the world. Immanuel Kant is a case in point. It has also become clear that reconstructionism, in spite of its merits, has little if any place for the transcendental, being basically naturalistic and to a certain extent relativistic: that is, particularly in its view of truth in terms of "social consensus." [29]

Whatever its weaknesses, perfectionism seems to be more all-inclusive and comprehensive in terms of its goal than all the others proposed—including that of Brameld. It aims at wholeness; it seeks to perfect man's highest and most truly human capacities; it recognizes the place and significance of the transcendental; and, whatever may have been true of certain of its classical formulations, some modern types do stress the social and the universal implications of the self. In short, as far as our own formulation of the final and all-inclusive goal is concerned, at least a broad, deep, and solid foundation has been laid upon which we may build. Perfectionism has immense potentiality.

5. Aspects of an Adequate Goal

The comprehensive, all-inclusive goal which we propose is largely the child of perfectionism and resembles its parent in many ways. Still, there are differences, among which is the difference in name. In other words, the terms *self-realization and perfectionism* are subject to serious misunderstandings, since the former suggests egoism while the latter sounds a bit stilted. Moreover, it has already become clear that Brameld's term "social-self-realization" tends to overemphasize the self's social aspects.

Really, in the final analysis, the goal which we envision is something of a combination of the ideal of self-realization and "social-self-realization." At the same time, however, while it is conceived as more social than the former, it also seeks to avoid the defects of the latter—that is, particularly its overemphasis on the social to the neglect of other vital aspects. For the lack of better terms

29. See *ibid.*, p. 456.

then, we shall designate the all-inclusive goal or aim as the *humanization of man*.

This concept serves us well for three reasons. First of all, it is surprisingly suggestive. To begin with, it suggests that, while at birth the child is not fully human, yet, by virtue of its unique capacities (which the brute does not possess), it is at least potentially human—a candidate for humanity. It also suggests that education is basically a refining, civilizing process. In the second place, it is clear that this concept of the goal is in harmony with that *ethical humanism* which serves as the common bond between the various conflicting educational philosophies. Finally, there seems to be nothing in this concept which conflicts with our criterion in terms of *critical analysis, consistency, inclusiveness,* and *fruitfulness.* We shall now proceed to clarify the goal in terms of its chief aspects.

a) THE DIGNITY OF MAN AS PERSON

Education as the *humanization of man* is, above all else, decidedly personalistic. This means a rejection of all behavioristic notions of the self. While animal psychology can throw light on human behavior, it cannot tell us much concerning the higher self-conscious, reflective processes; those distinctively human qualities which set man apart from the rest of creation.

Mind, then, must be understood primarily in terms of the conscious purposeful activities of a real self which appears to be something more than the sum total of its organic processes or the total effects of its environment, since it can stand over against both and, to a large extent, control them in the light of its own purposes.[30] While these conscious processes of the self may involve behavior, much more is present; indeed, behavior is often nothing more than deceptive surface appearance. In other words, there is nothing to prevent me from acting one way while my thoughts

---

30. For views of mind or personality similar to the above, see Allport, *Personality: A Psychological Interpretation,* pp. 549-66; and Herman Harrell Horne, *The Democratic Philosophy of Education,* p. 421.

are just the opposite. I may be speaking fair words to you while secretly, in my thoughts which you cannot see, I may be plotting your downfall. Furthermore, except for certain simple reactions which are mechanical and certain deliverances of the unconscious, the processes of self-conscious thought determine behavior, especially at the higher levels—as, for example, when a genius such as Einstein formulates a theory and explains it to his colleagues.

After all, to a remarkable degree, mind can transcend and control the body. Whatever, in the final analysis, the relations of the mind and brain may be, at least one thing is clear: without self-conscious minds, there could not be any awareness of brains whatsoever. The same also applies to the realm of the unconscious; man, in truth, would be entirely subject to the chaotic impulses emerging from its dark depths if it were not for the evaluating, organizing, and directing capacities of self-conscious mind. The latter is likewise presupposed in all scientific experiments as well as in philosophic reflection. In discussing creativity, we shall return to this vital matter of the nature of the mind and self.

Considerations such as the above naturally suggest the worth and dignity of personality.[31] Although man as a creature is undoubtedly influenced and to a large extent conditioned by many factors—mechanical, chemical, biological, subconscious, and social —to a certain degree he is capable of transcending them: that is, in terms of understanding, evaluating, and directing them. If this were not true and he were nothing more than an aspect of the various factors mentioned above, he might be treated impersonally as a thing, or subpersonally as a mere animal. This tendency, in fact, is always present when we deal with our fellows. If, however, man truly transcends impersonal processes and things, then he really has superior status and must be treated in this light.

---

31. Some naturalists, while denying that personality has any aspects which transcend nature, believe in human dignity. Indeed, Roy Wood Sellars speaks of "the *absolute principle* of the moral dignity of human beings." See Roy Wood Sellars, V. J. McGill, and Marvin Farber (eds.), *Philosophy for the Future* (New York: The Macmillan Co., 1949), p. 72.

Finally, it must be made clear that this larger view of man fits in much better than anything that naturalistic humanism can devise, not only with our heritage from Greece and Palestine, but also with the basic concepts and implications of democracy. As a matter of fact, even though we cannot be dogmatic here, it may well be, as the personalists insist, that human personality—in terms of self-conscious mind and will—affords our best clue to the dark riddle of existence. It is reasonable to hold that basically the universe is more likely to be like its highest products than like its lowest.

b) WHOLENESS OR INCLUSIVENESS

Education in terms of the *humanization of man* aims at wholeness and inclusiveness in the most comprehensive sense possible. Like self-realization, it seeks nothing less than the development of the whole man involving all the creative aspects of his total nature —physical, unconscious (how the latter can be trained within limits will be discussed later), social, esthetic, intellectual, moral, and spiritual. Moreover, the primary emphasis is on the development of these capacities in terms of man's quest for Truth, Beauty, and Goodness.

Similarly this concern for wholeness and inclusiveness seeks to embrace the values in all the ten goals that have been examined. As far as the first—*transmission of the cultural heritage*—is concerned, it is obvious that man cannot develop apart from, and in total ignorance of, his vast human heritage. Without this he could never rise to the human level and attain human dignity. He would be in a worse state than the brutes.

The second—*citizenship*—especially in terms of democracy in the very highest sense of the word, involves loyalties and values which are significant. After all, nations will be here for a long time. Many new nations, perhaps too many, have just come into being. Be that as it may, except where a narrow nationalism infects it, genuine love for one's own country, like love for one's home, need not conflict with a higher, universal, global loyalty.

Again, without the third objective—*discipline*—man could never attain that self-control so essential in learning, he could never successfully apply what he has learned, and he could never become truly creative.

Likewise the fourth end or goal—*religion*—cannot be ignored without loss. The truth of the matter seems to be that it constitutes a basic human capacity which, along with certain others, distinguishes man from the brute. Thus a *totally* nonreligious man— if there is such—would be to a certain extent less than human. It is also true that religion, as we shall show in a later chapter, has been amazingly creative. Besides furnishing many of the basic, structural ideas for the great civilizations in general, it must not be forgotten that it was high religion which awakened our ancestors from a long night of barbarism to an amazing creativity.

Nevertheless, if man is to be truly human, *secularism,* since it safeguards certain values, must not be ignored. Among these values are health, the scientific quest, and a sane regard for the present life. Secularism also tends to check the excesses of religious zealots and, in terms of the secular state, is able to perform certain important functions which a theocracy could not.

Again, since man cannot be truly human without refined tastes, *culture for its own sake* must be emphasized. Similarly, without *knowledge for its own sake,* not only would we lose the joy of knowing, but creativity in the very highest sense would also be dealt a shattering blow. Likewise the eighth—*growth*—as conceived by Dewey and others, by tying education in with the life process, keeps it from becoming stale and reaching a dead end.

In an age when even philosophers have often betrayed philosophy by stifling the search for unity and meaning on the vast cosmic scale, there can be no question concerning the significance of the ninth—*metaphysics.* Like religion, it constitutes one of those basic capacities which distinguishes man from the brute. It also means high adventure and creativity in a confused age in search of an adequate world view. Finally, the values of the tenth—*self-*

realization or *perfectionism*—are so obvious and so closely related to the goal we are discussing that any further consideration at this juncture would mean unnecessary repetition.

c) EXCELLENCE

While seeking the harmonious development of all of man's creative capacities, the supreme goal also involves excellence. In relation to education, excellence means two things in the light of our chief end or goal. First of all, it means, as it did for John Cardinal Newman, "intellectual excellence." This implies seeking truth with all the resources at our command and a profound dissatisfaction with anything short of the very best possible performance in terms of intellectual endeavor. It signifies that straining at our limits which leads to true greatness. All real scholars and teachers, in the light of excellence, abhor all that is shoddy and mediocre. They desire nothing more than ever to surpass themselves.

Today America is all but lost in the fog of anti-intellectualism. This fog is partly the result of the rather narrow type of pragmatism inherited from pioneer days and even more due to the confusion that has gripped our world. This anti-intellectualism, strange as it may seem, is prevalent in education. A recent writer on the subject, after conducting a rather thorough investigation, reports that not only are teachers as a profession and schools of education rated rather lowly, but many educators really believe that "intellectual ability is sometimes irrevelant to teaching, sometimes downright dangerous," and just "one of many abilities" needed by teachers.[32]

In the name of excellence everything possible must be done to combat anti-intellectualism on all levels. It must again be thought more important to make good grades as a result of real achievement rather than to be popular. Teachers, above all others, must

32. James D. Koerner, *The Miseducation of American Teachers*, p. 47.

find one of their greatest satisfactions in good teaching and writing based on sound scholarship.[33]

Closely related to "intellectual excellence" and in accordance with our goal, is the second and broader meaning of excellence: the attempt to perfect, not only the intellect, but, along with it, all the rest of man's creative capacities. Not all can be scholars; all, nevertheless, except a small group of unfortunates, have some creativity. In short, every possible effort must be made to perfect the truly human capacities—including the appreciations and the affections—of every person whether he be a potential ditchdigger or a scientist or statesman.

Above all else, every possible attempt must be made to banish ignorance. This is especially important in a democracy where the ditchdigger may also help to create public opinion, and where his vote will count as much as that of any intellectual. Democracies decay where the people are kept in ignorance.

d) SOCIAL RESPONSIBILITY

An inclusive goal worthy of the name must embrace the concept of social responsibility.[34] Brameld is absolutely right at this point. While the masses are usually inclined to be intellectually lazy and apathetic, it is easy for the educated genius to become either socially indifferent or selfish. Indifference usually means the way of the ivory tower, that is, using education as a means of escape while others toil and sweat. In contrast, the selfish intellectual uses his knowledge and superior ability to grasp power or wealth or both. Thus Joseph Paul Goebbels, an expert in psychology, became Hitler's minister for propaganda and national enlightenment. Similarly many scientists today leave the colleges in order to do research for the military or for giant corporations which are forging the missiles—on a mass production basis—

---

33. For some interesting observations on excellence, see Bertrand Russell, *Education and the Good Life*, pp. 37-38.

34. For a sense of social responsibility based on knowledge and love, see *ibid.*, pp. 190-92.

which tomorrow may wipe mankind from the face of the earth. They prefer fat salaries rather than the task of teaching the gifted young men and women who may, if properly stimulated and encouraged, build a new world.

In order to counteract these unsocial tendencies of many of the educated, everything possible must be done in our secondary schools, in our colleges, and in our universities to inculcate a sense of social obligation. After all, since education is a gift from society to the individual, the latter owes something to the former and to future generations.

One of the hopeful signs of the times is the fact that an increasing number of our scientists are beginning to sense the peril. Shocked by the nuclear threat which they have helped to produce, they are beginning to come down from their ivory towers. An increasing number of intellectuals, especially students, are also making common cause with the Negroes and other exploited groups. The response of our youth to the Peace Corps is likewise encouraging. In fact, in spite of scattered attacks by reactionaries, the growth of the Peace Corps is heartening. At any rate, if knowledge is power, then a heavy responsibility rests on the educated.

e) CREATIVITY

Since Part Three is devoted to creativity, it is not necessary to discuss it here. There are two reasons why an entire section of this book is devoted to this aspect of our general goal: creativity is and always has been important; and today we seem to be witnessing something of a revival of interest in this factor.

6. Two Possible Objections

Two possible objections might be raised against a general, all-inclusive goal. First of all, some might question its value by insisting that only specific aims are worthy of serious consideration. They forget, of course, that such a goal can be exceedingly valuable in terms of perspective and general direction; and, since this is lacking so far as the contemporary scene is concerned, it meets a real need. If one does not have a sense of the general direction in which one must go, all the little paths may be just so many ways of going astray. A general goal, like the North Star, may keep us from drifting aimlessly. More than this, since it also represents the unattained and even the unattainable in terms of a great ideal, it may challenge us to venture beyond the frontier as so many hundreds of lesser aims would not. It might give us a great excelsior.

Again, if inclusive enough, it would not only embrace the lesser aims (as ours most certainly does), but it would also serve as something of a norm or standard by means of which to judge the value and relevance of the lesser aims. Thus it might save us from needless preoccupation with the trivial and the irrevelant. Needless to say this is a common failing today.

There may also be critics who will insist that no real proof has been offered to convince them that the proposed goal is the most adequate. If by proof they mean absolute certainty in terms of demonstration, we will have to plead guilty. They need to be reminded, however, that here, as elsewhere, the most that can be hoped for is probability in terms of that which is the most reasonable in the light of all the facts.

Moreover, the chances are that, if these critics were called upon to offer a better alternative, they would attempt to do so either in terms of one of the more limited objectives or in terms of something not too far different from what has been attempted here. In short, the very inclusiveness of the goal that has been proposed is the best proof that can be offered for its adequacy. Therefore, while welcoming criticisms and suggestions concerning this very difficult question, we shall take the adequacy of this proposed solution for granted until shown otherwise. In the meantime an effort must be made to investigate this very important problem of creativity.

Part III

Perspectives for Creativity

VII

Creativity: Its Nature and Significance

1. Scope of the Inquiry

In spite of the decline of progressivism, nothing is more evident on the contemporary educational scene than the new interest in creativity. Getzels and Jackson report that of the 240 articles on "creativity" or "creativeness" that have appeared between 1927 and 1959, 20 per cent appeared during two years, namely, during 1958 and 1959. They also list a considerable number of books and various other publications dealing with the subject.[1] Moreover, the interest still seems to be high.

So far as this present venture is concerned, besides the frequent mentioning of the term in its various relationships, creativity received some consideration twice before. In Chapter I it was described broadly as one of the two significant aspects of the educational process seen in historic perspective. Likewise, in Chapter VI it was listed as an aspect of the general educational goal.

As the title of this chapter indicates, the aim is twofold. First of all, an attempt shall be made to define the term itself and to describe the basic human capacity involved in terms of its various characteristics. This will also mean a brief consideration of its relation both to intuition and the unconscious. The second aim,

1. See Jacob W. Getzels & Philip W. Jackson, *Creativity and Intelligence*, pp. 279-80, n. 16.

of course, is to show not only its relevance to these times, but also that it constitutes a necessity—even for bare survival.

This present chapter also serves as an introduction to this entire section. In the next chapter due consideration shall be given to the various obstructions to creativity. Then an effort shall be made to apply the concept of creativity to three vital disciplines, namely, science, religion, and philosophy. Here our purpose shall be not only to understand their nature, but also to reveal their potentialities in this age of confusion and crisis.

2. What Is Creativity?

Like all intangibles, creativity is very difficult to define. At this point, however, etymology may give us a hint. The term "creativity" is derived from the English word "create"—which in turn is derived from the Latin *creatus* constituting as it does the past participle of *creare* (to create). Basically it means to bring something into being, or to produce or originate something which did not exist before. As over against the process of merely putting things together, creativity involves *uniqueness* and *artistry*; and as such it is applied particularly to a certain capacity or ability resident in man—although it is by no means limited to the latter. Many, of course, see the highest manifestation of this capacity not in man, but rather in the Cosmic Mind or Will, that is, God. In short, creativity is that capacity which originates or at least is capable of originating something *unique, meaningful,* and *significant.* This is performed gracefully and artistically as well as skillfully.

First and foremost, creativity then means *originality* and *novelty.*[2] To these must also be added *variety.* The creative mind stands in sharp contrast to the merely reproductive or repetitive mind with its inclinations toward sameness; for, while the latter can memorize facts readily, it is surprisingly weak when it comes to the construction of something new—in terms of meaningful

2. John P. Wynne speaks of "the quality of creative originality" in his *Philosophies of Education,* p. 165.

patterns or adequate hypotheses—out of the deeper implications of these facts. Hence, since the creative mind is capable, by means of the play of the imagination upon experience, to entertain new ideas and thereby to transcend both the rigidness of custom and the stimulus of the immediate, it involves *resourcefulness* of a high order.

Nor is creativity in this sense limited to any one field of human endeavor. It involves all the great constructive fields. Great scientists, such as Newton, Darwin, and Einstein, face to face with a vast array of facts and theories both old and new, are able to grasp the relationships of these facts and by means of this insight to develop new and better hypotheses. Likewise the master musician, in the words of Robert Browning, is able "out of three sounds" to "frame" not merely "a fourth sound, but a star." Similarly painters like Rembrandt and poets like William Blake help us to see the glory of the commonplace as we have never seen it before. Thus Blake speaks of seeing

> . . . a world in a grain of sand,
> And a heaven in a wild flower.

Finally, the creative statesman, fully aware of what is at stake, instead of giving up when everyone else thinks the situation is impossible, is able to conceive new approaches that may not only prevent calamity now, but which may also actually mark a new direction—nothing short of a turning point in history.[3]

Closely related to the elements of originality, novelty, and variety, there is an interesting factor which many have observed, namely, a certain *freedom, spontaneity,* or *playfulness.* This playfulness is certainly clearly evident in many of Plato's dialogues, making them an added delight.[4] He plays with ideas like a cat with a mouse. Yet this playfulness, unlike that of the clown, is

3. On the creative element in relating facts and on the similarities of creativity in various fields, see Seymour M. Farber & Roger H. L. Wilson (eds.), *Man and Civilization: Control of the Mind; a Symposium* (New York: McGraw-Hill, 1961), p. 338.

4. This is especially true of the *Symposium* and the *Phaedrus.*

never a mere end in itself. Rather it is a mental process which often results in something of lasting significance.

Again, the creative mind, as Getzels and Jackson have pointed out, manifests " 'openness to the world.' " [5] Similarly Wynne speaks of *the expansion of experience.* [6] This openness and expansion likewise involve the element of curiosity and a willingness—again and again, in spite of the necessary effort—to take a fresh look at the facts. This also includes a certain amount of discontent and dissatisfaction with all that has been accomplished before. Hence, there is the possibility of continuous growth along with continuous discovery. Unlike the closed mind, the open, creative mind is always breaking out of the shell. Since this involves a certain amount of instability, it also involves dangers.

Moreover, as we observed in Chapter I, very closely related to the above is a certain daring or venturesomeness. The creative individual is by nature something of a rebel. Instead of accepting things as they are, he wants to reconstruct them in terms of what he thinks they ought to be. Theodore Brameld is a good example of this type of individual in our kind of world. To some, of course, the creative genius in any field appears to be maladjusted and even odd. The truth of the matter is that he is usually ahead of his times. Both Jesus and Socrates appeared eccentric to their contemporaries, and the same was true of Confucius.

Mention must be made at this point of what Toynbee has called "withdrawal-and-return." Although in his latest version he does not think that it is as universal as he once thought, yet he still thinks that many of the greatest men have followed this course—and he gives many examples. He even speaks of "withdrawal-and-return" as the "prelude," in many instances, "to outbursts of creativity." [7] The genius soon wearies of the crowds and retreats to the desert or to his ivory tower to meditate or ponder, and then, with renewed insight, returns to the market place. Nor can

5. See *Creativity and Intelligence,* pp. 112-15.
6. See *Philosophies of Education,* pp. 160-61.
7. See his *Reconsiderations,* pp. 263-66.

there be any doubt that this matter of "withdrawal-and-return" should receive much more consideration from our educationists. At any rate, our noisy, bizarre, materialistic age which demands spectacular efficiency—in the narrow pragmatic sense—from our schools, is pitifully deficient when it comes to the production of geniuses of the first magnitude.

In spite of the tendency toward originality, novelty, variety, and change, real creativity never signifies sheer novelty or absolute change. The mania for novelty and change as such and for eccentricity for its own sake is more the mark of the odd stick and the beatnik than of the creative mind. Though real insights may come in a flash, they are not mere freaks without order or continuity. High-grade minds, in fact, always have a real concern for both of these factors. In other words, what they aim at is not mere divergence without structure, but rather "some divergence in the structure." [8] Moreover, they are able to discern where the real frontiers lie and to advance beyond them because, instead of despising the past, they have made its wisdom their own, and, therefore, as it were, they stand upon its mighty shoulders.

3. Creativity, Intuition, and the Unconscious

This attempt to understand the nature of creativity is not complete without some consideration of two factors to which it is very closely related, namely, intuition and the unconscious. The reason why creativity seems to be vitally related to these two factors—in some mysterious manner—is that often, without any warning whatsoever, it flashes forth astonishing the individual himself. Suddenly the luminous thought appears and apparently out of somewhere. We shall begin with intuition followed by a discussion of the relations of the unconscious.

Although there are many philosophers as well as scientists to whom the term intuition is still taboo, it was Henri Bergson, one of the most creative and brilliant of contemporary philosophers,

8. See Farber & Wilson (eds.), *Man and Civilization: Control of the Mind; a Symposium*, p. 339.

who again made it philosophically proper to consider this factor. Bergson held that, since intuition arose out of instinct, it can give us something of a direct and immediate awareness of life, the process of time, and values. While he was by no means the anti-intellectualist which he appears to be on the surface, he did hold that intuition can give us a sense of immediacy which the intellect cannot.[9] Moreover, he stressed the place of intuition particularly in artistic creation and in high religion.[10]

By intuition as used here, we mean something closely akin to Bergson's view. The English word comes from the Latin term *intueri* which means to look on. By intuition, as used here then, we mean the mind's ability to grasp—more or less immediately— the meaning of anything. While in certain respects it is very closely related to Bergson's view, it differs in at least two ways: we do not contrast it as much with the intellect as he seems to do at times and, hence, cannot be charged with anti-intellectualism as he is by some; and we have broadened it to include all—more or less immediate—grasping of meaning. Thus, while reason is an- alyzing and marshaling the facts, intuition follows directly in its wake in seeing their relationships through flashes of insight. In taking this view of the intimate relationship existing between these two factors in the actual process of mental functioning, we also avoid the dualism which is apt to result from Bergson's view.

Nothing has been more destructive of real creativeness than the attitudes of some philosophers who, in their mania for analysis and precision, have treated intuition with contempt. While there is great merit in exercising due precaution, especially in view of the extremes to which fanatics have gone, yet they fail to see the real nature and relevance of intuition. For, along with reason, intuition constitutes a basic factor in all knowledge. This is true,

9. For Bergson's view of intuition, see his *Creative Evolution*, translated by Arthur Mitchell (New York: Henry Holt & Co., 1931), especially pp. 49, 176-79, 182.

10. On religion, see his *Two Sources of Morality and Religion*, translated by R. Ashley Audra & Cloudesley Brereton (Garden City, N.Y.: Doubleday & Co., 1956), especially pp. 207-317.

to begin with, in all ordinary experience. All sense experience, as when I say, "I see the cat," implies a kind of immediate grasping of meaning and, therefore, involves a measure of intuition. This is also true, in fact, in the case of grasping the meaning of any sentence that I read. Again, an element of intuition is likewise present in all unusual creative experiences. This is not true only in aesthetic and in moral and religious experiences, but also in scientific experience.

There are many illustrations which might be used to show the prevalence of intuition in the experiences of great scientists. A case in point is how, as in a flash, while in his bath pondering the problem, Archimedes discovered how to test King Hiero's crown for any presence of silver alloy.[11] There is also the famous story of how Sir Isaac Newton is supposed to have discovered the law of gravitation—in a flash—when an apple struck him on the head. While probably apocryphal, this story would not have appeared if such sudden experiences of illumination were not rather common among scientists. Thus Getzels and Jackson report a number of interesting experiences which happened to outstanding mathematicians.[12]

Since intuitions appear rather suddenly sometimes and since they must appear from somewhere, it is natural to arrive at the conclusion that they come from the unconscious—especially since they do show some relation to previous experience which may be conceived as leaving traces in the unconscious. Interestingly enough, among the mathematicians whom Getzels and Jackson quote is the famous Henri Poincaré, who attributes his experience of "sudden illumination" to the unconscious. Some of us have also had the experience of saying to ourselves before retiring, "I just must have that outline of that lecture before tomorrow noon," and the next morning, in an unguarded moment when we least

11. For the story, see Sir William Cecil Dampier, *A Shorter History of Science*, pp. 27-28.

12. *Creativity and Intelligence*, pp. 83-84.

expect it, suddenly and unannounced, it makes its appearance like a genie ready to do our biddings.

Although some, in spite of Freud and his disciples, reject the role of the dim unconscious in creativity—even insisting that it really serves only as a distorting factor[13]—it seems certain that there is some kind of intimate relation. Intuition or insight seems to involve the unconscious in some significant way. Yet many psychoanalysts magnify the role of the unconscious at the expense of the conscious mind. Chief among these is Freud who reduces the latter to little more than a puppet of the former.[14] Even C. G. Jung goes so far as to insist that "the unconscious is the ever-creative mother of consciousness."[15]

In spite of the importance of the unconscious, conscious mind seems to be the more significant for a number of reasons. To begin with, if consciousness did not exist, there could be no knowledge of anything whatsoever—including the unconscious. Freud himself could never have made his brilliant investigations of the unconscious if he himself had not been fully conscious of what he was doing. If man were not a self-conscious being, in fact, he could no more have explored the unfathomed depths of the unconscious mind than he could have explored the heights of the stellar universe. Thus, so far as significance and creativity are concerned, there can be no doubt about the primacy of conscious mind. All man's culture depends on reflective self-consciousness.

Again, so far as the unconscious and creativity are concerned, it is obvious that, if the unconscious were the most significant, extreme neurotics would be the most creative; but, as Jung[16]

13. See the discussion of L. S. Kubie in Getzels & Jackson, *Creativity and Intelligence,* pp. 94-97.

14. See "The Psychology of Dream-Processes," in A. A. Brill (translator & editor), *The Basic Writings of Sigmund Freud* (New York: Modern Library, 1938), pp. 542-45.

15. C. G. Jung, *The Development of Personality,* translated by R. F. C. Hull, Vol. 17 of his *Collected Works,* edited by Sir Herbert Read et al. ("Bollingen Series" [New York: Pantheon Books, 1954]), p. 115. Jung also speaks of consciousness as "like an island rising" out of the turbulent unconscious "sea." See *ibid.,* p. 51.

16. *Ibid.,* p. 115.

and others have made clear, this is most certainly not the case. While some geniuses, including the great Plato himself,[17] have had neurotic tendencies, this was not the secret of their greatness. Rather their creativity is manifest in the fact that they did not let these tendencies master them. Instead, they rose above them by continuing to go about their tasks and by continuing to strive for excellence through their achievements. Indeed, many have made the discovery that, if during periods of extreme depression, they will not give way to their moods but will continue with their work, they will find, more often than not, that a period of depression is apt to be followed by a period of supreme creativeness.

Along with the above, two more facts must be made clear. First, nothing important is apt to come up suddenly from the unconscious unless the individual pays the price. This involves study, reading, investigation, and hard thinking in the field or fields in which the individual is interested and wants to make a contribution. No lazy ignoramus is likely to become an Einstein overnight. This means that, to some extent at least, we can train our unconscious and our preconscious. What comes up, in most cases, is what we have stored there through long years of constant effort. Thus we can, to a surprising degree, turn our unconscious into an ally rather than an enemy. This does not mean, however, that we can ever hope to tame or civilize it completely. There is always the blind, instinctive, irrational aspect, the dangers of which Jung has described so graphically.[18] Yet these dangers become less real when the unconscious and the preconscious have been filled with material conducive to creativity.

The second fact is that what emerges from the unconscious through the preconscious to the level of consciousness cannot be accepted without examination. We must heed the advice of the New Testament writer: "Do not believe every spirit, but test the

17. See Earl D. Bond, *One Mind, Common to All* (New York: The Macmillan Co., 1958), p. 56.

18. In his *Psychology and Religion* (New Haven: Yale University Press, 1938), pp. 10-17.

spirits" (I John 4:1, RSV).[19] What breaks into consciousness from the depths below may be either a genuine insight or something trivial or even downright pernicious.[20] In short, every intuition must be judged in the light of reason and all the relevant facts drawn from man's *total* experience. Only if it can meet this test will it turn out to be genuine and truly creative.

At any rate, two conclusions emerge from this discussion. The first is that there is some intimate relationship existing between the conscious mind and the unconscious and, hence, likewise between the latter and the intuitions which are involved in creativity. The second is that real creativity is not primarily the work of the unconscious, but rather of the conscious mind. As we have seen, no unconscious process can become meaningful and significant until two conditions are fulfilled: it must break into consciousness, and it must be subjected to criticism. This brings the question: Just what is the relation of the unconscious to the conscious mind?

In this case, as in many others, the precise nature of the relationship is far from certain. Since the facts involved seem to show that both the unconscious and the conscious minds are real and that they interact, and it is doubtful that either causes or determines the other, perhaps it is best to take the moderate position that these facts may imply. It may well be that what is known as the unconscious mind, with its ability for at least some kind of mental activity, constitutes the nearest and the most intimate *environment* of the conscious mind.[21] As the *environment* of the conscious mind, it is more intimate than the brain; for, while the latter constitutes a material fact quite different from the thoughts

19. On the necessity of testing and criticism, see Wynne, *Philosophies of Education*, p. 164; also "Panel Discussion" in Seymour M. Farber & Roger H. L. Wilson (eds.), *Man and Civilization: Conflict and Creativity;* a Symposium, p. 60.

20. An illustration of the dirt that can come up from the unconscious comes from the life of Freud himself. One day he rushed from the consulting room shouting: " 'Why must I listen to such nastiness?' " See Albert William Levi, *Philosophy and the Modern World*, p. 173.

21. For this theory I am indebted to my teacher, Dr. Edgar Sheffield Brightman in his *Philosophy of Religion*, pp. 359-60 and n. 17.

which flit through the conscious mind, unconscious processes are definitely psychic. While protecting the integrity of both, this theory of the relation of the conscious to the unconscious accounts for their mutual interaction—including the fact that the former is able to draw upon the resources stored in the latter. Although this theory is by no means adequate, it is perhaps the best conceivable in the light of our present knowledge.

4. The Need of Creativity

Creativity has always been important. While the animals can depend safely on their instincts, that is, unless the environment changes too suddenly and drastically, man is dependent on the full use of those capacities which distinguish him most decidedly from the brutes. This was even true in Paleolithic times. Often a group survived simply because its wisest men made some new discovery. Thus any group that knew the secret of fire possessed a decided advantage.

So far as history as a whole is concerned, both John Stuart Mill in his famous essay *On Liberty* and Arnold Toynbee in his monumental *Study of History* have stressed the importance of creativity, especially in terms of outstanding men. Since our age faces greater *dangers* as well as greater *possibilities* than any previous age in all human history, and since its presence in sufficient quantities may spell the difference between doom or dawn, it is clear that creativity constitutes a very important need. Hence, we shall continue our explorations in the next chapter by attempting to deal with the difficult problem presented by the many obstructions.

VIII

Obstructions to Creativity

1. Factors in Modern Cultures

Aside from certain broad tendencies toward global unity, there is no such thing as a world culture. Instead there are still many cultures, ranging from the relatively primitive just emerging from the tribal stage to the most urbane, each trying frantically to maintain itself amid the clash of world forces. Hence, it is necessary to use the plural *cultures* rather than the singular *culture*. Yet, amid this mad welter, there are certain factors present—more or less common to them all—which obstruct and hinder creativity.

The first of these is *confusion* plus a general *aimlessness*. This confusion is very much in evidence in the new countries just emerging from tribalism. Seeing the inadequacies both of their old cultures and of the so-called ultramodern types, both of the right and of the left, the people—particularly the youth—find themselves profoundly perplexed.[1] Similarly, with the world knocking at their doors, the Latin American countries and such old countries as Japan, are witnessing a distressing confusion among their youth. Moreover, since even the most urbane cultures are subject to these same erosive forces, there is profound confusion in the West. Since the adults do not know where they are going, youth does not know

1. Karl Jaspers makes some interesting observations on cultural erosion; see *The Future of Mankind*, pp. 73-74.

either, and, therefore, often strikes out blindly. Even Russian youth is affected, far more than appears on the surface. This is one reason why juvenile delinquency is virtually world wide.

Although ultimately this collision of cultures may cause an amazing resurgence of creativity, for the time being at least it seems to act primarily as an obstructive force. The aimlessness prevalent among some of our more gifted young people is pitiful. This is one of the reasons why education must have an aim or goal that is inclusive and adequate.

Strangely enough, along with this general confusion, there is also a tendency toward *conformity* among youth as well as adults. This is evident most of all in Red China where the revolution is still young and where Marxian orthodoxy and dogmatism are strong. Even though there is far more creativity in Russia today than during the Stalin era, yet, due to the dogmatic temper of Marxianism, it languishes in the humanities. Little has come out of contemporary Russia in terms of great philosophy, poetry, or painting. While technical skill is much in evidence everywhere, creativity, in spite of some hopeful signs, is still lagging.[2]

Nor, in spite of the greater freedom, is the situation much better in this country. The fear of communism together with the fear of change has led to conformism. This was especially true during the McCarthy era when the tendency not only toward conformism, but —worse still—also toward fascism was surprisingly strong. At one time, during this period, the American Association of University Professors had so many cases of actual violations of academic freedom pending that it could not even issue its journal on time. Furthermore, for exercising their democratic right to differ, some of our most eminent scientists were fearfully persecuted.[3] Though

---

2. On the situation in Russian education, see George Z. F. Bereday *et al* (eds.), *The Changing Soviet School*, pp. 369-70. Also see "Panel Discussion" in Seymour M. Farber & Roger H. L. Wilson (eds.), *Man and Civilization: Conflict and Creativity*; a Symposium, pp. 236-37. For hopeful signs, see Fred Ablin (ed.), *Education in the USSR: A Collection of Readings from Soviet Journals*, Vol. I.

3. For a brief account by an outstanding scientist, see Ralph E. Lapp, *Kill and Overkill: The Strategy of Annihilation* (New York: Basic Books, 1962), pp. 19-20.

the situation has improved in some ways, extreme rightists, especially the racialists, are again busy, and a sharp turn for the worse, either at home or on the world scene, could increase their influence immeasurably.

Closely related to all this is the *pressure* exerted by the *mass* man. With the continual increase of the world's population at an alarming rate, this problem of mass pressure will also continue to increase. It involves three dangers, two of which are chiefly political and one cultural and educational. First of all, there is the danger of strong *tendencies away from democracy toward new forms of totalitarianism*. Both communism and nazism triumphed through the support given to certain leaders by the masses. The second danger, of course, as many have warned us, is *nuclear war*. In this respect, Red China constitutes a far greater danger than Russia—especially in view of our policy of nonrecognition.

The third great danger is the spread of *mediocrity* and *anti-intellectualism*. Swamped by the swarms of children who will be knocking at their doors tomorrow and whom they must accommodate, the great temptation will be for the schools to lower their standards accordingly. Along with all this, there will also be the danger of neglecting the gifted. While it may not make much difference for a time, ultimately this neglect of the creative can only mean social decay followed by irremediable ruin. Instead of producing more great theoretical scientists, philosophers with perspective, and statesmen with vision, we shall produce vast hordes of narrow-minded technicians fit tools for dictators.

There is also, of course, the vulgar *hedonism* and *materialism* evoked and nurtured by our affluence. As a very promising young high school teacher remarked recently: "What can I teach students who live in expensive houses and who drive sport cars?" According to press reports our list of millionnaires is growing by leaps and bounds (some think we may have 100,000), yet the great city of Detroit—due to the lack of funds—has not been able to develop a school system adequate to meet the needs. Toynbee

warns us that it is our "affluence" which is "estranging" us from
our ideals; so that America, once the guiding star of oppressed
people everywhere, is fast becoming the symbol of reactionism
standing guard over its money bags.[4]

And what does our affluent, decadent society demand of education? Not creativity, since that might mean a real attempt to take
our boasted democratic ideals seriously. Rather it tends to regard
our schools as the means to teach clever brains to invent new
gadgets or to devise new ways of getting rich quick. No wonder
that creativity is in jeopardy.

Finally, mention must be made of two opposite tendencies, both
of which are deadly to the creative spirit, namely, *archaism* and
futurism. Thus, while many in the democracies are archaists who
would like to turn the clock back to the nineteenth century, to
those wonderful days of white supremacy, the communists, who
are futurists by virtue of their creed, try to turn it forward to
that glorious future when the Marxian messiah (the chosen class)
will usher in the glorious new age foretold by their prophets.

Needless to say, both of these attitudes involve the impossible.
It is as ridiculous to attempt to defy history by trying to leap
back into the irrevocable past as to try to leap forward into a
future so full of contingencies. Moreover, in their vain efforts, both
may breed new types of fanaticism which may set the world afire.
Be that as it may, there is no other way of making the world
better than through creativity operating within and straining at
the limits of historic possibilities. Even Providence itself, as Kant
realized many years ago and as all religious liberals realize, has no
other way of promoting genuine progress.

2. Factors Within Our Schools

Having dealt with obstructive factors in the world generally
and with those in American culture more particularly, the time
has now come to take a look at our schools. Unfortunately, our
public schools tend to reflect our culture like a mirror. Not long

4. In his *America and the World Revolution*, p. 151.

ago, at a panel in Detroit on the very timely subject, "Positive Programs for Peace in the Schools," [5] Dr. Russell Brodhead, of the College of Education at Wayne State University, stated not once but several times that many public school teachers will not discuss controversial issues. Moreover, the representative of the Detroit Public Schools had little to report in terms of serious efforts at peace education. Undoubtedly, there is a marked tendency in our public schools toward *conformism;* and this may be one reason why so many creative minds refuse to consider the teaching profession.

Although the situation is much better in our colleges and our universities—especially since the scare during the Cuban crisis produced a new interest in world peace, in view of the marked interest in the Peace Corps, and perhaps, above all else, in the light of the number of students taking part in the freedom demonstrations—still, so far as students as a whole are concerned, there is a marked tendency toward *conformism.* While they are ready to rebel when there is any interference with their pleasures, few are ready to champion great causes.

In his book, *Changing Values in College,* Jacob has a chapter entitled: "The Myth of College Liberalism." [6] In this chapter he even goes so far as to say that "the social and economic attitudes" of college students are not much different from the attitudes of those who do not go to college. This undoubtedly in both instances shows the influence of social conditioning.

Jacob also insists that "college has a socializing rather than a liberalizing impact on values"; it tends to strengthen "respect for the prevailing social order." [7] This also tells something about col-

5. This panel discussion was held at the Central Methodist Church, Detroit, on June 14, 1963, and was sponsored by the following organizations: Detroit Women for Peace; Metropolitan Chapter, National Association of Social Workers; two chapters of Women's International League for Peace and Freedom; and Detroit Chapter, Committee for a Sane Nuclear Policy.

6. (New York: Harper & Row, 1957), pp. 50-53.

7. *Ibid.,* p. 53. As manifest in certain disgraceful instances involving some of our outstanding colleges and universities, youth is, however, quite ready to rebel against the moral code—another sign of decadence.

lege faculties. A college professor testifies that, although during his nearly twenty years of college teaching he has become acquainted with a considerable number of college and university professors in many institutions and has seen them perform under many different circumstances, he found only a few creative either in the social or in the intellectual sense. The causes seem to be fear plus the unwillingness to put forth just a bit more effort.

Closely related to the above is the *anti-intellectualism* which is rather marked in our schools today. Even though it is most marked in our public schools, our colleges, especially some departments and schools of education are infected with it. In his recent book—*The Miseducation of American Teachers*—James D. Koerner makes a vigorous attack on the prevalent anti-intellectualism. In fact, he returns to the subject again and again; and so far as education and educationists are concerned, he makes the following charges: that many seem to hold that intellectual ability is not very important for the teacher (p. 47); that textbooks used in education courses, and especially those in methods, are superficial and trivial (pp. 78-81); that the instruction in the educational courses is poor, and that the students manifest "an intellectually timorous attitude" (pp. 81-96); that the potential teacher has to take so many hours in education that he becomes a "technician" (p. 156); that both the Ed.D. and the Ph.D. (in education) are below the doctorate in the arts and sciences (p. 183); and, finally, that the subjects for the dissertations are mediocre and trivial (p. 185). This is an amazing list of charges; and, while Koerner is certainly a bit unfair, yet where there is so much smoke there is likely to be some fire. In short, the time has come for the educationists, if they want to promote real creativity, to set their house in order.

Last but not least among the obstructions, there is what may be called the cult of objectivity. This cult manifests itself in two ways. The first is in the stress that is placed on intelligence tests. While these tests have a certain value, they also have many defects and limitations. Among these is the fact that, while they can test intelligence in terms of the ability to recall and present factual knowledge, they are rather deficient in the discovery of "creative talent." Jacob W. Getzels and Philip W. Jackson have made this clear in their recent study, *Creativity and Intelligence*.[8] The great danger is that, in their stress on the intelligence tests, our schools turn out "quiz kids" who are virtually walking encyclopedias, but who do not really know how to think constructively and creatively.[9] Many others, including no one less than John Dewey, have questioned the whole concept of measurement back of the intelligence tests.[10] Again, while Gordon Allport recognizes that these tests have a certain value, he is also fully aware of their limitations and the dangers of abuse.[11] At any rate, too much reliance on intelligence tests is likely to hinder rather than enhance creativity.

In the second place the cult of objectivity is clearly evident in the widespread reliance on the so-called objective tests. One high school teacher confessed to me that he had given only one essay test during the entire school year. So far as many high schools are concerned, the basic trouble seems to be a shortage of teachers. If administrators spent more money on securing more and better teachers and less on buildings and gadgets, and if less clerical work were demanded of the teaching staff, there would be more time for grading essay-type tests and term papers.

Whether given in high school or in college, the so-called objective test is not likely to promote creativity. The reason for this is that it does not challenge students to think.[12] I began to realize this early in my career as a college teacher, and, as a result, abandoned the practice of giving objective tests. I also realized the value of term papers. Even though it takes more time to grade

8. See especially pp. vii-x, 1-12.
9. *Ibid.*, pp. 8, 127.
10. See the section in John S. Brubacher (ed.), *Eclectic Philosophy of Education*, pp. 404-11.
11. Gordon W. Allport, *Personality: A Psychological Interpretation*, pp. 449-451.
12. See also Koerner, *The Miseducation of American Teachers*, pp. 257-58. Mention must also be made again of James Bryant Conant's charge that in the vast majority of our high schools capable students are "not working hard enough." See his book, *The American High School Today*, p. 23.

essay-type tests and term papers, the student's gain in creativity is worth the extra effort.

3. Four Obstructive Dogmas

Besides the factors which have already been examined, there are four obstructive dogmas—*reductionism, determinism, illusionism, and relativism*—which must now be given due consideration. Although their roots go back to Greek philosophy, they are prevalent and influential in modern and contemporary education due in a large measure to science and technology in their various aspects.

We begin with *reductionism*. As we have already seen in our discussion of Dewey and in our discussion of naturalism,[13] by reductionism we mean the attempt to explain the higher nature and the higher capacities of man in terms of something lower. It usually takes one of two forms, namely, the biological and behavioristic or the Freudian. While behaviorism goes back to Ivan Pavlov (1849-1936) and his discovery of the conditioned reflex, John B. Watson is really the father of behaviorism as a theory. Ignoring consciousness, he tried to explain man as well as other animals purely in terms of a behavior system based on the stimulus-response mechanism. Thus man is reduced to a kind of complex machine. So far as Freud is concerned, it has become clear from our previous discussion,[14] that he made the self-conscious mind the puppet of unconscious factors and impulses. Suffice it to say, that both Watson and Freud tried to reduce man to merely impersonal processes.

Obviously reductionism is detrimental to creativity. The reason why it is detrimental is simply this: that while creativity is based on the belief in the efficacy and significance of man's higher capacities, including his reflective self-consciousness, behaviorism and Freudianism try to reduce these very capacities to virtual insignificance. In the final analysis, not only is man affected by what he thinks of himself (and to regard himself as nothing but a sum

13. See Ch. V, pp. 85-88, 98-99.
14. See Ch. VII, p. 148 and n. 14.

total of impersonal processes or a complex machine is not likely to inspire much great art, great poetry, or high religion), but he is also *not likely to put forth much effort to develop his higher capacities—upon which creativity depends—if he is convinced that they do not really amount to much.* This is one reason why the humanities languish today. Furthermore, since science itself, especially in its higher outreaches, is also dependent on the belief in the efficacy and significance of man's higher capacities, this view— taken seriously—will also eventually kill science. We shall have more to say about this later.

The dogma of *determinism* may arise in a number of ways. To begin with, it is obvious that it is closely related to reductionism. Rob man of his higher capacities by reducing them to simpler elements, and nothing remains except the body with its biological drives and mechanisms and the impulses surging up from that wild, turbulent sea known as the unconscious. Hence, it becomes easy for him to think of himself as nothing but a sum total of impersonal processes or as a kind of highly complex machine. Nor can there be any doubt that the invention of computers, these marvelous "thinking" machines, has greatly enhanced this view of man.[15]

The stress on the law of cause and effect or what is known as the uniformity of nature has likewise stimulated the growth of determinism. The chief point here is that, if thoroughgoing determinism is abandoned, and a measure of indeterminism or freedom is allowed, science will have to give up a doctrine that has proved so fruitful in the investigation of natural processes and even of man himself. Scientists, while admitting as they must that it has not been proved universally, try to defend it with three arguments: first, experience, as far as it goes, seems to justify our belief that under the same circumstances the same results inevitably follow; second, without this assumption, science would lose its power to predict; and, third, the pragmatic principle which has already

15. On the nature and influence of computers, see especially Norbert Wiener, *The Human Use of Human Beings: Cybernetics and Society* (second revised edition; paperback; Garden City: Doubleday & Co., 1954).

been mentioned, namely, that this acceptance of determinism has proved immensely fruitful in science.

The devastating effects of determinism upon creativity are evident. Since freedom and novelty are essential to creativeness and since thoroughgoing determinism denies the reality of these factors, it tends to cut the ground out from under the whole concept of creativity. The truth of the matter is that together reductionism and determinism have had nothing short of a devastating effect. Nothing is more frustrating than to feel that one is in the clutches of something over which one has no control whatsoever. It often leads to despair and a total failure of nerve. There is nothing creative about the belief that, regardless of all our efforts, what will be will be.

The third dogma—*illusionism*—is also closely related to reductionism and even to determinism. Illusionism is simply the attempt to look upon the higher capacities of man and all that they seem to discover or create as illusory. Although something resembling this is involved in some of the more extreme forms of the Hindu and Buddhist doctrines of *Maya*, so far as we are concerned, Freud is largely responsible for the prevalence of illusionism in its modern form. In short, in his stress on the primacy of the unconscious and in his attempt to explain all that arises in consciousness as largely the product of processes which take place in the former, he robs all values, including freedom, of their objectivity.

Religion fares worst of all at Freud's hands. For him it is nothing but one grand illusion. Finding life hard, man invented a kind heavenly Father who takes the sting out of misfortune by virtue of his providence—including the hope of a future reward in Heaven. While it would be "nice" if there were such a God, the brutal fact is that he just does not exist. He is merely the vast shadow cast by our desires and the product of our wishful thinking.[16]

16. On his views of religion, see his little book, *The Future of an Illusion*, translated by W. D. Robson-Scott (New York: Liveright Publishing Corporation, 1953); and also his *Civilization and Its Discontents* (translated Joan Riviere) (New York: Robert O. Ballou, 1930), especially pp. 23-24.

It is easy to see how illusionism stifles creativity. If our values are merely shadows cast by our wishes and our dreams, and if life itself really has no purpose, then there is nothing to strive for—at least nothing *significant*. Moreover, since religion has often been a primary source of the profoundest creativeness (as we shall see later), to reduce it to an illusion is to rob it of its ability to inspire men. With values reduced to shadows and religion to an illusion, Freud's world is indeed hard and bleak.

Finally, there is *relativism*. In general relativism means that there are no universally valid principles, standards, norms. Truth, beauty, and goodness lack objectivity. There are really two forms, namely, individualistic relativism and social or cultural relativism. While the first and most radical holds that everything is relative to the desires, whims, and impulses of the individual, the second holds that everything is relative to particular societies or cultures. So far as philosophers are concerned, there are relativistic tendencies present in certain versions of pragmatism, and relativism is very strong in logical positivism.[17]

The detrimental effects of relativism are perhaps not as clearly evident as those of the other three. Even though they are more elusive, in the long run at least, they are just as baneful. Since the relativist believes that there are no objective norms or ideals of truth, beauty, or goodness, he has *nothing*—transcending personal desires or whims or social conventions—toward which to strive. The results are especially deleterious to all efforts at *excellence*. Consequently, taken seriously, relativism can only lead to mediocrity and decay.

4. The Four Dogmas Examined

Reductionism is subject to many criticisms. The first is that it is guilty of what has been called the *genetic fallacy*. The fact that the simpler and less complex structure comes first is no sign that it is either more real than that which comes later or that it is

17. For the famous emotive ethical theory, see Alfred Jules Ayer's *Language, Truth and Logic*, especially pp. 106 ff.

capable of explaining the latter. While continuity is most certainly present in evolution, the principle of novelty is also operative. Emergents sometimes appear rather suddenly. Moreover, the real nature of a thing is probably more fully expressed in its fruits than in its roots. Therefore, although we can learn much about man from his lowly origin, he can be known most fully in terms of his very highest development. Hence, instead of spending so much time studying animal psychology as a means of understanding man, our psychologists had better spend more time studying man himself. The investigation of his higher mental capacities, such as what is involved in the mental operations of a genius like Einstein when he is investigating some important problem in theoretical physics, has been shamefully neglected.[18]

In the second place, reductionism, in its stress on continuity, has failed to see the significance of *uniqueness*.[19] As the emergent evolutionists have pointed out, with each new level in the evolutionary process—from matter to life and from life to mind—new characteristics (genuine novelties) appear which cannot be explained in terms of what appeared on the preceding level. The best example is the reflective capacity of man which enables him to transcend the limitations of instinct and of particularity and to rise to a perspective and a sense of freedom and creativity of which the animal is not conscious at all. The most significant thing about the human mind is that, although it is but a fragment of the universe, it has the capacity of trying to think in terms of the universe as a whole.[20] It likewise has the capacity of projecting itself into the vast future as well as looking back into the vast past.

The crucial instance of uniqueness is undoubtedly *reflective self-consciousness* which psychologists—both in the behavioristic camp and in the Freudian camp—have tried to belittle and to ignore,

18. For some interesting observations on anti-intellectualism in psychology, see "Panel Discussion" in Seymour M. Farber & Roger H. L. Wilson (eds.), *Man and Civilization: Control of the Mind; a Symposium*, pp. 126-27.

19. For some interesting observations on uniqueness, see Gordon W. Allport, *Becoming* (New Haven: Yale University Press, 1955), pp. 19-24.

20. On this point, see Errol E. Harris, *Nature, Mind and Modern Science*, p. 45.

but which they have had to *use* in the very act of attempting to ignore or disprove it. Even though animals can solve problems, they never rise to the level of reflective self-consciousness. Nor can the reductionist prove his case by an appeal to computers. While they do many wonderful, even uncanny things, yet they can only operate within the limited fields provided by their structure; they have to be provided with facts; and, most important of all, they are certainly not self-conscious.[21] Again, men invent them, order them to do certain things, and supply them with the means; and it is the human mind which has to interpret the answers which they give. This last fact is especially important: the answers which they give have no real significance until they *appear in* some human mind and are *interpreted by* that mind.

Finally, so far as man is concerned, the reductionists in both camps leave little place for *growth* or the process of *becoming*. While the behaviorists overstress conditioning during childhood, the Freudians overemphasize especially the first three years, that is, the traumatic experiences which might occur during that period. Although no psychologist in his right mind will underestimate either the influence of powerful conditioning factors or the significance of infancy for later life, yet today many believe that both the behaviorists and the Freudians have gone too far.[22] Among other things, no one can deny that there are many crucial stages of human life when radical transformations take place. One of these stages is the adolescent. Another, so far as college students are concerned, is about the time they become seniors or begin their work in graduate school. Nothing is more evident than man's capacity for growth—as Dewey truly recognized.

While there must be considerable truth in *determinism*, since man is so largely conditioned by his heredity and his environment and the thousands of subtle factors which these embrace, yet

21. On computers, besides Wiener, *The Human Use of Human Beings,* see especially the following pages in Farber & Wilson (eds.), *Man and Civilization: Control of the Mind;* a Symposium, pp. 127-28, 219-232.

22. See Allport, *Becoming,* pp. 31-33. For the importance of later influences, see also his *Personality: A Psychological Interpretation,* pp. 207-12.

thoroughgoing determinism falls far short of the mark. It is at its worst a dogma and at its best a hypothesis that has never been proved. To begin with, the *thoroughgoing* determinist assumes to possess knowledge which we do not have. If nature has again become a profound mystery (since the modern physicist has reduced the seemingly solid matter to a mysterious something which he calls energy), the same is even more true of man himself. Some years ago, in fact, one of America's most outstanding medical experts, Alexis Carrel, wrote a book entitled *Man, the Unknown*—in which he expressed his conviction that, in spite of all the marvelous discoveries that science has made in the physical realm, our knowledge of man himself is "still rudimentary." [23]

In the second place, *thoroughgoing* determinism is basically self-contradictory and even absurd. The *strict* determinist, if he is philosophical enough to examine his presuppositions (which most scientists, particularly psychologists, are not), finds himself confronting a dilemma from which there is no escape. Either, on the one hand, he must accept a certain amount of freedom in human thought and action—which destroys his case—or, on the other hand, he must accept the fact that all *thoroughgoing* determinism destroys the very basis of *all objectivity,* including not only the basis of all science, but also the basis of his own judgment that determinism is true. In other words, if *thoroughgoing* determinism is true, then the conclusions of the scientist and the determinist are also determined, and, therefore, no better and no worse, no more true or untrue, than those of anyone else. No determinist has yet tried to face this dilemma, with all its implications, seriously.[24]

In the third place, *thoroughgoing* determinism cannot give an adequate explanation of certain very significant facts. Foremost among these is the fact of deliberation. All sane, rational men, in spite of the fact that they often act like fools and "rush in where

23. (New York: Harper & Brothers, 1935).

24. While the classic statement of the case for determinism is found in Spinoza's *Ethics* (see especially Prop. XLVIII), William James, along with Bergson, was a champion of free will. See his classic essay, "The Dilemma of Determinism."

angels fear to tread," at times deliberate and make decisions on the basis of the actual evidence. This is as true of the "hard-boiled" scientist as of the ordinary individual. *Thoroughgoing* determinism would make this process meaningless; it reduces the process, in truth, to a kind of subtle game or even to nothing but shadowboxing.[25] Attention must also again be called to the facts of growth, development, change, novelty. Facts like this led the great philosopher Henri Bergson away from his earlier mechanistic views to indeterminism and freedomism.[26] Closely related to all that has been stated above is also our experience of the self as an agent, that is, especially when we will to act with a certain aim and purpose—and not only will the act subjectively, but really carry it out with actual changes taking place in our environment in direct accordance with our aim or purpose.[27] There is likewise the sense of guilt which is difficult to explain on deterministic lines. Although there are times when we feel guilty without reason, there are other times when there are good reasons for feeling guilty. Moreover, since a sense of guilt for actual wrongdoing can lead to repentance and the fruits of repentance, it can be *profoundly creative*. If Hitler had possessed a real sense of horror at the slaughter of human beings, instead of killing millions of Jews, he might have used his power over the masses to promote global understanding and peace.

Fourthly, although so far as natural phenomena in the mass is concerned determinism does seem to apply in terms of the law of cause and effect—thus making prediction possible—yet, in terms of the famous principle of uncertainty, this does not seem to be true on the subatomic scale. Again, along with this, there is also a marked tendency to regard scientific laws as largely statistical.

25. On this point, see also indeterminist psychologist Carl Rogers' account of his exchange with determinist psychologist, B. F. Skinner, in Farber & Wilson (eds.), *Man and Civilization: Conflict and Creativity; a Symposium*, pp. 271-72.

26. See Ralph Barton Perry, *The Thought and Character of William James* (Boston: Little, Brown & Co., 1935), p. 623.

27. On this point, see also John Macmurray's *The Self as Agent* (New York: Harper & Row, 1958).

While these tendencies in science by no means prove human freedom, they have shaken the old nineteenth-century totally mechanistic view of nature to its very foundation.[28] At any rate, there seems to be a certain degree of freedom within the realm of nature itself, thus enabling the human mind to act into the latter creatively. The belief of Baruch Spinoza and others that nature really constitutes an unending causal chain certainly remains unproved. The truth of the matter seems to be that in many situations the human will can itself function as a determining cause; not by defying nature and its laws, but rather by using them consciously and purposefully as a means toward freedom. This is what Bacon had in mind when he stated in his *Novum Organum* that "nature to be commanded must be obeyed." Furthermore, it seems to be evident that, in many situations at least, the thoughtful individual may have a choice of causal chains; but once having accepted one or the other, he will have to accept the consequences involved until the time comes when the consequences can be changed by some new creative act of self-conscious freedom based on knowledge. A case in point is the individual contemplating suicide by means of some kind of poison. As long as he is merely thinking about it and weighing the consequences, he is still free between two possible causal chains; but once he swallows it, he is subject to the effects. If his friends, however, appear in time and call the doctor, the man of science, by virtue of his knowledge and his desire to save life, may act creatively into the situation and thus produce a new chain of consequences.

Finally, there can be no doubt that *thoroughgoing* determinism is contrary to democratic conceptions of freedom and human dignity. Determinist B. F. Skinner freely admits this, but still affirms his faith in science.[29] Gordon W. Allport, however, as a

28. For various points of view from the standpoints of both science and philosophy, see Sidney Hook (ed.), *Determinism and Freedom in the Age of Modern Science* (paperback; New York: Collier Books, 1961).

29. See his *Science and Human Behavior* (New York: The Macmillan Co., 1953), pp. 446-49.

moderate, views this trend in science with alarm and ventures to predict that psychology is on the verge of setting forth a view of man more in accord with democratic beliefs and aspirations. Facts seem to show that the latter has his hands on the larger truth. His attack on the mechanists is especially telling when he points out the contradiction which exists between their zealous espousal of democratic ideals, on the one hand, and their affirmation of *thoroughgoing* determinism, on the other.[30] Undoubtedly the truth lies somewhere between *thoroughgoing* determinism and *thoroughgoing* indeterminism. Within *limits* man does seem to be free— free enough, if he would only realize it, to become truly creative.

Like reductionism and determinism, *illusionism* fails to do full justice to certain facts. Among these, first of all, is the fact that every level of the evolutionary process seems to be real in some sense, and, hence, more than an illusion. More than this, some levels are clearly more important than others. Foremost among these is the fact of self-consciousness. For in spite of its dependence upon the brain and the unconscious in certain vital respects, consciousness in terms of thought and will constitutes the primary datum of experience. If we were not self-conscious, we would not know that we possess either a brain or an unconscious mind. Hence, it would seem that the former is, in truth, more real than the latter. It has also become clear that the self has a certain executive power over both the brain and the unconscious. Again, whatever else may be true of parapsychology, Joseph B. Rhine seems to have shown that telepathy does actually occur;[31] and, if this is true, this fact, since it implies that mind can sometimes act across space without the use of any material medium whatsoever, is deadly to any epiphenomenalistic view of mind that tries to reduce it to a nonentity or an illusion.

Strangely enough, as Albert W. Levi points out, although Freud

30. Allport, *Becoming,* pp. 82-88, 99-101. Allport, of course, is not an indeterminist in the extreme sense. He takes a moderate view.

31. Joseph Banks Rhine, *New World of the Mind* (New York: William Sloane Associates, 1953), pp. 23-32.

never doubted the reality of the external world, he denied that religion and the arts have any objective basis in the nature of things.[32] Instead he condemned them as being essentially the products of blind, instinctive forces surging up from the dark depths of the unconscious. Yet today the new physics has found it necessary to replace the hard, solid matter of ordinary sensation with dynamic processes. In short, if Freud had seriously studied the concepts of the new physics, he would have found that the type of realism which he called scientific and upon which he built his faith had been undermined by science itself;[33] and that, since the stuff out of which the external world is composed is now viewed as reducible to something intangible, it is not necessarily unscientific to believe in such great intangibles as religion or ideals. After all, not *tangibility* but *coherence* is the test of truth.

Again, Freud's view of religion itself was hopelessly onesided and defective. His crudely anthropomorphic conception of the nature of religion reminds one too much of the college sophomore in the first stages of his rebellion against his fundamentalistic background. Obviously, he had not studied the history of religion seriously and, therefore, knew little about its higher forms. Nor, since most of his patients were mentally ill, did he know much about the religion of normal people. Besides this, there was his dogmatic devotion to the scientific mechanism and determinism which was rampant and which ruled out both freedom and all spiritual reality, but which, as we have seen, is today becoming obsolete.

At any rate, his attempt to derive religion from the pleasure principle is particularly naïve. Although much religion has been crudely hedonistic, some of it even resembling "an endless amatory flirtation," [34] this has not been true of religion at its best. It has

32. Albert William Levi, *Philosophy and the Modern World*, pp. 152-53.
33. For his rather naïve faith in the scientific empiricism of his day, see his *Future of an Illusion*, pp. 95-98.
34. This is William James' famous description of St. Teresa's mysticism; see his *Varieties of Religious Experience* (New York: Modern Library, 1902), p. 340.

often, in fact, meant a cross. The symbol of Christianity itself, as everyone knows, is the Cross. Moreover, some individuals—either because they do not want to assume the responsibility which belief in God implies or because God constitutes an offense to their egotism and pride—wish atheism to be true with all the fervor and zeal of the pious religious believer.

Finally, in spite of a few references to famous philosophers, Freud, while making pronouncements in this realm, seems to have known very little either about philosophy in general or about the philosophy of religion in particular. Levi has shown how much he was the product of "nineteenth-century science," and how greatly he was influenced by "the materialism of Mach and Helmholtz." [35] As a result, while condemning religion and the idea of God with all the zeal of the dogmatist, he never made an attempt to look at all the facts involved. His contention, of course, that, in view of the hard facts of life, the old orthodox view of God—as a kind of omnipotent magician who tampers with nature's laws occasionally when his favorites are in trouble or when he wants to punish his enemies—must be dismissed as absurd, will be readily accepted by all religious liberals today. Freud's great fault is that he never took the time to consider seriously all the evidence for God's existence.[36] Nor did he consider the new versions of theism which, in view of the facts of evil in general and in view of the implications of the theory of evolution in particular, have abandoned the concept of an omnipotent God for that of a God who must struggle with wild, dark, capricious forces in order to create.

We have dealt with Freud's attack upon religion somewhat at length because, in striking at this important form of human endeavor and condemning it as "a universal, obsessional neurosis" destined for oblivion as soon as man matures, he was striking at the heart of one of the primary sources of human creativity. Later

---

35. *Philosophy and the Modern World,* p. 151. On Freud's basic philosophy Levi is superb.

36. For some of these facts, see Ch. V, pp. 97-98.

in this venture, we shall deal with this question of the significance of high religion.

In *relativism*, as in determinism, there is a large measure of truth. Although truth, beauty, and goodness as norms and ideals which the mind must accept seem to be objective in some meaningful sense, our human *conceptions* of each one of these great three are largely relative. No human mind can possibly fathom the ideal in all the richness of its totality. Again, any particular effort to realize the ideal through human creativity, no matter how excellent, since it must always fall short, is, therefore, always more or less relative. The fact of the relativity of all *human concepts* of truth, beauty, and goodness does not mean, however, that these norms themselves are of necessity relative.

Relativists usually advance two arguments. The first is the "emotive" made famous by Ayer and the logical positivists. They contend that, since values cannot be verified like ordinary empirical facts, they are not facts at all but matters of feeling. The second argument, especially common among sociologists, appeals to the fact of diversity. Since there are so many diverse standards among the various cultures and societies, values are purely relative; universal standards simply do not exist.[37]

In spite of the apparent strength of these arguments, *thoroughgoing* relativism, like *thoroughgoing* determinism, is subject to many strictures. To begin with, the former, like the latter, is really self-contradictory, and, therefore, self-refuting. The relativist finds himself in the unpleasant predicament of asserting, on the one hand, that there are no universally valid principles, yet, on the other, he tries to make a universally valid principle out of

37. For defenses of relativism, see Ayer, *Language, Truth, and Logic,* pp. 102-20; Hans Reichenbach, *The Rise of Scientific Philosophy* (Berkeley: University of California Press, 1951), pp. 276-302; and Edward Westermarck, *The Origin and Development of the Moral Ideas* (New York: The Macmillan Co., 1906), I, 4 ff. For criticisms, see James B. Pratt, *Reason in the Art of Living,* pp. 51-75; Peter A. Bertocci & Richard M. Millard, *Personality and the Good* (New York: David McKay Co., 1963), pp. 271-91; and Arthur W. Munk, *Perplexing Problems of Religion,* pp. 47-56.

his own relativism. This is especially evident when he tries to convince others. Further, in the same vein, if truth itself is really relative to feeling, as the logical positivists seem to say, or to the "social situation," as Karl Mannheim and the sociologists of knowledge seem to say, then, their own theories—since they are subject to these same forces as everyone else's—are also purely relative and wholly without objectivity.[38] Moreover, as Bertocci and Millard have shown, while the emotivists have a decided preference for truth as over against falsehood, they actually have no way whatsoever of justifying this preference.[39] Thus, it would seem that, from the standpoint of logic in terms of the principle of contradiction, *thoroughgoing* relativism is impossible.

But there is more still to come. So far as the logical positivists are concerned, their principle of verification, by means of which Ayer hoped to banish all the great intangibles, seems to be faulty. For, if verification means direct observation, then science itself, as Blanshard has shown, would become impossible.[40] The reason for this is the fact that, while the scientist may begin with the facts of sense experience in his quest for universally valid laws, he soon finds himself driven beyond all that is directly observable or tangible. This is particularly true, as we have observed before, of the new physics. It was facts like these which drove Ayer himself, in his "Introduction" to his second edition of *Language, Truth and Logic* to revise his verification principle so that he seems to have passed beyond logical positivism. Be that as it may, today, at any rate, it is not so easy to condemn the great intangibles as subjective, relative, and even meaningless.

It may also be contended that to insist that the great ideals or norms are mere matters of feeling or convention rests on a false analysis of their real nature. Truth, for example, stubbornly resists all attempts to reduce it to mere feeling or convention. Not

38. See Brand Blanshard's devastating criticism of Mannheim, in his *Reason and Analysis* (LaSalle, Ill.: Open Court Publishing Co., 1962), pp. 41-42.

39. *Personality and the Good*, p. 271.

40. Blanshard, *Reason and Analysis*, pp. 226-27.

only are some things really true regardless of how I or even the whole human race may feel or think about them, but the various truths also tend to form a system of meaning. If this were not the case, the concept of natural law would be utterly meaningless. Again, so far as the Good is concerned, in order to do my duty I may actually have to go against my own feelings or the conventions of the particular social group to which I may belong. This has most certainly been true of the very greatest teachers of mankind. While they were careful to conserve the real values in their various traditions, yet they were not known for their conformity.

Furthermore, although there has been great diversity in terms of both moral principles and practices, the widest diversity exists at the primitive level. As man advances toward civilization, it is surprising how similar concepts appear everywhere. On basic principles, the greatest teachers the race has known are virtually in agreement. The latest confirmation of this fact of unity is the adoption by the United Nations of the Universal Declaration of Human Rights.[41]

Mention must also be made of the fact that man's capacities for truth, beauty, and goodness are not something that he himself creates. He may develop or refuse to develop them, but it is the Universe that has bestowed them upon him. Moreover, in spite of the presence of disvalue and evil, the Universe provides him real opportunities to use these capacities: not only as merely a means of survival, but also as a means of enriching life. In view of these reciprocal facts plus the fact that man, as the highest known product of the Universe, may well be—as the personalists insist— the best clue to its inner nature, *the Universe itself may be on the side of values.* In short, if this is really the case, then the objectivity of values is assured.

Finally, it may be urged that *thoroughgoing* relativism is basically absurd. If there are no objective standards, then Einstein was

41. On the vast amount of unity and agreement in terms of basic principles, see also Bertocci & Millard, *Personality and the Good*, pp. 290-91.

really no better and no worse as a scientist than the most ignorant
primitive, Pope John XXIII was no better and no worse than
Adolf Hitler, and democracy is no better and no worse than
fascism. While such a state of affairs is conceivable, it is too
ridiculous to be taken seriously.

5. Conclusions

From this brief survey, analysis, and criticism of the chief obstructions to creativity, two important conclusions emerge. The
first is that obstructions—both practical and theoretical—actually
exist and are more detrimental than most educationists realize.
The second is the fact that by means of a thorough analysis and
criticism plus effective action, their influence can be greatly de-
creased. In the light then of these two chapters on creativity, we
shall now proceed to look at three important disciplines, namely,
science, religion, and philosophy.

IX

Toward Creativity in Science

What follows is by no means a thorough or an adequate treatment of science as an educational discipline. To obtain that the reader must look elsewhere. The purpose is rather to promote creativity in science by viewing it through broad historical and philosophical perspectives, and also in terms of the demands of this new age into which man has stumbled.

1. Science Yesterday and Today

There was a time when one could pursue science only at a great personal risk. Giordano Bruno, "the first martyr to science," was burned at the stake in the year 1600, Copernicus was regarded as stupid as well as subversive for giving the world his heliocentric theory, while, as everyone knows, Galileo was forced to recant for insisting that the earth moves. Most surprising of all, from the standpoint of the curriculum itself, almost until the very dawn of the twentieth century, science was treated like an unwanted stepchild.

Today, however, the tables are turned. Modern man has become so fascinated by the siren voice of science that on both sides of the Iron Curtain the scientist is regarded as a miracle man, and is often venerated in a manner strikingly reminiscent of the homage given to the kings and priests of old.[1] There is real danger, in fact, that science may virtually monopolize the curriculum to the detriment of the humanities.[2] The unwanted stepchild of yesterday may actually usurp the throne.

2. The Nature of Science

At this juncture we are confronted with an important question to which we must try to find an answer before we can go further. This is the question of the nature of science itself. Since there is no absolute distinction between the scientific and what may be called the nonscientific, it is not easy to find an adequate answer to this question.

The English word science comes from the Latin *scientia* which is derived from *scire* (to know). Science, in the very broadest sense, really signifies any body of organized or systematized knowledge. Taken in this broad sense, science would embrace most of the material comprised in the other disciplines—including most of philosophy itself. Strange as it may seem today with so much emphasis being laid on the centrality of science, there was a time when the latter was really regarded as an aspect of philosophy. Indeed, historically speaking, philosophy is the mother of the sciences. Beginning as the latter did in the speculations of the philosophers, the various sciences gradually developed and differentiated themselves when they attained a certain degree of maturity.

At any rate, in view of the fact that they have differentiated themselves from philosophy, science (which comprises the various sciences) must be defined much more precisely than we have thus far attempted. Philosophy, of course, aims at a type of knowledge that is more synoptic, comprehensive, and all-embracing than that which is attempted by the various sciences. Indeed, something

1. On the Soviet emphasis on science and technology, see Alexander G. Korol, *Soviet Education for Science and Technology*.

2. For an excellent discussion of science and its educational import and significance, see Philip H. Phenix, *Philosophy of Education* (New York: Henry Holt & Co., 1958), pp. 321-423. For perspectives on the place of technical education, see Alfred North Whitehead, *The Aims of Education*, pp. 52-68.

can be said in favor of the notion that there is nothing that can be called science, but that there are only sciences—that is, the various specialized disciplines.

Again, if taken in the broad sense of any systematized knowledge whatsoever, science would also include much of what is known as common sense. Thomas H. Huxley, that ardent champion of science, went so far as to call science "nothing but trained and organized common sense." This conception is not, however, adequate. Even though it is true that any and all investigation of the nature of things had to begin, historically speaking, with common sense, it is also true that the investigator —sooner or later—discovered that he was forced to leave the deliverances and concepts of common sense far behind. In fact, he found himself in the grip of an intellectual discipline whose concepts transcend all ordinary experience. The truth of the matter is that such biological concepts as evolution, and even more such concepts of modern physics as energy and relativity, based as they are on many facts and on very complex processes of induction and deduction, constitute something other and something more than what is usually called common sense.

A. S. Eddington is probably right in his insistence that the real "cleavage" between the "scientific" and the "extra-scientific" or nonscientific lies primarily in the necessary distinction between the "metrical" and the "nonmetrical." [3] Thus, basically, science is a certain method of approach to reality. The aim is to understand and to predict by observing, measuring, and describing (if possible in mathematical terms or formulas) the nature of any phenomenon. Moreover, the ideal involved is *precision*. Hence, wherever possible, the scientist uses mathematics as his tool.[4] This is especially true in such sciences as physics and astronomy.

3. A. S. Eddington, *The Nature of the Physical World* (New York: The Macmillan Co., 1933), p. 275.

4. For a provocative discussion of the relations of mathematics to science, John G. Kemeny, *A Philosopher Looks at Science* (New York: D. Van Nostrand Co., 1959), pp. 14-35, is suggested.

As over against philosophy, science does not concern itself with ultimates. The basic terms involved are not *why* (which suggests the metaphysical and the ultimate) and *ought* (which suggests the normative), but rather *how* and *what*—both of which suggest the descriptive. Leaving ultimate explanation to the philosopher, the scientist is more in quest of an immediate explanation of *how* things behave or *how* they may be expected to behave: that is, he tries to explain what is now happening and what is likely to happen by means of certain fundamental uniformities or laws—which he assumes will function in the future in much the same manner as they have in the past. Thus astronomy tries to describe how the universe began, how a star or a galaxy behaves, and what may happen in the future so far as the affairs of the vast sidereal system are concerned. Similarly, though far less accurately, psychology and sociology seek to describe mental and social processes and individual and group behavior, and on the basis of these facts, they attempt predictions in terms of widely observed uniformities; while history tries to give an account of what has happened, is happening, and is likely to happen in the future. At any rate, in his search for *how* things operate, the scientist bypasses the more basic question of *why* they operate thus or *why* they exist at all.

It must also be added that, along with the desire to understand in order to predict, there is also the closely related desire to control. Here, in fact, we approach the problem of *pure science* (so dear to the Greek philosopher) versus *applied science* or technology. Insofar as the attempt is made to understand out of sheer intellectual curiosity, we have pure science; but insofar as the attempt is made to understand and predict in order to control, we, of course, have technology—that ambitious son of the scientific enterprise which today tends to dominate the scene.

Some attempt must now be made to classify the sciences. While this is difficult, it is true that they all seem to fall—more or less naturally—under three general heads: first, the *formal* (including logic along with the various forms of mathematics); second, the *natural* (embracing everything from astronomy and physics to biology); and, third, the *human* (comprising everything from anthropology and sociology to psychology and history).

Although a thorough discussion of science is beyond the scope of this venture, yet something more is in order relative to the question of scientific method. First of all, in terms of method, all the various sciences have the following in common: (1) they all begin with problems pertaining especially to their particular fields—though most of these problems, sooner or later, also tend to involve other fields; (2) they all *aim* at strict impartiality and objectivity and precision; and (3) they all try to build up bodies of reliable knowledge through a correct formulation of the facts and laws which govern their various fields. Second, in spite of these and other basic likenesses, and, in spite of popular opinion to the contrary, not all the sciences find it possible to use exactly the same methods.[5] Thus, while mathematics is decidedly abstract and deductive, biology is largely empirical and inductive. Third, even though a revolution has been taking place in mathematics in terms of the new non-Euclidean geometry,[6] a large measure of certainty and precision is still possible—especially in arithmetic; whereas the social sciences have to operate almost altogether in the realm of probability. Finally, while some sciences, such as chemistry and physics, make extensive use of laboratory experiments and procedures, others, like history and political science, find them quite useless.

From this brief consideration of the nature of science at least the following have become evident: that science is chiefly interested in that aspect of things which can be more or less pre-

5. For an excellent discussion of various sciences by a number of authorities, see James R. Newman (ed.), *What Is Science?* (paperback; New York: Washington Square Press, 1961).

6. On the significance of the non-Euclidean geometry, see the following: William Kneale & Martha Kneale, *The Development of Logic* (New York: Oxford University Press, 1962), p. 381 ff.; and David Eugene Smith, *History of Mathematics* (paperback; New York: Dover Publications, 1953), II, 335-37.

cisely measured; that, instead of being concerned with ultimates, it is concerned with the *how* and *what* of things; that it assumes a large amount of order in nature and on this basis it develops hypotheses and makes its predictions; that it aims both to understand and to control nature—this latter giving birth to technology; and that many sciences (especially astronomy and physics), in their attempt at precision, rely heavily on mathematics. After this effort to understand the nature of science, in order to obtain further perspective, we turn to its historic relations to education.

3. Historic Relations [7]

The relations of education and science go back to antiquity. The priests of ancient Egypt, Sumeria, and Babylon were greatly interested in astronomy, mathematics, and medicine. In spite of strong otherworldly tendencies, the Hindus also made important contributions, particularly to mathematics and medicine.

Unlike Americans and Russians, the ancient Greeks were interested primarily in the theoretical aspects of science, that is, in pure science rather than technology. Both Plato and Aristotle, in fact, had a certain contempt for a merely practical education.[8] Yet, regardless of this, Plato in his Academy carried on discussions not only in speculative philosophy and in mathematics, but also in political science, in astronomy, and even in biology and in geology.[9] Moreover, not only was Aristotle much more empirical than his great teacher, but Graves even goes so far as to say that modern biology, physiology, physics, mechanics, and psychology owe their original impetus largely to him.[10]

The medieval ideal, of course, was so otherworldly that little

7. For this section the following are helpful: Frederick Eby, *The Development of Modern Education;* Frank Pierrepoint Graves, *A History of Education;* and James Mulhern, *A History of Education.*

8. See, for example, Aristotle, *Politics,* Book VIII, 1338*b.* This contempt of Greek intellectuals for the practical must be listed as one cause of the decline of Greece; for, as a result, technology never really developed and slavery was condoned.

9. See John M. Warbeke, *The Searching Mind of Greece,* p. 160.

10. *A History of Education,* I, 198.

attention was given to science as such; but, as Alfred North Whitehead has shown, in the stress placed on the concept of law and order in nature, the foundations of the modern scientific movement were laid.[11] The Moslems and the Jews also made progress in astronomy, mathematics, medicine, and in some of the other sciences. Furthermore, in the bold rationalism of Abelard (1079-1142), and even more in the empirical and inductive spirit of Albertus Magnus (c. 1193-1280) and Roger Bacon (c. 1214-1294), one can detect the first faint glimmerings of the coming scientific revolution.

This revolution owes much to four men, namely, Copernicus (1473-1543), Galileo (1564-1642), Newton (1642-1727), and Darwin (1809-1882); and, so far as education itself is concerned, the "germ" of the idea of introducing science into "the content of education" finds its source in Rousseau.[12] Again, even though Johann Friedrich Herbart's chief aim in education was moral and cultural: he made considerable use of psychology.[13] Yet, in spite of the enormous progress in science, it was given little place in the curriculum until toward the very end of the nineteenth century and the beginning of the twentieth.

The two great champions of science in education were Herbert Spencer (1820-1903) and Thomas Huxley (1825-1895). While the former insisted that, in comparison to all other knowledge, the scientific is of most worth, the latter exposed mercilessly the shortcomings of the classical schools of his day and demanded that science be given a place in the curriculum *comparable* to that of the other disciplines. Thus Huxley was by far the more moderate of the two.[14]

With the coming of the Nuclear and Space Age, there has come an even greater interest in science. Not only does science

---

11. In his *Science and the Modern World*, pp. 18-19.

12. Graves, *A History of Education*, III, 320.

13. See Eby, *The Development of Modern Education*, pp. 474-85. Herbart also was the first to formulate a real science of education.

14. See his *Science and Education* (New York: Appleton-Century-Crofts, 1900).

practically dominate the curriculum, especially in some of our colleges and universities, but the scientific method has also been applied to the educational process itself in many ways. Earlier experimental schools in Europe inspired many similar projects in this country. John Dewey was, of course, one of the leaders in the experimental movement. Others began introducing various scientific techniques. Educational research and measurement became something of a fad.[15] In fact, standardized tests almost became a "mania" in some quarters.[16] The present stress on vocational training and technology likewise tends to enhance science. The same is also true of the policy of the federal government which, through various inducements, makes scientific careers attractive to gifted young men. The chief object here, unfortunately, is the development of more and more deadly weapons.

In spite of this continued emphasis on science, there are signs that a change may be in process. John Dewey sensed this "revolt against science." [17] Today many thoughtful people no longer look upon science as a virtual Moses ready to lead mankind into the Promised Land. Some have even come to distrust it profoundly. Extreme as some of these protests undoubtedly are, they are all indicative of one significant fact: that, both from a philosophical and a practical standpoint, the time is ripe for a new evaluation of science in terms of its place in education.

4. Limitations and Dangers [18]

There was a time when men had supreme confidence in science as the way to ultimate truth. Strange as it may seem, during the

15. For an illuminating discussion of scientific education and techniques in this country, see Harl R. Douglass & Calvin Grieder, *American Public Education* (New York: The Ronald Press Co., 1948), pp. 483-508.

16. See *ibid.*, p. 490.

17. In his *Philosophy of Education*, pp. 160-63. He viewed this trend with alarm.

18. On this section, see the following: Eddington, *The Nature of the Physical World;* Max Planck, *The Philosophy of Physics;* J. W. N. Sullivan, *The Limitations of Science* (New York: New American Library, 1949); Lecomte du Noüy, *Human Destiny;* and Ralph E. Lapp, *Kill and Overkill.* See also my chapter, "Personalistic Religion and Science," in Edwin Prince Booth (ed.), *Religion Ponders Science*, especially pp. 164-68.

nineteenth century, most physicists were convinced that their mechanistic scheme—based upon the old atomic theory—was little short of final.[19] Some thinkers, such as Ernst Haeckel, built their philosophies confidently upon the sciences, fondly believing that they would soon tear the veil from life's last mystery. Even in some contemporary philosophers, though somewhat chastened by the course of events, one can still detect something of this extreme confidence in science.

There is, however, the increasing realization that science is in no sense absolute, that it too has its limitations. Philosophical analysis discloses the fact that science rests on certain presuppositions that can never be completely proved. Among these assumptions, there is not only the existence of other minds and of an external world, but also the belief that this world is knowable by human minds. As every philosopher knows, these assumptions—though reasonable—involve profound epistemological considerations which science really bypasses.

Closely related to the above is the fact that science assumes the constancy of natural law. Simply because the processes of nature have always been dependable, however, is no absolute proof that they will always and everywhere meet our expectations. David Hume showed this long ago.[20] In short, here, as elsewhere, there is most certainly an element of faith involved.[21]

That scientific knowledge can never be absolute and final is also abundantly proved by the history of science; for, not unlike religion, science also has had its orthodoxies and its heterodoxies, and often the latter have displaced the former. Thus, the defenders

19. For a graphic account (by an outstanding physicist who lived through the experience) of the consternation that the new, dynamic physics produced, see Robert Andrews Millikan, *Evolution in Science and Religion* (New Haven: Yale University Press, 1927), pp. 10-11. The old mechanistic physicists were confounded.

20. See the interesting passage from his "Inquiry Concerning Human Understanding" in Benjamin Rand (ed.), *Modern Classical Philosophers* (second edition; Boston: Houghton Mifflin Co., 1936), p. 324.

21. On the place of faith in science, see Planck, *The Philosophy of Physics*, pp. 119-25.

of orthodoxy, holding to the fixity of the species, opposed Darwin, but were finally completely defeated. Similarly, the new, dynamic physics displaced the old, classical type. Moreover, there is the question of origins (cosmogony) which today is in a state of virtual chaos. There seem to be as many theories as there are astronomers.[22] There is also the disgraceful struggle in psychology between the behaviorists and the psychoanalysts. Recently a psychologist told of a department of psychology in a well-known institution of higher learning where the two leading members—belonging to these two opposing schools—were not even on speaking terms most of the time.

Again, the scientific approach to reality is, for the most part at least, analytical and, therefore, piecemeal. Instead of there being one discipline called science, there are really, as we have already seen, many sciences. There is no doubt, of course, that the analytical approach to reality is important and fruitful; for reality is, in truth, so vast that only a Don Quixote would be foolish enough to attack it all at once. The strategy of divide and conquer possesses certain decided advantages. One can surely learn much about wholes by studying the parts.

Still, it must be admitted that analysis is but the first step in sound method. Left by itself, instead of going from less to more, it tends to go from more to less; for, it tries to explain the more complex and more significant in terms of the simpler and less significant—thus falling into the error of reductionism. There is a "togetherness" in things and in the structure of human personality which analysis misses. Mental processes, as the Gestalt psychologists have shown, tend to function as integrated structures, patterns, configurations. Hence, if there is to be a real understanding of the nature of mind, there must be much more

22. Compare, for example, George Gamow, *The Creation of the Universe* (New York: The Viking Press, 1955) with Fred Hoyle, *The Nature of the Universe* (paper back; New York: The New American Library, 1950) For the many different theories that have been held, see also Milton K. Munitz (ed.), *Theories of the Universe* (Glencoe, Ill.: The Free Press, 1957). See also *The Monist*, Vol. XLVII, No. 1 (Fall, 1962) on developments in cosmology.

of a synoptic approach than orthodox psychologists are willing to allow.

Nor can the problem of the *many* sciences (each with its own field and often contradicting one another) be forgotten. The great need in science today is a coordination of the findings in the various fields; for after all, every science (from psychology to astronomy) has something important to add to our knowledge of the universe. More than this, there is real need of a *scientia scientiarum* (a science of the sciences) to coordinate not only the findings of all the sciences, but also the latter with the best insights of the great religions. We need wholeness in terms of a world view that makes sense.

It also became clear at the beginning of this chapter that, since the chief aim of the sciences signifies a real attempt to measure and to describe, their primary concern is with the tangible and quantitative aspects of reality rather than with the intangible and qualitative. This means that the intangible and the qualitative aspects of reality are largely beyond the reach of science—that is, at least in the strict sense of the word. One may, of course, take seriously the dogma that whatever exists can be measured, and then begin throwing out as unreal whatever does not fit this Procrustean bed. This, however, is sheer arbitrariness—a very unscientific way to get rid of a difficult problem. Moreover, it has already become clear that there are aspects of reality which, if they can be measured at all, certainly cannot be measured with precision. Among these are creativity, individuality, uniqueness, thoughts, ideals—in fact, all the higher reaches of the mind which our psychologists have so largely neglected. How long or short or light or heavy is a thought or an ideal? While these certainly must be studied *critically* and *synoptically* (in the light of all available knowledge to which all the sciences can make a contribution), they cannot be measured with anything even remotely approaching precision and, therefore, science cannot speak the last word. This does not mean, however, that it cannot throw any light on them.

Mention must also be made of the fact that value norms such as justice and ethical love are not derived from the sciences. The *ought* cannot be derived from the *is*. While the sciences can aid greatly in terms of providing the means necessary to the realization of ideals, they can never prescribe the ideals themselves. Those scientists who possess ideals—and most of them certainly do—bring them to the sciences rather than deriving them from the sciences.[23] Those scientists who have protested against the misuse of science by the politicians, working hand in hand with the militarists, have derived their ideals from their democratic environment[24] and, ultimately, from their Hebrew-Christian-Greek heritage.

Similarly, when it comes to the question of goals or ends, the sciences have no answer. They deal with effective means not ends. Neither analysis as such, nor the limited synthesis which science entails, can ever envisage an adequate goal for education or for life and make it function as an imperative. This can only be done through a synoptic process, capable of doing full justice both to the demands of intuition and of reason and of grasping something of a total vision of life and of its highest possibilities. The sciences can never really deal creatively with ultimates, since they lack the necessary *wholeness* of outlook which this necessitates. The whole meaning of life can, of course, never be completely comprehended by any mortal; but the best insights are not likely to be obtained from any disciplines which approach it from a mere aspect. As a matter of fact, the chief function of science, it has already become evident, is to deal with the *how* rather than the *why* of things.

Finally, the dangerous aspects of science must not be overlooked. Not only is it incapable of giving us moral ideals, but

23. For a defense of the idea that scientists can derive moral judgments from science, see Abraham Edel, *Ethical Judgment* (Glencoe, Ill.: The Free Press, 1955), pp. 243, 246; and for criticisms, see the review by John Ladd, in *The Philosophical Review*, Oct., 1956, pp. 550-56; also my review in *The Personalist*, Summer, 1956, pp. 287-88.

24. For the damaging effects of determinism, as found in some of our psychologists, see previous discussion, Ch. VIII, pp. 167-68.

it is also capable of creating conditions that will lead to the destruction of democracy. A great nuclear scientist in a recent book has an entire chapter entitled "The Tragedy of Science." [25] He especially deplores the fact that so many scientists have sold themselves to the military and use their minds to develop new and more destructive weapons. The tragic situation pictured in George Orwell's *Nineteen Eighty-Four* is not beyond possibility. Both Hitler and Stalin have shown the world what a terrible instrument science can be in the hands of the new barbarians. Equipped with modern scientific techniques, there are hardly any limits—however fantastic—to which a modern dictator may not go. Worst of all, there is the nuclear threat hanging over our uneasy heads like a mighty sword of Damocles.

5. Science as Indispensable

In spite of its limitations and in spite of the dangers, the fact remains that science is indispensable, and must, therefore, occupy an important place in the total educational enterprise. In what follows, we shall briefly present the reasons why it is and why it shall continue to be significant.

To begin with, the quantitative aspect of reality is very important. By all means, since it gives us the power to predict and control a capricious nature for man's benefit, let us continue to describe and to measure all that is measurable. Again, the various sciences represent large bodies of tested knowledge. To say that this knowledge is not final and absolute is not to question its worth as far as it goes. Furthermore, it is subject to constant increase. Nor can there be any doubt that philosophy itself, since this knowledge tells us something about the nature of reality, must make the fullest possible use of all that science has to offer. Not only, as the Greeks realized long ago, can science serve to satisfy man's intellectual curiosity, but it can also serve to broaden his vision. This is particularly true of astronomy.

25. See Ralph E. Lapp, *Kill and Overkill*, pp. 15-22. Every educator and every scientist, in particular, should read this chapter.

Similarly, from an intellectual standpoint, man owes much more than he realizes to the mental discipline which comes from the use of the scientific method. It has taught him the difficult task of thinking empirically, impartially, and in experimental terms. This has helped to liberate him from authoritarianism and from a thousand errors and superstitions with their accompanying horrors. Due in part at least to science, we no longer burn helpless old women for witchcraft or attempt to "beat the Devil" out of the insane.

Nor must it be forgotten that ideals cannot be realized, at least on a large scale, without the means that science provides. The Greeks paid dearly for their cold disdain for the practical aspects of science. Thus, John Dewey was fully justified in his protest against the "disparagement of effective means." [26]

In an hour when mankind has stumbled to the very edge of the precipice, no one will deny the importance of the age-old longing for peace. Yet, paradoxical as it may seem, while science holds the diabolical means of mass annihilation in her left hand, with her right she graciously offers us the means toward the realization of this ideal. Peace means, among other things, effective governments both on the national and on the international levels; and this involves the knowledge offered by the social sciences. Peace also means a vast increase of the world's food supply plus a rational program of birth control. As long as half of the human race goes to bed hungry every night, and as long as population increases outrun food supplies, there can be no peace. [27] Yet, for effective solutions to these problems, where else can we turn except to science?

As a final justification of science, an appeal may be made to the scientific educational movement itself. Psychology and sociology

26. See his *Quest for Certainty*, p. 270.
27. On the necessity of a sane birth control policy, see Eby, *The Development of Modern Education*, pp. 677-78. For the problem as it exists today, see also the article (which has stimulated considerable discussion), "How Many Babies Is Too Many?" in *Newsweek*, July 23, 1962, pp. 27-33.

have facilitated the learning process considerably. In many ways, in fact, they have helped us to understand the learner better. Moreover, even though the measurement movement has become something of a fad at times, still, within certain limits and in certain respects, it has proved its worth.

6. Scientific Creativity for the Future

In this chapter we have considered five things: the status of science today; its general nature; its relation to education historically speaking; its limitations and dangers; and its indispensability. All this is for the purpose of attaining perspective—the kind of perspective that is conducive to that creativity which is so badly needed today. It remains to summarize our conclusions relative to this very important matter.

To become truly creative in the very highest sense of the word, it is clear that science must set its house in order. This means not less than four very significant things.

First of all, science must liberate itself from bondage to the militarists—in all countries. Militarism means Prussianism and totalitarianism. There can be no doubt that these are contrary to the scientific spirit of free inquiry. More than this, subservience to the militarists, if continued much longer, will destroy science itself as well as the human race. It is this subservience, in fact, that has given science a bad name.

Second, for the maximum creativity, it must give equal attention to its two chief aspects, namely, the pure or theoretical and the practical or technological. The first is important for no less than three reasons: it gives a certain intellectual satisfaction—which the Greeks prized so highly; it supplies philosophy with new facts and perspectives; and it provides the foundation for the practical or technological. The benefits of the latter are obvious to everyone.

Third, scientists must realize the limitations as well as possibilities of science. A due regard for its limitations will cause them to beware of dogmatism and of that strange new faith—*scientism*, the child of scientific dogmatism. At the same time, however, a true realization of its immense possibilities, both in terms of increasing our knowledge of the universe and in its ability to minister to human needs, would present challenges which would continue to attract many of the best minds.

Finally, to become really creative in this the Nuclear Age, science must itself become *humanized* and thoroughly *responsible*. This means that, instead of spawning more deadly weapons, scientists must become more vocal in their demand for disarmament and a new world order. A few of the greatest—among them Albert Einstein (while he was still alive), Bertrand Russell, Linus Pauling, Ralph Lapp, etc.—have caught this greater vision. What is needed is a mass awakening of scientists all over the world. This could mean a new era for science as well as a new day for mankind.

From this consideration of creativity in science we now turn to that aspect of human endeavor with which science has often warred, namely, religion. For, if man is to live richly as well as survive, it is not enough for him to try to understand and control nature, he must also worship.

X

Toward Creativity in Religion

1. The Nature and Significance of Religion

Religion exhibits such variety that it is even more difficult to
define than education or science.[1] In terms of its essence, it is
probably best defined as a vital concern for whatever is believed
to be of *supreme worth*.[2] This involves two factors, namely, a
Supreme Object or objects of devotion, and the devotees with their
various ways of expressing their regard and concern.

Although the *Supreme Object* of devotion has been conceived
both in personal and impersonal terms, the former has been predominant—particularly in the West. While on the primitive levels
this has meant animism and polytheism with the gods conceived
in a rather crude anthropomorphic fashion as glorified men, gradually, as man gained a larger perspective, this belief gave way to
theism with its highly moralized and spiritualized conception of
God. In short, in terms of Cosmic Mind and Will, God came to be
regarded as the supreme Person. Hence theism is closely related to

---

1. On the nature of religion see: Winston L. King, *Introduction to Religion* (New
York: Harper & Row, 1954), pp. 6-8; and Edgar Sheffield Brightman, *A Philosophy of
Religion*, pp. 13-18.
2. This was suggested by Wieman's concept of the "Supremely Worthful"; see
Henry Nelson Wieman & Bernard Eugene Meland, *American Philosophies of Religion*
(Chicago: Willett, Clark, & Company, 1936), p. 299.

philosophic personalism. Among other things, theists stress the dignity and worth of human personality, the objectivity of truth, beauty, and goodness, the conflict with evil, and the possibility of triumph over evil through a creative faith in the Divine Love.

It is not true, of course, that all religion is creative. There is definitely a debit side.[3] That is why it is necessary to make a distinction between high and low religion. By high religion we mean the great faiths of mankind—Christianity, Judaism, Buddhism, Hinduism, Islam, and Zoroastrianism—at their *best*. As over against low religion, this means thoughtful, ethical, enlightened religion: the faith that is in line with the very highest aspirations of the human spirit.[4]

Arnold Toynbee gives four reasons why high religion is so important. Among these is the fact that it has had a very important effect on human affairs both through its mighty deeds and through the institutions that it has created.[5] Likewise Brightman speaks of "the coalescence of religious values with other values." [6] By this he means that during its great creative periods, instead of confining itself to the narrowly religious, it also expresses itself mightily through art, music, architecture, education, the healing of the sick, etc. Moreover, Alfred North Whitehead shows that it was the concept of order taken from Christianity, Judaism, and Greek philosophy which made the modern scientific movement possible.[7] Finally, there is William Ernest Hocking with his insistence that high religion is nothing less than "the *mother of the Arts*." [8]

There are two reasons why religion at its best has been so creative: first, through all its great forms it has stressed values—including the transcendental; and, second, through all its great

---

3. On the debit side, see C. J. Ducasse, *A Philosophical Scrutiny of Religion* (New York: The Ronald Press Co., 1953), pp. 168-94.

4. On high and low religion, see also my *Perplexing Problems of Religion*, pp. 95-96.

5. See his *Reconsiderations*, p. 97.

6. See *A Philosophy of Religion*, pp. 104-105.

7. In his *Science and the Modern World*, pp. 18-19.

8. In *The Meaning of God in Human Experience*, p. 14. For the great art inspired by Hinduism and Buddhism, see Jack Finegan, *The Archaeology of World Religions* (Princeton: Princeton University Press, 1952).

theistic forms it has stressed the idea of God as Cosmic Mind and Will. This latter is very important since it emphasizes the idea of a *Purpose* running through the universe and human life, so that our human creativity, in spite of the effects of time and change, is not ultimately in vain.

Since our primary interest so far as this venture is concerned is educational rather than religious, it is not necessary to attempt to prove the superiority of any specific form which religion has taken. One thing, however, is certain: by virtue of its influence and its potentialities (regardless of his personal views), no fair-minded educational philosopher can afford to neglect it. He has it on his hands and must, in some sense, relate it to the total educational process. This will become even more evident in the light of the section which follows.

2. Historic Relations [9]

In Chapter II it became clear that the relations between education and religion were remarkably close during primitive times. Primitive culture was permeated by religion. The dominant figure in prehistoric times—the shaman or medicine man—was really the forerunner of the priest and the prophet as well as the teacher.

Religion also played an important part in the educational systems of the ancient world. In Egypt, Sumeria, Assyria, and Babylon, the temples served as vital centers of learning, while in China Confucianism dominated the educational system for some two thousand years. Moreover, in both Palestine and India, the end and goal of the entire educational process was provided by re-

9. A considerable part of what follows is based upon an article of mine—"A Synoptic Approach to Religious Education"—which appeared in *Religious Education*, May-June, 1958. I am grateful to the publisher, The Religious Education Association, for allowing me to make use of this material. For perspective in religious education, the following are suggested: J. Donald Butler, *Religious Education: The Foundations And Practice of Nurture*; Marvin J. Taylor (ed.), *Religious Education: A Comprehensive Survey*; Howard Grimes, *The Church Redemptive*; and Philip Henry Lotz (ed.), *Orientation in Religious Education* (Nashville: Abingdon Press, 1951). Although the latter is a bit out of date so far as the present situation is concerned, in terms of historic perspective, Part I is still valuable.

ligion. Again, while there were strong secular influences in Greece, some of the greatest philosophers—including Plato himself [10]— were deeply concerned about religious education. Nor can there be any question about the place of religion during the Middle Ages. As "the Queen of the sciences" theology, in fact, constituted the crowning glory of the entire educational structure.

With the decay of Scholasticism, the advent of the Renaissance, and eventually the rise of the new science, secularism began to revive and to reassert itself. Four chief factors are involved in this process: (1) the overthrow of the traditional Christian *Weltanschauung* by modern science (while Copernicus and Galileo began the process during the sixteenth century, Darwin finished it during the nineteenth); (2) the French Revolution (which marked the first real modern attempt to overthrow and replace religion—and which also resulted in the establishment of the secular state); (3) the advent of the Industrial Revolution with its promise of material abundance (beginning during the latter part of the eighteenth century in England and spreading gradually over the world); and (4) the rise of what Paul Tillich calls the "quasi-religions," [11] chief among which is Marxianism (this young, aggressive, atheistic faith which is challenging all the great religious systems). With the dawn of the twentieth century, education was well on its way toward secularization.

In spite of this, religion has and still plays an important role in education. To begin with, most of the centers of higher learning in the West have been in some way connected with religion—at least in their beginnings. One has only to mention Oxford and Cambridge, Harvard and Yale; and that there are still a few live coals beneath the ashes is evident from some of the things which have occurred at Harvard through the policies of President Nathan M. Pusey.

---

10. See A. E. Taylor's comments in his Introduction to his translation of *The Laws of Plato* (London: J. M. Dent & Sons, 1934), pp. xviii-xix.

11. In his little book, *Christianity and the Encounter of the World Religions* (New York: Columbia University Press, 1963).

While both Roman Catholicism and Protestantism have exercised a profound influence on modern education, the influence of the latter is particularly noteworthy. Even though many Protestants actually opposed public education, it is probably true that, if there had been no Protestant Reformation, there would not have been any public school system: for, in its stress on the rights of conscience and on Bible reading by the laity, Protestantism made imperative the enlightenment of the masses.

Although, as Eby points out, Luther had no real desire for popular education as it is understood today, as a reformer, he set in motion certain "liberalizing forces" which were bound to have an effect sooner or later. Among these were his break with the autocratic Roman hierarchy, his translation of the Bible into high German (the language of the people), and his inclusion of *all* children, regardless of class, in his plans for religious education. At this point then, despite his political reactionism, Luther made an outstanding contribution.[12]

John Knox, the Scottish Calvinist, went further than Luther. In his *First Book of Discipline*, he proposed a system consisting of everything from elementary schools to universities.[13] This idea bore fruit in 1646 when the Scottish Parliament passed an act requiring a school in every parish, supported by public taxation and under the supervision of the Presbyteries; and, while this particular legislation was not put into effect due to the English tyranny, after the Revolution of 1688, Scotland actually set up a system of national schools.[14]

Mention must also be made of the Protestant Sunday school. Beginning in England in 1780, when Robert Raikes conceived the idea of employing a teacher to instruct the children of the poor who worked every day except Sunday, it soon spread all over the kingdom and even across the sea to America. Whatever the faults of

12. See Frederick Eby, *The Development of Modern Education*, p. 79.
13. *Ibid.*, p. 120.
14. *Ibid.*, pp. 214-15.

the Sunday school may be today (and they are many), its historic significance as a medium of mass enlightenment remains.[15]

Equally important is the religious concern of the great, modern educational pioneers. John Amos Comenius (1592-1670), Bishop of the Moravians, and Johann Heinrich Pestalozzi (1746-1827) both had a profound regard for religion.[16] Similarly, Friedrich Froebel (1782-1852) held that the aim of education is nothing short of an understanding of one's self, of mankind, "of God and nature," and the living of "a pure and holy life." [17]

Consequently, while it is true that some educators are indifferent to religion, this was not true of the giants who paved the way for so much that is best in contemporary educational schemes.[18] Even Rousseau—rebel that he was against all institutions, even the church—believed in God and had a profound respect for the Christian faith. Again, today, even though the tides of secularism are running strong, many educators are not only personally interested in religion, but some are also seeking ways of making it a part of the curriculum and of integrating it more effectively with the educational process as a whole. History then serves to illustrate the close relations existing between education and religion.

A few remarks, however, are in order at this juncture concerning modern and contemporary trends in religious education.[19] Religious education in this country has gone through three chief

15. For an illuminating account of the rise and development of the Sunday School, see Butler, *Religious Education*, pp. 53-67.

16. For Pestalozzi's view, see *How Gertrude Teaches Her Children*, translated by Lucy E. Holland, Francis C. Turner, & edited by Ebenezer Cooke (third edition; London: George Allen & Unwin, 1915), especially pp. 190-97.

17. See his book, *The Education of Man*, p. 5.

18. Perhaps the best illustration of the lack of interest in religion on the part of some educationists is still the famous Report of the Harvard Committee, *General Education in a Free Society* (Cambridge: Harvard University Press, 1945). It virtually ignores religion.

19. On these trends, see especially Butler, *Religious Education*, pp. 113-21; and Taylor (ed.), *Religious Education*, pp. 30-33.

stages and is probably approaching a fourth. The first may be termed the traditional with its emphasis on discipline, authority, and transmission. It was centered on the Bible which was regarded as an infallible book. Although the second or liberal period began with Horace Bushnell's *Christian Nurture,* later, through the influence of men such as George Albert Coe, it took on many of the features of John Dewey's naturalism and pragmatism—along with his stress on social democracy. Hence, while there was little theological content, it centered on ethics. This led to the third period, namely, due largely to influences from Europe, a stress on theology at the expense of ethics. Later, in dealing with the religious outlook, we shall have more to say about this concern for theology.

At any rate, since the present stress on theology seems to be as extreme as the former emphasis on ethics to the neglect of theology, and, since many educators look at it askance, we seem to be rapidly approaching a fourth stage: that is, a stage of confusion. The truth of the matter seems to be that, in view of the lack of an adequate overall aim or goal, there is as much confusion today in religious education as in education as a whole. The great need is a creativity which will do full justice to both ethics and theology, and which will, at the same time find common ground with education as a whole. In an age when the great danger is the brutalization and the barbarization of man (especially in an hour when the tides of reactionism are running high again) perhaps our suggestion of the *humanization of man* will prove helpful. We shall have more to say about this is later chapters.

3. The American Dilemma

It is evident that democracy has religious roots: concepts such as justice and the dignity of human personality, which lie at the basis of genuine democracy, are derived largely from the great Hebrew-Christian tradition. Again, while both Catholicism and Protestantism have made significant contributions to American democracy, the latter, in particular, with its emphasis on the individual conscience, set the basic pattern. Both Puritanism (through its firm belief in the rights of conscience and the duty of resisting tyranny)[20] and the so-called left-wing churches— that is, Quakers, Baptists, etc.—(through their devotion to religious freedom), have made outstanding contributions.

Indeed, not only were the churches pioneers in higher education, but they also played a part in the development of the public school system itself. The early colonial schools were, for the most part, the products of the church; and in them the religious emphasis was dominant.[21] Nor is it true that reformers such as Thomas Jefferson and Horace Mann advocated a strictly secularized education. While for them the doctrine of the separation of church and state meant the ending of all sectarian control, it did not mean that absolute divorce between religion and education of which modern secularists dream. They not only recognized that democracy has a religious foundation, but they would also have made provision for the actual teaching of religion in public educational institutions.

Although, in his plans for the University of Virginia, Jefferson opposed all sectarian control, he favored instruction in religion. Indeed, he even went so far as to propose that the various sects establish schools of divinity on the campus.[22] Likewise, in a letter, Mann, far from advocating the exclusion of all religious instruction from the public schools, insisted that he favored as much non-sectarian religious education as possible. He also made it clear that the consequences of extreme secularism are as dangerous as those arising from narrow sectarianism.[23]

So far as the present situation is concerned, in spite of certain strong secularistic tendencies, there is no reason to suppose that our public schools are nearly as godless and materialistic as their foes would have us believe. This is one of the conclusions of one of

20. On the contributions of Puritanism, see Ralph Barton Perry, *Puritanism and Democracy* (New York: Vanguard Press, 1944).

21. See Harl R. Douglass & Calvin Grieder, *American Public Education*, pp. 13-15.

22. See Henry P. Van Dusen, *God in Modern Education*, pp. 105-106.

23. This letter is in J. Paul Williams, *The New Education and Religion* (New York: Association Press, 1945), p. 45.

the best recent surveys.[24] Not only do many teachers and administrators have a real interest in religion, but there is also considerable
religious teaching, both direct and indirect, and, if it were not
for the jealous rivalry of the many competing sects, there would
be much more. In short, sectarianism is probably doing more to
secularize our schools than all the schemes devised by atheists and
agnostics.

Be that as it may, regardless of the religious foundations of democracy, and regardless of the significance of the religious factor
in education, today the dominant trend in our schools is toward
secularization.[25] Consequently, this is essentially the dilemma in
which our public schools find themselves: teachers are free to tell
our youth about Hitler and even about Stalin (at least in communities where the superpatriots are not too active), but in many
places Jesus and the prophets are taboo.

Why this conspiracy of silence concerning our foundations? It
cannot excuse itself in terms of neutralism, since, by this very
silence, secularism and materialism are given the very opportunity
which they seek. Thus a nation whose very foundations rest on religious idealism finds itself in the embarrassing situation of ignoring
vital elements of its own heritage. The great danger is the creation
of a generation which knows not Joseph—which would mean the
downfall of the democratic system.[26] That this is already in
process is clear from the large crop of barbarians which we are
producing, some of whom turn away from democracy to an
American brand of fascism, while others resort to crime.[27]

24. R. H. Dierenfield, *Religion in American Public Schools* (Washington, D.C.:
Public Affairs Press, 1962), especially p. 106.

25. For an interesting sketch of the relations of church and state and the advance
toward secularization, see A. D. C. Peterson's book, *A Hundred Years of Education*,
pp. 31-52.

26. For the dangers inherent in secularization, see Luther A. Weigle, "The Aim and
Scope of Religious Education," in Lotz (ed.), *Orientation in Religious Education*,
pp. 87-98.

27. Recently, Police Supt. O. W. Wilson of Chicago warned that, if present crime
rates continue, "every street will become a jungle."

4. The Religious Outlook [28]

Since the primary purpose of this venture is educational and philosophical rather than theological, we shall be brief. Yet, since every educational and philosophical problem has ultimate and hence theological implications, this section is necessary. Our purpose then in what follows is to sketch the chief aspects of the religious situation in bold relief. We begin with those which are negative and downright discouraging.

There is, to begin with, the current confusion. It has already become evident that many of our educational leaders are confused: lacking a clear vision of basic aims and objectives, like so many politicians, they seem to be content with a shortsighted pragmatism. Moreover, lacking any sense of absolutes, they wander in a fog of relativism and fail to see the value of religion. If there is confusion in education, it is still worse in religion. The scandal of religion is and always has been this sorry spectacle of the many competing sects, each claiming to have—if not the only way— the surest way to headquarters in heaven. Besides this, today as usually in the past, the theologians are almost as confused as the laity. If one were to gather together the theologians of all religions and sects for a public discussion, that would be *babel* indeed. No wonder that there is so much skepticism.

> Myself when young did eagerly frequent
> Doctor and Saint, and heard great argument

28. For the beginner seeking general perspective, the following are suggested: Butler, *Religious Education*, pp. 113-35; Taylor (ed.), *Religious Education*, pp. 30-33; William Hordern, *A Layman's Guide to Theology*; John A. T. Robinson, *Honest to God* (Philadelphia: The Westminister Press, 1963); and a stimulating article, "The Time Has Come," by Deane William Ferm, in *The Christian Century*, July 15, 1964, pp. 903-906. The following will help the student who wants to go deeper: John Macquarrie, *Twentieth Century Religious Thought*; T. Alec Burkill, *God and Reality in Modern Thought* (Englewood Cliffs: Prentice-Hall, 1963); Paul Tillich, *Christianity and the Encounter of the World Religions*; L. Harold DeWolf, *The Religious Revolt Against Reason* (New York: Harper & Brothers, 1949); Kenneth Cauthen, *The Impact of American Religious Liberalism* (New York: Harper & Row, 1962); Sarvepalli Radhakrishnan, *Recovery of Faith* (New York: Harper & Brothers, 1955); Nathaniel Micklem, *Ultimate Questions* (Nashville: Abingdon Press, 1955); and Edgar Sheffield Brightman, *The Problem of God* (New York: The Abingdon Press, 1930).

About it and about: but evermore
Came out by the same door where in I went.

So far as Christianity is concerned, most of its theologians are failing to give much light to an age when mankind has stumbled within an inch of the abyss. In spite of certain creative trends, Roman Catholic theologians are still too much confined by the narrow circle of dogmas within which they must operate. They are also still weighted down by an obsolete terminology inherited from the Middle Ages. Although there is much more creativity among the philosophers (which includes such names as Jacques Maritain, Étienne Gilson, and Louis de Raeymaeker), even here one is often bewildered by the preoccupation with archaic terms.[29]

The failures of much contemporary Protestant theology may be stated in three words: *dogmatism, fragmentariness,* and *vagueness*. Speaking of the Barthians, Paul Tillich has rightly observed that, while under Barth's leadership, the European Protestants were able to resist Hitler, the end result was "a theological and ecclesiastical narrowness" which fails to realize the creative possibilities existing in today's world.[30] The fragmentary thinking of these theologians is especially evident in their failures in three areas, namely, their rejection of natural theology,[31] their failure to deal creatively with the ultimate meaning of such important scientific concepts as evolution and the intriguing dynamic theories of the new physics, and their sectarian attitude to the challenge presented by the other religions.[32] Probably the best illustration of vagueness is no one less than Tillich himself. Thus Burkill has pointed out

29. While this is true to some extent of Maritain, *Preface to Metaphysics,* New York: New American Library, 1962), it is especially true of de Raeymaeker, *Philosophy of Being,* translated by E. H. Ziegelmeyer (St. Louis: B. Herder Book Co., 1954).

30. Tillich, *Christianity and the Encounter of World Religions,* pp. 45-46.

31. See John Wild's criticism in his article, "Questions Philosophers Ask Theologians," in *Religion In Life,* Summer, 1964, pp. 367-68.

32. Although Niebuhr has been more liberal than Barth, see E. A. Burtt's "Some Questions About Niebuhr's Theology," in Charles W. Kegley & Robert W. Bretail (eds.), *Reinhold Niebuhr* (New York: The Macmillan Co., 1956), p. 361.

the ambiguities inherent in his concept of "ultimate concern." [33] This is even more true of Tillich's conception of God. A case in point is his insistence that "it is as atheistic to affirm the existence of God as it is to deny it." [34] Indeed, his concept of God is so vague that he has been accused of everything from pantheism to atheism.[35]

Again, religion, both Christian and otherwise, has failed to meet the demands of the social and political crisis. While Christianity, for the most part, has been more alert and has contributed more than the other religions, yet, in comparison to the demands of its ideal and the demands of the hour, it has done far too little and often it has been too late. During the summer of 1962 (just three months before the Cuban Crisis), some of us who attended a conference of theologians at Oxford University were amazed that there was so much preoccupation with matters of doctrine and form and so little social concern. Three months later (back in this country during the Cuban crisis), this writer was even more amazed when he was told by one of the theologians that the destruction of the human race by means of a nuclear war might be God's will! Moreover, there is more than a grain of truth in the statement that the eleven o'clock hour on Sundays is the most *segregated* of the entire week. It is the moral and social indifference of the masses that comprise the Church which puts the sting into Szczesny's charge that there might have been a *bit* more suffering if our savage ancestors had not been converted to Christianity.[36]

33. See *God and Reality in Modern Thought*, p. 206.

34. See his *Systematic Theology* (Chicago: University of Chicago Press, 1951), I, 237.

35. Now that the third vol. of his *Systematic Theology* has appeared (University of Chicago Press, 1963), it seems that Tillich's idea of God as "Spiritual Presence," since he rejects theism, constitutes a mixture of pantheistic and naturalistic notions. Interestingly enough, some years ago the following question was seriously debated at the annual meeting of the Western Division of the American Philosophical Association: "Is Tillich an Atheist?"

36. See Gerhard Szczesny, *The Future of Unbelief*, translated by E. B. Garside

Coming back to the state of contemporary religion in America, it seems that the much advertised, so-called religious revival (which was based to a large extent on the reactions of American nationalism to the Communist challenge) has just about run its course. There are even signs of a counterattack: not by a native brand of Marxianism, but rather by the forces of American secularism. While the importance of the Supreme Court ruling relative to Bible reading and prayer in the public schools has been greatly exaggerated, it does make two things clear: that American secularism is *strong*, and that it is taking the *offensive*.

In spite of the negative factors in the present religious situation, there are also many positive factors to which we now turn. To begin with, it must be repeated that many public school teachers and administrators have a real religious concern. It may even happen that the Supreme Court ruling will actually lead toward a more creative approach to the whole problem of religious education. We shall, in fact, make certain suggestions in the next section of this chapter.

In the second place, there has never been a greater desire to do something constructive about the problem of religious unity. Not only have many religious denominations merged, but the National Council of Churches (which now includes thirty-one denominations) and the World Council of Churches are exerting an increasing influence.[37] Due both to foresighted Roman Catholic leaders (chief among which was the late Pope John XXIII) and to foresighted Protestant leaders, these two great divisions of Christendom are coming closer together. Another hopeful sign was the meeting sponsored by the Religious Education Association which met in Chicago in November, 1962. Nearly a thousand representatives of the three major religious groups in this country (Roman

---

(New York: George Braziller, 1961), p. 195. This book constitutes one of the most bitter recent attacks on Christianity.

37. On the recent New Delhi meeting of the World Council of Churches, see W. A. Visser 't Hooft (ed.), *New Delhi Speaks* (New York: Association Press, 1962).

Catholicism, Judaism, and Protestantism) spent three days taking "a look at the moral climate of America." [38]

In the third place, and closely related to the above, there are also signs of a new creativity among Christian theologians. This is especially evident in the followers of Pope John XXIII. Many thoughtful Protestants who attended the meeting in Chicago called by the Religious Education Association were, in fact, amazed at the new outlook and frankness of some of the Roman Catholic scholars. [39]

Following in the wake of Rudolf Bultmann, Protestant scholars, in their attempt to get at the "vital essence" of Christianity, are trying to cut away the jungle of mythology which has so long covered and hidden it. [40] Even more important is the concern with "ultimate questions" rather than the more sectarian and superficial. There are also signs of the appearance of a new and more adequate liberalism. [41] Similarly, there are stirrings within the Barthian camp. This is certainly evident in Barth's little book, *The Humanity of God*. [42] Besides being less dogmatic, his conception of God, in this book, is less Calvinistic and he is even willing to acknowledge a certain indebtedness to philosophy. Christian theologians are also showing a greater and friendlier interest in the non-Christian religions. The best illustration is Tillich's very stimulating and illuminating little book, *Christianity and the Encounter of the World Religions*.

Finally, there are signs of another great social awakening. In the Roman Catholic Church these stem largely from former Pope John XXIII. There is even hope that the Roman Church will change its view on birth control. In the light of the frightening

38. On this meeting, see the special issue of *Religious Education*, March-April, 1963—which contains a complete report.

39. On Roman Catholic thought, see Macquarrie, *Twentieth Century Religious Thought*, pp. 278-300.

40. See Bultmann's *Jesus Christ and Mythology;* and also Schubert M. Ogden, *Christ Without Myth*.

41. See L. Harold DeWolf, *The Case for Theology in Liberal Perspective*.

42. (Richmond, Virginia: John Knox Press, 1960).

"population explosion" which could lead to a war which would wipe every trace of mankind from the face of the earth, the sooner it changes its stand the better.

One of the clearest signs of a social awakening among Protestants is the appeal of the Third Assembly of the World Council of Churches "to all governments and peoples." [43] Equally important is the creative response of the Negro clergy under the able leadership of Martin Luther King, Jr.[44] That an increasing number of white clergymen are joining his movement is likewise encouraging.

Yet, in spite of these creative factors, the total situation in this country remains critical. Among other things, morally we seem to be going backward.[45] No less frightening is the appearance of a type of reactionism that may open the door to fascism. In short, we are in deadly peril in spite of our might.

5. The Problem of Religious Education

In terms of the perspective furnished by the two preceding sections, it is clear that the relation of religion to public education poses a major problem in this country. Worse still, in view of the dominance of dogmatic sectarianism matched by an equally dogmatic secularism, this constitutes a very *thorny* problem. Neither is it safe to ignore it. This, as in the case of cancer, only serves to aggravate it. What is necessary at present is a real advance in the direction of a solution: that is, an advance which will not only improve the present situation, but which will also pave the way for further advances. Hence, our method of dealing with the problem must, of necessity, embrace two complementary processes: while, on the one hand, it must be critical and analytical, on the other, it must also be synoptic and constructive.

Now it seems obvious that there are two answers to the prob-

43. Visser 't Hooft, *New Delhi Speaks,* pp. 22-25.

44. See Dr. King's *Stride Toward Freedom* (New York: Harper & Row, 1958).

45. The Seminar on "Sex and Family Relations" (at the meeting sponsored by the Religious Education Association) reported that the "increasing laxity" is seriously threatening "the norms of chastity and faithfulness enjoined by the Judaic and Christian tradition"; see *Religious Education,* March-April, 1963, pp. 194-99.

lem which must both be rejected. The first is that of the religious dogmatist who favors a return to outright indoctrination. This would raise more problems than it would solve. Chief among these would be whose scheme to adopt amid the many jealous, competing systems, and on what basis to make the selection. Indoctrination, in fact, would work only if the public school were replaced by various types of parochial schools. While parochial schools have a place, to rely on them alone would result in the following evils: instead of one efficient system, there would be many competing systems totally incapable of handling the vast problem of mass education; there would be a mad scramble for public funds; and, amid this chaos, the quality of education would deteriorate.

The second answer is that of the thoroughgoing secularist. As an attempt at a solution, it might even prove worse than that of the religious dogmatist for the following reasons. To begin with, since so much that is best in the humanities is profoundly saturated with high religious concepts and meanings, our youth would not be able to appreciate much of the world's greatest literature, art, music, and historical writings. Again, religious illiteracy on the part of the younger generation would make it impossible for the young people to understand the older generation, including their parents. This would stop the flow of the stream of continuity, and thus make exceedingly difficult that creative form of cooperation so essential to the proper functioning of a dynamic, growing democratic society. Furthermore, since religion has been and still is important in many cultures, it would make it impossible to understand the people of other countries and races. A generation so culturally and morally and spiritually naked would, in all probability, hasten to sew on the fig leaves of some American brand of fascism; and the crass materialism and behaviorism which this would entail would produce a condition not unlike that pictured in Aldous Huxley's *Brave New World*—or, worse still, like that found in George Orwell's *Nineteen Eighty-Four*.

Some will contend, of course, that, since the home and the church or synagogue will rise to the occasion, this will not happen. That this contention is pitifully naïve is clear in the light of four significant facts: first, neither the home nor the church or synagogue have the influence today that they once had; second, since the public school tends to monopolize the pupil's time with its many activities (a fact to which any minister, priest, or rabbi can testify), there is really little time left to do a thorough job; third, the very facts that religion has no place in the curriculum and that—worse still—discussion of the subject is discouraged leave the impression that it is either *insignificant* or even downright *perverse;* and, fourth, the school's failure to include religion in its curriculum makes it virtually impossible for the pupil to integrate it with the rest of his studies—resulting in that bane of our "senate culture," namely, fragmentary thinking and living.

Having shown the inadequacies of the two extreme answers to the problem of religious education, we shall now proceed to discuss a proposal which is at once *moderate* and *synoptic.* Moderate in that it seeks to find the *mean* between the two extremes which we considered above, and synoptic in that it seeks the *broadest* and *most adequate approach* to the problem. Moreover, since these ideas have been gathered from many sources, and since our proposal has already been tried in a limited way in various places, we make no claim of uniqueness or originality.[46]

Our proposal includes four chief aspects. The first is that the process of religious education, *today as always,* must begin in the home. Though most parents are not equipped to do much in terms of the formal religious education of their children, still, *today as always,* they are capable of exerting an enormous influence, both by means of personal religious living (the power of example

46. For perspective on the problem, the following have proved helpful: Dierenfield, *Religion in American Public Schools,* pp. 39-61; Taylor (ed.), *Religious Education,* pp. 87-98, 226-32, 294-315; Lotz (ed.), *Orientation in Religious Education,* pp. 352-78; Van Dusen, *God in Modern Education,* pp. 113-14. The meeting in Chicago called by the Religious Education Association also proved very stimulating. See especially the reports of the seminars on "The School" and "The College," *Religious Education,* March-April, 1963, pp. 208-216. For further perspective, see also *Religious Education,* July-August, 1964. In this issue the Symposia, "Christian Education in Retrospect," and, "Where Are We with the Supreme Court?" (pp. 283-337) are *superb.*

stressed by all the greatest teachers of mankind) and also their support of the church or synagogue.[47] As a matter of fact, it has been shown again and again that without the support of the home, little can be accomplished by the various agencies engaged in formal religious education. *This fact very strongly suggests the need of classes for the religious education of parents.* Altogether too little has been done. Under the general direction of the Religious Education Association a joint program might be launched involving all three major religious groups.

The second aspect involves the churches and synagogues. So far as the specific religious educational programs of each group in general and each congregation in particular are concerned, suffice it to say that they should be broadened as well as intensified— with due regard both to theology and ethics, but with special stress on the latter.[48] More than this, explorations should be made of the possibilities of fruitful cooperation by means of "the released time" program.[49] This usually means that pupils are released from the public school for an hour or more each week to engage in religious studies either under the supervision of their own particular denomination or, as is often the case, under the direction of a group of cooperating churches or denominations. According to some estimates not less than four million children are enrolled in these released time programs annually.[50] Although released time has been criticized,[51] its defects can be removed. As one who has seen such a program in operation and is convinced of its merit, I suggest that it be utilized in the best possible sense wherever it is feasible.[52] Above all else, everything possible must be done to secure

47. See Wesner Fallow's article, "The Role of the Home in Religious Education," in Taylor (ed.), *Religious Education*, pp. 143-51.

48. The chief stress of the meeting in Chicago was on *ethics*.

49. On the nature of "released time," see Dierenfield, *Religion in American Public Schools*, pp. 75-82.

50. Taylor (ed.), *Religious Education*, p. 97.

51. See Theodore Brameld, *Education for the Emerging Age*, pp. 163-64.

52. Under Supreme Court rulings "released time" is permissible if the classes are not held in school buildings and if tax money is not used; see Dierenfield, *Religion in American Public Schools*, p. 33.

well-qualified teachers who are capable of challenging gifted youth. The third aspect of the synoptic approach has to do with the secondary schools. As I have written elsewhere:

A minimum of not less than three courses is suggested, to be taken in high school. They should be elective, or at least not compulsory. They should also be flexible rather than stereotyped, planned in such a way as to meet best the conditions prevailing in any particular school or community.

The first course might well begin with matters close to home, that is, with Christianity and Judaism. Here considerable use might be made of broad-minded local religious leaders (Catholic, Jewish, Protestant). The next course should deal with the other great religions. The approach should be biographical and practical, with special attention being given to the lives and teachings of the founders. Students should also become acquainted with some of the outstanding passages from the scriptures of the various faiths. Again, if intelligent representatives of these religions are available, they might be invited occasionally to present their point of view. The third course should be definitely synoptic in the very highest sense. An attempt should be made to tie together what was learned in the other two courses and to relate the most significant aspects of the total subject matter to democracy, and also to other courses in the curriculum such as history, literature, science, music, etc.[53]

Furthermore, as in the case of the courses under "released time," the teachers should be well qualified. As over against the "released time" program, however, these teachers should be part of the regular high school staff.[54]

Fourth, and, finally, every youth fortunate enough to gain entrance into some institution of higher learning should have the opportunity of exploring religion further. Many colleges and uni-

53. "A Synoptic Approach to Religious Education," reprinted from the May-June, 1958 issue of *Religious Education,* by permission of the publisher, The Religious Education Association, New York City.

54. Similar programs are being tried in various places. One of the most interesting is in operation at West High School, Denver, Colorado. See also Dierenfield, *Religion in American Public Schools,* pp. 55-58; and Brameld, *Education for the Emerging Age,* pp. 166-73.

versities—*public* as well as church-related—are offering courses in religion. The former include the University of Michigan, the University of North Carolina, the University of California (though the latter has little of a *specific* religious nature), Oklahoma State University, and the State University of Iowa.[55] Suffice it to say that as a bare minimum, there should be at least three courses, namely, one in the history of religion, one in the Bible, and one in philosophy of religion.

Although a synoptic scheme such as the one outlined above is far from perfect, and would have to be subject to revision as conditions changed, there is reason to believe that it really might constitute something of an advance. It might even mark the beginnings of a real effort to halt the decay and degeneration which is so evident today.

6. Can Religion Again Become Creative?

Some, particularly the Marxians and the Freudians, would answer this question with a resounding no. Pointing both to its many shortcomings and to the increasing inroads that science seems to be making on its territory, they would insist that it is destined to disappear as mankind matures and as science succeeds in satisfying more and more human needs. In short, a scientific age just has no place for God.[56]

It has already become clear, however, that religion has been one of the greatest sources of human creativity. All of the great faiths have also had their periods of outstanding creativity. This was certainly true of Buddhism during the reign of King Asoka who came to the throne in 273 B.C., of Islam for over a century after the prophet's death, of Hinduism during the time of the brilliant Sankara, and of Christianity when it conquered the Roman Empire, when it converted the northern Germanic bar-

55. See Taylor (ed.), *Religious Education*, pp. 310-13.

56. For an attempt to answer this objection, see the chapter, "Has Science Made God Unnecessary?" in my little book, *Perplexing Problems of Religion*, pp. 64-78. On the relations of science and religion, see also Edwin P. Booth (ed.), *Religion Ponders Science*. This book provides a broad perspective.

barians, and when, during the nineteenth century, it spread all over the globe.

Today, however, religion seems to be sick—not only in one land but also in every land, and not only in terms of one of its many forms but rather in terms of all forms. Although some of the ancient faiths, after lying dormant for centuries, seem to have come to new life, this seems to be due to a shot in the arm by that powerful new stimulant, namely, nationalism. While dealing at length with Christianity, Szczesny is also critical of such systems as Hinduism and Buddhism; for, he charges that, in their unconcern for the world (a consequence of their doctrine of Maya), they have greatly hindered progress.[57]

There are many reasons why religion is sick today. At least three of these are due to the spread of science and technology. The first has also affected art and the humanities generally, namely, the process of dehumanization which scientism inevitably causes. The wonders of science and technology fascinate many to the point of bewitchment. So impressive, indeed, are the possibilities of nuclear power that all but the most profoundly philosophical find themselves spellbound and strangely overwhelmed. In the presence of stupendous physical forces such as these, the things of the mind and spirit seem to shrink into utter insignificance. In fact, as we have seen, many of our scientists—particularly many psychologists —preach a *reductionism,* a *determinism,* an *illusionism,* and a *relativism* that, ultimately, if taken seriously, will be just as detrimental to democracy as to religion itself. Therefore, we have seen fit to subject these factors to criticism.[58]

The second and even more basic reason is the fact that science and technology, with their powerful battering rams, are demolishing large sections of the world views of the ancient faiths. So far as Christianity is concerned, this process began with the Copernican Revolution, it received new impetus from Darwin, and, with the advent of the Nuclear Age, it was again accelerated. At the same

57. Szczesny, *The Future of Unbelief,* p. 209.
58. See Ch. VIII, pp. 162-76.

time, however, the other religions are just beginning to feel the full impact of this process. The result, of course, is that state of moral and spiritual nakedness among vast masses of people which give secularism and materialism their opportunity.

A third reason why religion is sick today is the collision of cultures. This too is largely the result of the spread of science and technology—that is, insofar as they have annihilated time and space as it were and have brought mankind close together. As we have observed before, while ultimately this will probably prove to be a blessing since it will make possible—for the first time—the development of a real global society, yet, today, this babel of creeds and doctrines is creating confusion. *Confusionism* is, in truth, the most flourishing creed—along with the skepticism that it inevitably breeds.

Finally, there is the failure of the religionists to respond with a creativity adequate for these times. While, on the one hand, they have failed to respond in terms of theological and philosophical adequacy, on the other hand, they have failed just as decidedly socially and educationally.

In spite of everything, it is clear that—while sick—religion is far from dead. Not only has it been creative in the past, but even today there are live coals beneath the ashes—coals which a touch of human creativity could cause to burst into flame. If religion is to become creative, however, religionists must prepare themselves to meet the theological and philosophical and the social and educational challenges. Creativity, despite all the glamorous hopes of our apocalyptists, will not fall—like manna—from heaven. In what follows we hope to make a few suggestions.

To begin with, without committing the mistake of trying to oppose science itself—as fundamentalists and some existentialists have done—there must be continued criticism of the four fatal dogmas of scientism. This means that the theologians must drop their quarrel with reason and with philosophy itself. Instead they should make reason their weapon and all religiously minded philosophers their allies. This is no time for an internecine war between the two groups.

In the second place creative theologians and creative philosophers must cooperate in the great task of building an adequate world view. Although Dr. Albert Schweitzer is much more interested in ethics than in metaphysics, he has recognized this need of "a theory of the universe" as a foundation for civilization.[59] Similarly, John Wild pleads for "an integral world-view" as a basis of the philosophy of education.[60]

How shall the theologians begin? Let them first come out of their bomb shelters of irrationalism and dogmatism. Next by means of critical analysis let them dispose of all archaic elements and penetrate down to the "vital essence" of their various religious systems.[61] Getting down to base rock, they might find that the many things which they have in common are far more important than their differences.[62]

After having determined the "vital essence" of their systems, the next step is to look at the implications not only in the light of man's total religious experience (insofar as this is available), but also in the light of the facts that science has disclosed. Let it be repeated that, while the scientist can neither dictate to the theologian nor to the philosopher for obvious reasons,[63] yet, in building an adequate world view, no significant and relevant scientific fact or theory must be neglected. The reason for this is clear: seen in its proper perspective, it may shed light on the nature of the universe.

Moreover, the theologians, along with their philosophical allies,

59. In his book, *The Decay and the Restoration of Civilization*, translated by C. T. Campion (London: A. & C. Black, 1923), pp. xii-xiii.

60. In an article, "Philosophy of Education in the West: A Desperate Present Need," in *Harvard Educational Review*, XXVI (Spring, 1956), 183.

61. For an attempt both at a statement of Christianity's "vital essence" and an answer to Szczesny, see my article, "Is Christianity Adequate for These Times?," in *The London Quarterly & Holborn Review*, July, 1963, pp. 219-28.

62. Though this does not necessarily mean all religions are *equally true*. See my *Perplexing Problems of Religion*, pp. 94-107.

63. See Ch. IX, especially pp. 182-85.

must ever keep their eyes on the object of their quest: that is, the possibility of discovering a magnificent new world view great enough and comprehensive enough to do full justice to all the creative aspects of existence—including man with his marvelous capacities. They must also keep in mind the fact that neither the old traditional views of the various religious systems nor scientism and materialism have done full justice to creativity. For, while the dogmas of the former crippled man's scientific creativity, the dogmas of the latter have tried to cripple man himself by reducing him to a machine or to a mere process. In view of these facts, an effort must be made to avoid both of these extremes; and this leaves the way open for the theologians to take a good look at the new theism and personalism with its concept of a struggling God.

Finally, in this process of quest for an adequate world view, two principles which have already been discussed [64]—*change* and *continuity*—must constantly be kept in mind. Whitehead has truly stated that, if religion is to "regain its old power," it must be as fearless of "change" as science is.[65] How else can it continue to be relevant in a dynamic age such as ours? But, as in the case of art, mere change, instead of resulting in something genuinely creative, can only produce oddities and monstrosities. The truth of the matter is that today in religion, as well as in art, one hears of all kinds of reversions to primitivism.

Socially speaking, religion has three great challenges which it must meet. The first is the challenge of integration. If it fails to be effective in helping the Negro to obtain his rights, the great danger is that extremists on both sides will gain control resulting in bloodshed and chaos. The second is the nuclear challenge. It must do all in its power to save man from a nuclear holocaust. Indeed, in this high hour when the possibilities for a lasting peace are greater than ever before, it must rise to the occasion. Among other things, there should be a world conference of all the great faiths in an effort to

64. See Ch. VII, pp. 142-45.
65. See his *Science and the Modern World*, p. 270.

place the power of religion behind the peace movement on a world scale. Moreover, in view of the rise of a dangerous form of reactionism in this country which may actually open the door to an American brand of fascism, religion must raise its voice of warning. There is no time to lose. This country must not be allowed to sell its birthright for a mess of pottage.

The third challenge involves the problem of an adequate religious educational scheme. In terms of a creative solution of the problem of religious education, something resembling the synoptic approach is necessary. The most important aspect of our approach consists of the suggestion of high school classes in religion. Both in his recent book, *Education for the Emerging Age,* and still more in a recent article,[66] Brameld has stressed the significance of such classes. Most interesting of all is his suggestion of "pilot projects" in carefully selected communities. Everything possible must also be done to encourage and strengthen such existing projects as the one which is being conducted at West High School, Denver, Colorado.[67]

There are three reasons why these projects are so important. First of all, they enhance the importance of religion. Second, they reach some who show little or no interest in the various sectarian approaches. Finally, and most significant of all, they help to prevent fragmentary thinking and living by integrating religion with the various other phases of human life and thought.

We conclude then that religion can again become creative in the highest sense of the word. This creativity, however, is only possible as religionists rise to meet the challenge. We now turn to take another look at philosophy.

66. "The Place of Religion in Educational Theory: A Reconsideration," in *The Philosophical Forum,* XX; see especially 75-76.
67. On the project at West High School, Denver, see Dierenfield, *Religion in American Public Schools,* p. 57.

XI

Toward Creativity in Philosophy

In this chapter, we can afford to be brief. Not only have philosophy and philosophy of education appeared in some form or fashion in all the preceding chapters, but Chapter III dealt specifically with the nature and significance of philosophy and the philosophy of education. In this present chapter then, we shall consider three problems primarily: the present state of philosophy; the need of philosophy; and some suggestions that may serve to stimulate greater creativity.

1. Eclipse of Philosophy

In spite of the appearance of certain favorable signs, it is still true that philosophy is in eclipse. There are three chief reasons why it is in eclipse. First of all, like religion and the humanities generally, it is subject to the unfavorable influence of certain factors present in the general cultural situation. These conditions, as we observed in the last chapter, are largely due to the spread of science and technology.

While science itself is by no means hostile to philosophy and while it may even actually spur philosophers to greater creativity through its experimental attitude as well as through its findings, it has, nevertheless, given rise to certain conditions that are not favorable to the philosophical enterprise. Among these are vulgar materialism, hedonism, and pragmatism which want results quickly and which have arisen from the multiplication of things. Interestingly enough, this attitude is just as detrimental to the higher reaches of science (that is, theoretical science) as it is to philosophical inquiry and speculation.[1] Moreover, science has given birth to *scientism* with its four obstructive dogmas—*reductionism, determinism, illusionism,* and *relativism*—which have tried to ignore, to minimize, and even to deny the significance of man's higher creative capacities. Since all the humanities represent the natural flowering of man's higher capacities, and since they are in certain respects intangible (which is highly distasteful to the narrow empirical attitude so often engendered by science), they all naturally suffer. This is especially true of philosophy: for ever since Aristophanes, in *The Clouds,* caricatured Socrates as suspended in a basket, it has been the fashion of many to dismiss philosophers as eccentric, idle dreamers. The predominance of both a narrow native pragmatism and an imported irrationalism has created an atmosphere in contemporary America in which philosophy can hardly breathe.

Closely related to all this is also the *confusion* caused by the collision of cultures. Along with many other things, this collision of cultures has also meant the collision of philosophies. Amid this maze of conflicting philosophic systems, creeds, and theories, it is very difficult to believe that it is possible to develop a world view that is really any better or any worse than any of the others. Hence, the impulse toward metaphysical creativity is crushed in the bud.

The second reason why philosophy is in eclipse is the indifference and even hostility of certain groups. This is certainly true of many theologians—especially of the Barthians. It is also still true of many scientists. Although those engaged in the older sciences, particularly physics, are beginning to see the need of philosophy since they have themselves—in their own fields—encountered certain prob-

1. On our failure to produce our share of creative minds, see Brand Blanshard's article—"Quantity or Quality?"—in *Harvard Educational Review,* XXVI (Spring, 1956), 199-202.

lems which have profound philosophical implications, many in the younger sciences, such as psychology and sociology, still tend to scoff at philosophy.

Worst of all, many professional educationists seem to be indifferent to philosophy. The truth of the matter is that most of these who are indifferent know very little about it. In a very stimulating "Symposium" in the *Harvard Educational Review* some years ago, one of the participants protested that, while "many professors of education like to use the word *philosophy*," they neither study it themselves nor encourage their students to study it.[2] The loose way in which many professors use the term reveals the fact that, throughout their entire college career, they were never exposed to a first-class course in philosophy taught by a first-class teacher. Besides teacher's colleges, there are, in fact, liberal arts colleges which require courses in physical education but not a single course in philosophy! Later in this chapter, we shall look at the dire consequences of this philosophical ignorance.

Yet it is not enough for philosophers to protest against this modern tendency of treating philosophy as a stepchild. The time has come for considerable heart searching on their part. The third reason, in fact, why philosophy is in eclipse is nothing less than the failure of so many of the philosophers themselves to measure up to what is required of them in this strange new age so full of unparalleled opportunities as well as unparalleled dangers. The situation in philosophy today is, in certain very important respects at least, just as discouraging as it is in education and in religion.[3]

If nineteenth-century idealism went to extremes in its dogmatic metaphysical assertions and thereby blocked creativity, both the leading contemporary tendencies—existentialism and the analytical

2. Louise Antz, "Some Thoughts on Philosophy in and of Education," in *Harvard Educational Review* (Spring, 1956), p. 163.

3. For a general perspective of the contemporary situation, see the following: Morton White, *The Age of Analysis*, William Barrett & Henry D. Aiken (eds.), *Philosophy in the Twentieth Century* (New York: Random House, 1962), especially Vols. 2 and 3; and James L. Jarrett & Sterling M. McMurrin (eds.), *Contemporary Philosophy* (New York: Henry Holt & Co., 1954).

philosophies—have also gone to extremes and blocked creativity. Therefore, at this juncture, it is imperative that we look at their limitations and weaknesses again.[4]

To begin with, by virtue of its extreme vagueness, existentialism sins against the principle of clarity. This vagueness, especially in thinkers like Heidegger and Tillich, surrounds it like a fog. Although philosophy by its very nature can never be absolutely precise, yet without a determined effort toward all the precision that is possible, there can be no creativity. Sartre and his disciples and some of Kierkegaard's devotees are also irrationalists with a special interest in the morbid. Moreover, in the former, individualism has almost gone to the verge of nihilism. Not only do these tendencies not make for creativity, but they also give grounds for the charge that existentialism is to a considerable extent pathological and flourishes best in a sick society.[5]

It has already become clear that the limitations and weaknesses of the analytical philosophies, including what is known as logical positivism or logical empiricism, are just the opposite of those which are characteristic of existentialism. In the light of our discussion in Chapter VIII, it is evident that much contemporary philosophy is guilty of scientism with its dogmas. This is particularly true of logical positivism and of the whole analytical movement. Cases in point are Alfred Jules Ayer and Gilbert Ryle, both of whom are *basically* behaviorists.[6] Along with all this, there is the habit of running away from the great metaphysical problems and the consequent narrowing of the scope of the entire philosophical enterprise. The latter, as the history of philosophy shows, really serves to make philosophy appear unimportant.

Closely related to the above is a narrow empirical and analytical method which leads from more to less and less. The intense desire

4. See also previous discussion, Ch. V, pp. 107-8.

5. See George F. Kneller, *Existentialism and Education*, pp. 152-53.

6. See particularly Ayer's *Language, Truth and Logic;* and Gilbert Ryle's *Concept of Mind* (New York: Barnes & Noble, 1949). Ryle's attempt to wiggle out of his general behavioristic position (see p. 328) sounds unconvincing.

for precision among the analysts has led both to a preoccupation with trivialities and to a style of writing that tends to repel the reader.[7] One is painfully aware of these facts as one tries to read Ludwig Wittgenstein's *Tractatus Logico Philosophicus* or his *Philosophical Investigations*.[8] At any rate, these tendencies of the analysts give real point to Lewis S. Feuer's criticism that the attempts of analysts such as Kingsley Price and Israel Scheffler to develop an " 'analytic philosophy of education' " lead "to a kind of involuted scholasticism." [9]

In some instances among analysts, there are also evidences of what may be called a kind of skeptical dogmatism. A recent book, in which the author tries to use Wittgenstein's statement—"all the facts are in"—as a basis for deriding all attempts at theology and philosophy, affords an excellent illustration.[10] The truth of the matter is that "all the facts" are *never* in. In short, this kind of attitude—that we already know everything that is really relevant and significant—stifles the spirit of quest and what may be called the experimental attitude, which are as essential for real creativity in philosophy as they are in science.

In its reaction against nineteenth-century idealistic dogmatism, most contemporary philosophy is too timid. It never achieves much simply because, in its concern for precision and in its horror of mystification, it never ventures very far. Thus, instead of scaling Olympus and at least acquiring a much wider perspective, in the attempt to play safe there is the danger of landing, in the bitter end, on an ant hill in a dead-end street.[11]

7. As an example of becoming highly technical in dealing with unimportant problems, see Brian Medlin's article, "The Unexpected Examination," in *American Philosophical Quarterly*, Jan., 1964, pp. 66-72. Some analysts tend to make an esoteric cult of philosophy.

8. They are, however, worth reading.

9. See Feuer's article, "The Aims of a Philosophy of Education," in *Harvard Educational Review*, XXVI (Spring, 1956), 112-13.

10. Joseph Margolis (ed.), *Philosophy Looks at the Arts* (New York: Charles Scribner's Sons, 1962), p. 2.

11. For further criticism with specific instances, see my article, "What Ails Our Philosophers?" in *The Hibbert Journal*, LX (July, 1962), 271-74.

Contemporary philosophy has also, for the most part, evaded the great social, political, and ethical issues involved in the present world crisis. Peter Laslett has even gone so far as to insist that at present "political philosophy is dead." [12] While this, of course, is not altogether true, Paul Arthur Schilpp is entirely right in his charge that the scientists have been much more alert and much bolder in their pronouncements than the philosophers. [13] At both the Fifth Inter-American Conference on Philosophy and the Third East-West Philosophers' Conference, an attitude of social complacency prevailed. Although at the latter Sarvepalli Radhakrishnan delivered an address which revealed remarkable social insight and concern, so great was the influence of the conservatives who were in control, that it was impossible to get a mild resolution on the nuclear crisis to the floor of the conference. [14]

2. Creative Tendencies

Yet, as in the case of religion and theology, the picture is by no means hopeless. Mention must be made, first of all, of the fact that we have observed before: that both existentialism and the analytical philosophies have made and are making important contributions—to which we must again turn. [15]

As a corrective to the narrow and often trivial attitude of the analytical philosophies, existentialism has brought us back to that most basic source of all philosophical endeavor, that is, the fact of existence itself with all its wonders and dangers. Closely related and very important indeed, in an age when so many forces— social, political, and scientific—are threatening to depersonalize and

12. See his *Philosophy, Politics and Society* (New York: The Macmillan Co., 1956), p. vii.

13. See his presidential address before the fifty-seventh annual meeting of the Western Division of the American Philosophical Association, in *Proceedings and Addresses of the American Philosophical Association*, (Yellow Springs, Ohio: Antioch Press, 1959) 19-39.

14. In some respects, however, it was a great conference; see my article: "Philosophers' Conference in Retrospect," in *The Hibbert Journal*, LVIII (Jan., 1960), 135-41.

15. See also previous discussion, Ch. V, pp. 107-8.

to dehumanize man, is also its stress on man himself as the center of creativity. Here, in fact, it has something in common with all the great personalistic systems.

Among the contributions of the analytical philosophies, three are outstanding: they have done much to correct the habit of idealists of indulging in fantastic, unempirical speculation and of regarding it as metaphysically valid; they induced a real desire for precision in philosophy; and, in stressing analysis and criticism (in spite of their social unconcern *as philosophers*), they have forged a weapon for us to use against totalitarianism masked in the guise of freedom. It is also clear that these movements are involved in a process of creative change—as the result of which they are becoming more moderate.

As important illustrations of the type of philosophical ferment which is going on among philosophers generally today, we shall consider very briefly four outstanding presidential addresses. The first which has already been referred to is Dr. Schilpp's presidential address—"The Abdication of Philosophy"—which he delivered before the Western Division of the American Philosophical Association.[16] Besides attacking the obvious weaknesses of logical positivism, especially its lack of social concern, he presented a call to philosophers to become fully responsible in this time of peril. The second—"The Exploration of the Life-World"—was given by John Wild before the Eastern Division of the American Philosophical Association.[17] Basically it constitutes a plea for a type of philosophy which is at once empirical and synoptic. The third— "Freedom and Creativity"—was delivered before the Western Division by A. Campbell Garnett.[18] It is important both for the attempt to define creativity and to link it with the concept of freedom. Finally, the fourth—"The Power of Positivistic Thinking"—was presented before the Western Division by Herbert Feigl

16. See Schilpp, in *Proceedings and Addresses of the American Philosophical Association,* XXXII (1958-1959), 19-39.

17. See Wild, in *Proceedings and Addresses of the American Philosophical Association,* XXXIV (1960-1961), 5-23.

18. See Garnett, in *ibid.,* pp. 25-39.

(a leading analyst and one of the original members of the famous Vienna Circle).[19] It came as a revelation of the creative change that is going on within this movement.

So far as a creative approach to the world situation is concerned, mention must also be made of the formation of the Society for the Philosophical Study of Dialectical Materialism. The East-West Philosophers' Conferences have also made contributions.

There are also signs of a new metaphysical awakening. In Germany this came with philosophers such as Karl Jaspers and Martin Heidegger. The best evidence of metaphysical ferment in England is the book edited by Ian Ramsey of Oxford—*Prospect for Metaphysics*—which consists of twelve essays by various philosophers and theologians.[20] In this country the following three books suggest a similar tendency: Errol E. Harris' *Nature, Mind and Modern Science;* Edgar Sheffield Brightman's posthumous *Person and Reality;*[21] and Brand Blanshard's Paul Carus Lectures, *Reason and Analysis.* This new interest in metaphysics is likewise evident in the activities of the Metaphysical Society of America. A recent announcement reports that it now has over six hundred members and that it "continues to grow very rapidly."

3. The Cost of Philosophical Neglect

While it is true that philosophy gives no promise of immediate reward, yet, ultimately, the cost of neglect is very high indeed. This neglect accounts for much of the current vagueness concerning goals. Many of our educational leaders do not seem to know where they are going. Their preoccupation and fascination with the splendid and efficient means which science has placed at their disposal has caused them "to lose sight of the end." [22] Is there any wonder that confusion and chaos reign?

19. See Feigl, in *Proceedings and Addresses of the American Philosophical Association,* XXXVI (1962-63), 21-41.
20. (London: George Allen & Unwin, 1961).
21. (New York: The Ronald Press Co., 1958)—edited by Peter Anthony Bertocci, Jannette Elthina Newhall, & Robert Sheffield Brightman.
22. Jacques Maritain, *Education at the Crossroads,* pp. 2-4.

Moreover, this same neglect makes for inadequate and superficial goals. Many of our institutions of higher learning are obsessed with a narrow vocationalism, a bread-and-butter theory of education.[23] Such a materialistic motivation results in a kind of shortsightedness and a selfish grasping which can only serve in the bitter end to wreck and ruin the American Commonwealth. Any society which prizes education primarily as a means toward wealth and power is already far advanced on the road to decadence and final disaster.

This neglect of philosophy also involves a narrow specialization together with a devotion to the cult of scientism. In some colleges the tendency toward scientific specialization (especially in view of the material rewards that it may bring) is so strong that the end products are little more than dehumanized mechanisms— with little knowledge of the broader aspects of human life. Furthermore, so far as education is concerned, in the name of a so-called "science of education" advocated by psychometricians such as C. H. Judd, educators have too long been subject to the cult of scientism with its four dogmas.[24] The result has been disastrous.

Finally, such disregard for philosophy means a knowledge of myriads of facts without seeing their larger relationships. It signifies a lack of perspective. Worse still, it leads to that fragmentary thinking and fragmentary living which is the curse of our modern culture. This is why we have constantly stressed synopsis, wholeness, totality, and an all-embracing goal. Similarly, Brameld speaks of the educational philosopher as "interdisciplinarian" and, finally, as "the maker of *Weltanschauungen*." [25]

From the standpoint of education then, the value and significance of philosophy may be summarized in terms of three statements. First, like science, though in a much more comprehensive and

---

23. On this and other defects, see Robert Maynard Hutchins, *The Higher Learning in America* (New Haven: Yale University Press, 1936). See also "Symposium: Philosophy of Education," in *The Journal of Philosophy*, Oct. 25, 1962, pp. 629-47.

24. On scientism, see James D. Koerner, *The Miseducation of American Teachers*, pp. 29-31.

25. In his *Education for the Emerging Age*, p. 214.

ultimate way, it signifies the excitement of high intellectual adventure. Second, instead of a piecemeal view of life and of the universe, philosophy seeks wholeness on a cosmic scale, that is, in terms of an adequate world view. Third, it means a concern for values and norms, ends and goals.

4. Toward Greater Creativity

Although we may be witnessing the beginnings of something of a philosophical awakening, this is no time for philosophers to rest on their oars. If there is to be genuine creativity, certain things are necessary. In what follows, our aim is to point out and to clarify the most significant.

First of all, philosophers must beware of *narrowing* the *scope* of philosophy. In Chapter III, it became clear that, as the science of the sciences (*scientia scientiarum*), philosophy is synoptic by nature. If there were no discipline of this nature, we would certainly have to invent one. At any rate, if logical positivism has proved anything, it is the fact that the best way to kill philosophy is to narrow its scope. Important as analysis undoubtedly is as a vital aspect of philosophy, it is still only an aspect. Concentration on this aspect has meant fragmentation, a preoccupation with the trivial, and that turning "inward upon itself" [26] which has led to a peeling of the onion until there was nothing left to peel.

In the second place, in order to be truly creative, the philosophers must come down from their ivory towers long enough to take a *serious look* at our *world*—as Socrates did in his day. The great problem today is how to deal creatively with a *pluralism* that causes the confusion and chaos that may bring destruction. In terms of perspective, the philosophers have two outstanding contributions to make.[27] The first is metaphysical and theological. Philosophers must employ their energies—as never before—to help bring order out of this threatening chaos. This means that once

26. See Feuer, *Harvard Educational Review*, Jan., 1964, p. 113.
27. On this question of the contributions of philosophy, see also my article, "Philosophy in the Nuclear Age," in *The Philosophical Quarterly* (India), XXXI (Oct., 1958), 157-62.

more they must use their capacities in order to develop a world view that is at once reasonable in the highest sense of the word and which will also serve to challenge man to creativity in all the great realms of human endeavor.

The trouble with modern man is that he does not feel at home in the universe. He feels strangely lost perched as he is on this grain of sand surrounded by the dizzy vastnesses of these oceans of space. He also feels lost when he contemplates the fact that he lives this fast fleeting moment in the presence of two other vastnesses, namely, the vastness of the past that seems gone and the vastness of the uncertain future. To make him feel still more insecure, science and technology not only have made possible the destruction of all his works almost within the twinkling of an eye, but they have also made his old beliefs seem childish and absurd. Hence, difficult as the task may be, philosophy has never had a greater challenge. Moreover, since it has the wisdom of the ages, including the insights of man's total experience in all times and cultures to draw on, it is not without resources. If it is willing, with these resources to draw upon, it may develop some day a world view which may look like a cathedral or a palace in comparison with all that has been accomplished thus far.

In order to be truly creative metaphysically speaking, two extremes must be avoided. The first is that of a *dogmatic certainty*. Whether it is religious or secular and naturalistic (as in the case of Marxianism), dogmatic certainty is neither reasonable nor does it make for creativity. It is unreasonable because we simply do not know enough to be absolutely certain, and it stifles creativeness, since it leaves no place for any further search. If we are sure we have the truth absolutely and completely, there is no reason or motive for any further quest. The other extreme is *dogmatic skepticism*.[28] Not only is thoroughgoing skepticism self-contradic-

28. In his *Thoughts*, Pascal made the interesting observation that the Greek skeptic, Arcesilaus "became a domatist"; see *The Harvard Classics*, XLVIII, 124. In this he is certainly correct. It is easy to forget sometimes that the spirit that denies can be just as dogmatic as "the true believer."

tory, since—while denying all possibility of certainty—it affirms its skepticism to be true, but, as in the case of its opposite, we also know too little to be skeptics in any absolute sense. Nor can there be any doubt that it cuts the nerve of creativity. If we are absolutely certain that nothing is possible, it is not likely that we will do anything that takes effort—much less aim at the ideal of perfection or excellence.

Difficult as creativity in metaphysics undoubtedly is, since it deals in world hypotheses, yet it is not impossible. By finding his way between the two above extremes, there is nothing to prevent the philosopher from advancing more and more adequate world hypotheses. Nor should it worry him that he cannot prove them in terms of demonstration. Even the scientist, especially as he goes beyond the frontiers, has to be satisfied with reasonableness and probability. Theories, such as the Theory of Evolution, cannot be demonstrated, but rest on coherence and probability.

One other thing must be emphasized so far as this matter of an adequate world view is involved: there must be *teamwork*. While philosophers must keep their eyes on the scientists, on the one hand, to see what new light they may be shedding in terms of new facts and theories, on the other, they must also watch the theologians—dealing as they are with the profoundest experiences and aspirations of the human spirit. Each has something to contribute toward an understanding of the nature of the universe and of man. Suffice it to say that, if man is to live creatively as well as survive, the insights and energies of all three types of thinkers must be employed to their maximum capacity.

The other contribution which philosophers can make toward a solution of the world crisis may be termed ethical and social. This involves three things. To begin with, philosophers, by the very nature of their discipline, can present the problem of peace and global order in the very broadest perspective. This will help to correct the shortsighted day-by-day view which the politician is inclined to take. Thus, while rejoicing at the possibilities of the test ban, they would also warn leaders and people alike that the Chinese problem must be faced now before it becomes insoluble. Closely related is the critical and analytical function which the philosophers may exercise. This would involve a critical examination of popular slogans, including the assumptions of nationalism and racialism. Finally, something can also be done in terms of more direct action. Besides making pronouncements, philosophers should be found in all organizations which are attempting to do something constructive towards solving the problem of peace, the problem of social justice, and all other related problems. Nor need they fear that in so doing they are dishonoring their profession. Anyone who knows the history of philosophy at all is aware of the fact that most of the greatest philosophers from Plato to Kant and from Kant to Dewey tried to do something constructive about the stirring problems and issues of their day.[29]

Again, as in the case of religion, if philosophy is to become creative, it must be given a more significant place in education. More experiments should be conducted on the high school level.[30] Obviously, in order to avoid a distaste for philosophy, the deeper, more intricate, and more complex aspects of metaphysics, epistemology, theology, and logic should be avoided. Yet, there is no good reason why there might not be elementary courses in ethics, in logic, and also explorations into the lives and basic teachings of some of the greatest and most interesting of the philosophers— beginning with Socrates. Some way might also be found of correlating these courses in philosophy with the courses in religion mentioned in the last chapter. In spite of certain objections to the teaching of philosophy in high school, there are three good argu-

29. See my article, "The Philosopher as Reformer," in *The Personalist*, XI (Autumn, 1959), 380-87.

30. The American Philosophical Association's Committee on Philosophy in Education has issued an excellent report on this subject. See "The Teaching of Philosophy in American High Schools," in *Proceedings and Addresses of The American Philosophical Association*, XXXII (Yellow Springs, Ohio: Antioch Press, 1959), 91-137. This deals both with arguments for and against such schemes and with courses now being offered. See also Brameld, *Education for the Emerging Age*, p. 57.

ments in its favor: (1) many students never take philosophy in college simply because they were not introduced to it in high school, and among these are some who might be outstanding; (2) many students mature early, especially under the influences of modern life, and begin asking the great questions, but receive very little guidance; and (3) there have actually been successful experiments. The great problem, of course, is securing capable teachers.[31]

As far as the college level is concerned, at least two courses should be required of every student. These courses should include a course in the history of philosophy besides the general introductory course which usually takes the problems approach. To implement this program properly, a real attempt should be made to staff every department adequately. As a minimum, there should not be less than two men.[32]

Finally, the philosophers themselves—as teachers—must awaken to a new sense of responsibility. Like Socrates of old, they must look upon their task with something of a sense of mission. Of all men, the philosopher can least afford to be flippant or cynical. Teaching philosophy is serious business.[33]

31. For an interesting project conducted by Dr. W. D. Nietmann and designed for teaching philosophy to public school teachers, see my article, "Sign of Creativity: A Unique Educational Experiment," in *The Journal of Teacher Education*, Sept., 1964, pp. 316-18.

32. On some suggestions by the Committee on Philosophy in Education of the American Philosophical Association, see their report, "Criteria for the constituting of a Department of Philosophy," in *Proceedings and Addresses of The American Philosophical Association*, XXXII, 85-90.

33. Operating from a much broader perspective than most historians, political scientists, and sociologists, a course in social philosophy affords the philosopher an unusual opportunity to bring students face to face with the problems of this very crucial age. On what I have attempted on a small scale, see my article—"Social Philosophy in the Nuclear Age"—in *The Philosophical Quarterly* (India), XXXI (July, 1959), 113-16. This article serves as a companion article to the one mentioned on p. 225, n. 27.

Part IV

Conclusion

XII

Education in This Age of Transition

1. A Turning Point in History

The advent of the Nuclear Age constitutes a major—perhaps *the* major—turning point in history. There have been many other significant turning points: when primitive man invented tools and discovered the use of fire; the rise of the great civilizations and the development of great religious and philosophical systems; the fall of Rome and the rise of medievalism; the invention of the fast sailing vessel and the discovery of America; the advent of the new science with its substitution of a heliocentric for a geocentric perspective, and the consequent shattering of the medieval world view; the Industrial Revolution with its vast implications, including the rise of the masses and the appearance of Marxian communism; the great Depression (for the first time almost world-wide) plus the two World Wars—all these and many others like them may be called to mind.

When all is said and done, however, the fact remains that mankind has never faced an age of transition with these factors: the cracking of the nucleus of the atom and the availability of atomic energy; the invention of bombs capable of reducing the earth's largest cities to cinders in a matter of minutes; artificial moons circling around the earth; space ships—perhaps sooner than we think—capable of visiting the moon and other planets in our solar system; and all this plus a population explosion so great that, unless it is checked soon, it will most certainly bring war, the final war—Armageddon.

Amid all this din and confusion, one thing at least remains certain: instead of standing still, things will *rush* on, and at an ever-increasing speed. Moreover, these forces that make for change will continue to produce repercussions educationally and otherwise. Today, in fact, we are like a group of desperate men stranded on a barren shore. Close to their feet there is a raging sea which threatens to engulf them, while a high ridge of mountains—rising almost from the water's edge—separates them from a fair and peaceful land. They know that they must climb those mountains, but they are far from sure that they will be successful.

Today that ridge of mountains represents all the factors that make the future seem so grim and uncertain. Among these factors is the danger that some homegrown brand of fascism may destroy our democratic heritage. There also looms the vast shape of Red China and the possibility that she may emerge as the leader of all the world's colored people. This together with the West's short-sightedness, especially in refusing her a seat in the United Nations may, in fact, set the world on fire.

There are not less than four reasons why Red China represents the *number one* problem: (1) unlike that of the Russians, her revolution is still young and belligerent; (2) her resentment of over two centuries of Western aggression;[1] (3) she, as no other nation, represents the underprivileged colored nations—and she may make a real impression on them if they become disillusioned with both the West and with Moscow; (4), most ominous of all, along with the fact that she is now a nuclear power, Red China represents the perplexing population problem at its worst.[2] She is literally bursting at the seams and hence is likely to continue to

1. On the iniquitous Opium War, see Arnold J. Toynbee, *Civilization on Trial*, pp. 89-92.

2. One of the best books on Red China is still A. Doak Barnett's *Communist China and Asia* (New York: Harper & Row, 1960)—published for the Council on Foreign Affairs.

cause trouble. The Chinese Dragon, in truth, if aroused to anger, may set the stage for Armageddon.

At this juncture at least two things are certain. The first is the fact that this is really an age of transition—we are on our way somewhere and going fast. The second is that at this time the result is far from clear; it is still in the lap of the gods. We may climb that high ridge of mountains and reach a new land of promise, or we may fail and fall into the treacherous waves. It is also certain, however, that we are not being forced in either direction by a blind Fate. It is up to us: if we fail, it is our fault.

2. The Crisis in American Education

In spite of the great Depression and two World Wars, and in spite of the stern warnings from sensitive observers both domestic and foreign, the American people continued to worship their Golden Calf, still certain of the superiority of their "know how" and all things American.[3] Whenever doubters appeared and ruffled the Olympian calm, the soothsayers—from the halls of government, from editorial offices, from the marts of trade, and even from classrooms and pupils—instantly aroused themselves to give new assurances. Indeed, when not handed over directly to the Inquisition (twentieth-century American style), critics were given the cold shoulder or laughed out of court.

When, however, the bitter truth was out at last and in a manner that none could doubt (that is, of course, with Sputnik, the Soviet man-made moon, revolving around the earth) the first reactions— for the most part at least—were more hysterical than thoughtful. There were those, including some in high government circles, who wanted to scrap our whole educational system and substitute a cheap "crash program" based on that of our totalitarian rivals.[4]

3. In this connection, the student will find it illuminating to read Arnold J. Toynbee's *America and the World Revolution.*

4. It soon became evident, however, that the Soviets themselves were changing "many of the features" which some Americans praised; see Gaither McConnell, "Shall Soviet Practices Govern Changes in American Schools?" in *Educational Administration and Supervision,* XLV (May, 1959), 141.

Many also began beating the tom-toms in search of scapegoats. For some, indeed, the great game was pouring their vials of wrath on John Dewey and the progressives.

Fortunately, despite the tremendous pressures coming from above, saner voices—with whom the hope of the future lies—began to speak out. Interestingly enough, they all seemed to stress four very significant points.

First and foremost, they were frank enough to admit that there is something seriously wrong with the American educational system, especially at the point of discipline—educationally and otherwise. Second, they made it plain that nothing could be more disastrous to democracy than the attempt to ape our totalitarian opponents by imposing a regimented system top-heavy with the natural sciences at the expense of the humanities. Third, they pointed out that what is needed is not the complete overhauling of our educational scheme, which would produce chaos, but rather finding and eliminating the weak spots. Fourth, in harmony with the synoptic approach advocated in this book, they emphasized the need of strengthening our total educational program in all its vital aspects.[5]

3. The Greatest Single Need

The chief defects and weaknesses of American education as a whole may be summarized as follows: (1) a deplorable confusion and shortsightedness due to the lack of an adequate overall aim or goal;[6] (2) its obvious mediocrity in certain respects;[7] (3) its tendency toward conformity and its lack of social vision;[8] (4) an overemphasis on science and technology (particularly due to the

5. For expressions of the National Council for the Social Studies, see *The New York Times*, Nov. 28, 1957, p. 28; and *Senior Scholastic*, Dec. 13, 1957, pp. 1T-2T. On the views of educators, see also *The Education Digest*, Dec., 1957, p. 53 ff.

6. On this vital matter, see Ch. VI, pp. 113-14.

7. See especially *my* summary of James D. Koerner's book, *The Miseducation of American Teachers*, in Ch. VIII, p. 157.

8. On this point, see especially Theodore Brameld's recent book, *Education for the Emerging Age*.

pressure of the military and other interested groups)[9] at the expense of the humanities; and (5) a narrow, pragmatic, and sensationalistic attitude which is far more ready to spend for buildings and other equipment than for good teachers[10] and (this applies particularly to colleges and universities both public and private) for more and larger scholarships for gifted students from the lower income groups.

Really the greatest single need of American education can be expressed in the word *adequacy*. If we are to help mankind scale that forbidding range of mountains, our whole educational system must become more *adequate*.[11] With this in mind, in the next and final chapter, we shall attempt to sketch in bold relief the most important aspects of a more *adequate* educational approach.

9. Here it is well to look again at the chapter, "The Tragedy of Science," in Ralph E. Lapp's recent book, *Kill and Overkill*, pp. 15-22. See also my review in *The Christian Century*, May 1, 1963, p. 382.

10. On this problem, see A. D. C. Peterson's illuminating remarks in his little book, *A Hundred Years of Education*, pp. 307-308.

11. On this point, see also the address of Commissioner Francis Keppel delivered at the spring conference of the Magazine Publishers Association, Washington, D. C. It is found in *Higher Education*, May, 1963, pp. 7-10, and bears the interesting title, "The Changing Face of Education"

XIII

Aspects of a Synoptic View

What follows is based on four well-recognized principles, all of which are related to the overall goal, the *humanization of man*. First and foremost, there is the concept of synopsis—inclusiveness, wholeness. While this principle goes back to Plato's view of the philosopher as the synoptic man, it has also been stressed by modern and contemporary Hegelians and personalists. Since it seeks to exclude nothing of real value in man's total educational experience and experimentation, it needs no further justification.

The second is the principle of the mean which signifies the sense of balance, moderation, and proportion. It really means taking a middle course between extremes, and of excesses in nothing. The mean is found in Eastern as well as Western philosophy: it was stressed as much by Confucius as by Aristotle. In a time when man is constantly being pushed from the verge of one abyss to the verge of another by wild, elemental, irrational forces, this principle has real relevance.

The third is the empirical, experimental approach. Though present in Eastern thought, particularly Confucianism, it is especially a child of the West. Since it means a certain ventureness which, in ever pressing on beyond the frontiers, has greatly added to the store of human knowledge, it has more than proved itself. Indeed, in one form or another, most of the world has borrowed it.

Finally, and, in some respects, most important of all, there is the democratic principle of freedom based upon a profound belief in the value and dignity of human personality. While the latter finds its genesis in the great Hebrew-Christian tradition and in Greek thought, modern progressives, personalists, and existentialists also emphasize it. The importance of belief in the value and dignity of personality and its corollary—freedom—is only fully recognized when we consider the fact that they lie at the basis of creativity in the very highest sense of the word as well as at the basis of all ethics worthy of the name. Rob man of his dignity as a person and of his freedom, and the stream of creativity begins to dry up.

In what follows no attempt shall be made either to prescribe a rigid system or merely to throw certain prinicples together in a loose disjointed fashion. Our purpose rather is to set forth certain basic aspects of a synoptic view in bold relief, leaving it to every reader, regardless of his educational philosophy, to develop his own system and to revise it as he sees fit. To put it in another way, what follows is not proposed as a set of rigid principles to adhere to at all costs, but rather as clues and guides to serve as a basis for creative discussion and effective action.

1. A Realistic Idealism [1]

A philosophy of education adequate for times such as these must contain both realistic and idealistic elements. Let us first consider what realism has to offer.

From realism we can learn the necessity of objectivity, of the critical attitude, and of the dangers of escapism. Instead of running away from problems just because they are unpleasant, students must be taught the facts just as they are, including the facts about themselves, their country, and their world. There is always the danger that the gullible public may fall for some pleasant illusion,

1. What follows in this chapter is largely an expansion and a thoroughgoing revision of a part of my article—"Educational Philosophy for Today"—which appeared in *The Philosophical Quarterly* (India), XXXIV (July, 161), 95-101. I am grateful to the editor, G. R. Malkani, for permission to use this material.

made thrice pleasant by the siren voice of skillful propagandists with ulterior motives. This is the way to totalitarianism in its most monstrous forms—on whose heels follow, sure and swift, the hell-hounds of total war and self-destruction.

Toynbee has made it clear that in a decadent society in fear of disintegration, desperate people tend to follow "the savior with the sword" (the strong man, the military hero), or "the savior with the time machine" ("the archaist" who wants to carry them back to some idealized past), or "the futurist" (who intoxicates them with visions of a golden future).[2] Against these illusions, the hardheaded realist offers protection, confident as he is that his more critical, honest, fearless approach will—in the long run at least— result in a better future.[3] No democracy can last long unless the schools take very seriously their obligation to teach youth—with its enthusiasm—to be *critical* and *discerning*. This alone protects a country against the illusions spread by demagogues who, once in the seat of power, will destroy democracy itself, while, at the same time, brazenly mouthing its slogans.

The painful truth, however, as we have noticed before, is that whatever may be true of many of our colleges and universities, the vast majority of our secondary schools are not ready for this task which the Nuclear Age has made imperative. The administrators have neither the foresight nor the courage; and the same thing is true of most of the teachers. Disgraceful as it is, they drift— like dead fish—with the tide. Some of our more foresighted educators fear the influence of the military on our universities and colleges.[4] Among other things, this makes for conformism in the worst sense of the word.

2. Arnold J. Toynbee, *A Study of History*, abridgment of Vols. I-VI by D. C. Somervell, pp. 534-40.

3. See Frederick S. Breed, *Education and the New Realism*, pp. 221-26. Breed, of course, has been one of the outstanding realists among American educational philosophers. Mention must also be made of the fact that the analysts, who are basically realists of a sort, also stress this critical attitude as we have observed before; see Ch. V, pp. 108-9.

4. See, for example, the article by Allan Brick, "Why Have ROTC on Campus?,"

As forms of essentialism, both realism and idealism, of course, emphasize the value of man's cultural heritage. In an age such as ours, which is obsessed with contemporaneousness, this emphasis is invaluable. It is as dangerous to neglect the past as it is to glorify the future at the expense of the present. In either case there is a loss of perspective and of proportion.

At any rate, ancient history and the classics are at least as important as mathematics and the natural sciences; for, after all, our basic problems are primarily human rather than technological; and, since human nature has not changed much during the last two thousand years, we can learn much from Plato, Aristotle, Pericles, Thucydides, and Cicero. Among other things, they can teach us much concerning the burning social issues of our times. Counts points out that the Marxians borrowed heavily from Plato.[5] One of my students whose father knows something about politics at first hand, upon reading Aristotle's *Politics* for the first time, was amazed to discover how strangely modern he sounds. Similarly, while reading Thucydides, Toynbee came to the conclusion that the former's world is really "philosophically contemporary" with our own.[6]

Besides this interest in man's legacy from the past and other similar matters which it shares with essentialism in general, idealism, especially in the form of personalism, is capable of making certain important contributions of its own. Among these, three are outstanding.

The first is the significance of the belief in the objectivity of ideals or norms. In Chapter VIII the weaknesses of relativism as one of the obstructions to creativity became evident, and we need not repeat them here. Something more, however, is in order regarding the practical effects. A generation imbued with utter relativism would be capable of any act, no matter how barbarous

AAUP Bulletin, XLV (June, 1959), 218-22. This is the official journal of the American Association of University Professors.

5. George S. Counts, *The Challenge of Soviet Education,* p. 10.

6. See his *Civilization on Trial,* pp. 18-19.

or frightful. One of the maladies from which many of our youthful gangsters suffer is a lack of any sense of moral obligation or value. When one youth was asked recently why he killed a certain person, his answer was, "I felt like it." When utterly devoid of principles, the feelings themselves function as absolutes. Suffice it to say that our youthful gangsters are conditioned by a culture and an age that has lost sight of anything really *great* and *worthy*.

The second principle which idealism stresses, especially in its personalistic forms, is the dignity of man which was duly examined not only at the beginning of this chapter as the basis of freedom, but also in Chapter VI as an aspect of the overall goal.[7] The third is the philosophical conviction that self-conscious mind, as the highest product of the evolutionary process and hence of the universe, constitutes our best clue to Ultimate Reality. In other words, this implies theism. Even though some may reject it sincerely and honestly due to the presence of evil on so vast a scale, yet it should not be rejected lightly. If easy belief is a crime, so is easy unbelief. Theism is important and deserves due consideration, particularly its newer forms, for many reasons. Chief among these is the fact that it holds that man, instead of being just so much flotsam adrift on a vast cosmic ocean, is part of a purpose far greater than he can ever completely envision. After all, it was this splendid thing which served to awaken our ancestors from the long night of barbarism.

2. A Daring Experimentalism

Noteworthy as the contributions of realism and idealism most certainly are, the time has now come to deal with the place and role of experimentalism. In a dynamic situation such as ours, there can be no question about its importance. It is not enough to admire the old, we must have the courage to try the new; and at no time in history has man ever faced greater challenges. There are, in truth, three great challenges which face all thoughtful men.

7. Existentialists, of course, along with idealists stress this principle. This is especially true of Jaspers. Indeed, the latter is probably more of an idealist than an existentialist.

The first is the scientific challenge, involving both the theoretical and the practical, technological aspects. By all means let us compete with the Russians scientifically, but in a peaceful and constructive manner. Perhaps, in spite of all past failures, we shall yet be successful in our attempt to scale that forbidding ridge of mountains which stand between us and a better tomorrow.

Closely related to the first is the second, namely, the social challenge. It consists primarily in contriving ways to kill those four hellhounds: war, hunger, ignorance, and prejudice. Creativity in the accomplishment of this Herculean task will require the services of historians, political scientists, philosophers, psychologists, sociologists, ministers of religion, and, above all else, teachers and statesmen with broad perspectives, as well as mathematicians and physicists. What good will the sheer power which nuclear physics has thrust into our hands do, in the final analysis, if there are no socially responsible and socially creative minds to dirct it?

Finally, there is the metaphysical and theological challenge. John Dewey and his followers, in ruling out the intangible and the transcendent due to their naturalistic inclinations, conceived the experimental principle altogether too narrowly. Man is the metaphysical and the theological animal as assuredly as he is the political animal. Besides the wonder of this mysterious universe—a wonder which stares at him from every side and becomes even greater when he begins to explore it—there are also still the even greater mysteries of life and death, of which the existentialists have been reminding us during these latter days.

Thus, in spite of all our efforts to be good materialists and secularists, these age-old problems begin to disturb us anew.

> Just when we're safest, there's a sunset-touch,
> A fancy from a flower-bell, some one's death,
> A chorus-ending from Euripides—
> And that's enough for fifty hopes and fears.

Nor is it too much to say that these problems, since they involve the very meaning of man's strange adventure on this planet, are the most *basic*—if not the most urgent. Hence, in this attempt at a philosophy of education, we have not tried to dodge them. In short, it is evident that the new experimentalism must be at once bolder and more existentialistic than the older forms.

3. Specialization Without Fragmentation

The problem of specialization versus general education has bedeviled the modern situation. Thus, it has often set the generalist, including the educationist, against the experts in the various disciplines—to the detriment of both. Perhaps it is well to add that, in a real sense, the synoptic philosopher is a kind of generalist of generalists. Be that as it may, the chief difficulty in this dispute has undoubtedly been the tendency to go to extremes.

There have been some, particularly in the sciences, who have pursued the ideal of specialization to the very brink of atomism. After all is said and done, the truth gradually dawns that in some sense both life and the universe are one. Although they carry it to an extreme, there is considerable truth in the contention of Hegelians that "truth is the whole." [8]

So far as the sciences themselves are concerned, it is becoming clearer every day that the boundaries are by no means fixed and rigid. Every science—pursued far enough—seems to involve every other science. Even mathematics and physics cannot exclude psychology altogether: for both involve the use of the mind with all its creative capacities. Similarly, since it has to make use of it in any attempt at mental tests and measurements, psychology cannot function without mathematics. Again, since the mind is dependent upon the physical world in many ways, psychology cannot, ultimately at least, avoid certain involvements with physics and chemistry.

Moreover, the biologist knows that he cannot study any animal

8. For an outstanding attempt by a contemporary Hegelian to apply Hegel's concept of wholeness to the present scene, especially in the light of scientific developments, see Errol E. Harris' *Nature, Mind and Modern Science.*

or even a single organ in isolation. Likewise, broad concepts such as evolution not only have biological significance, but also sociological, psychological, political (especially in relation to the concept of power politics), and even, as we have pointed out before, profound philosophical implications. Most interesting of all, the physicists who gave us atomic energy are beginning to realize that, even though the natural sciences in themselves as basic disciplines are politically and ethically neutral, yet, at the same time, they have far-reaching consequences which in turn involve moral as well as political implications. Thus, physicists, together with chemists and biologists, who only yesterday, as a result of their devotion to a fragmentary, atomistic specialization were not only politically neutral but even naïve, are becoming increasingly more vocal.[9] A similar process also seems to be taking place in the Soviet Union.

In spite of all the evils that arise from specialization run riot, it cannot be denied that it must have an honored place in any educational system worthy of the name. The great danger inherent in some of our "general education" schemes and courses is superficiality. The student gets a smattering of everything without much of anything. It is this danger that the specialist fears.

More than this, specialization is imperative because no human mind can take in the whole province of knowledge or even a large part of it at any one time. The field of knowledge is now so vast and the problems involved are so complex that, if one is to make any headway at all, the tactics of divide and conquer become absolutely necessary.[10] Finally, from a practical standpoint, the specialist or expert is indispensable. When one must have a delicate brain operation, he does not go to the general practitioner.

As far as the more technical aspects of the problem of specialization versus general education are concerned, these must be left to

9. See especially the issues of the *Bulletin of the Atomic Scientists: A Magazine of Science and Public Affairs.* There is also the *SSRS Newsletter,* published by the Society for Social Responsibility in Science, with headquarters at Gambier, Ohio.

10. It is at this point in particular that the analyst, with his stress on analysis, has something important to offer—that is, along with his stress on precision and the critical attitude.

those who have taken the time to study all of the important details involved in the light of any particular situation. Even a philosopher, however, may be permitted a few general suggestions. First and foremost, the mean must be applied: that is, every possible effort must be made to find a way between the two extremes of a specialization that means fragmentation, atomism, chaos, and a general education that can only result in shallowness, superficiality, and incompetence. Second, much more must be done to get the specialists and experts in the various fields together, and not only to share each other's knowledge, but also in order to launch vast cooperative attacks on common problems. Third, so far as undergraduates are involved, a generous liberal education with due emphasis on the social sciences and the humanities should —always and everywhere—precede specialization in any field. This is in accordance with the basic, overall goal, namely, the *humanization of man*.

Furthermore, along with all this, since philosophy, as the *scientia scientiarum*, is the great integrator among the various disciplines and fields of knowledge, far more stress must be placed upon it. Experiments with courses in philosophy, as we suggested, should be conducted in many high schools. Nor should any student be allowed to graduate from any college or university without some acquaintance with philosophy. At any rate, one thing is becoming increasingly certain: as long as we continue to treat philosophy as a kind of stepchild, and as long as too many philosophers—on their part—stress the details of an analysis that has overstepped its bounds, we shall continue to be the victims of fragmentary thinking and living.

4. Authority Without Authoritarianism

Strange as it may seem, the American is both a notorious lawbreaker and a conformist. His disregard for the ordinary proprieties of law and order has injured our reputation abroad almost beyond repair. At the same time, nevertheless, he is willing to accept authority blindly, especially if it comes from the "miracle man" who claims to have the "know how." Amaury de Riencourt goes so far as to say that "hero worship and bossism" are natural features of American life, and that "circumstances" rather than "conviction" have made Americans "nonmilitaristic" in the past.[11] The blind acceptance of peace time conscription, in spite of the fact that it is contrary to our basic democratic traditions and in spite of the fact that it is archaic, serves to confirm this view.

One thing is, however, becoming increasingly clear, namely, that lack of respect for authority is as dangerous to democracy as unthinking conformity and blind submission. Without a certain healthy, sane respect for law and order and common decency, any society breaks down; and, after a period of anarchy and chaos, tyranny, in terms of the strong man (Toynbee's "savior with the sword"), rides into power.

Coming back more directly to education itself, it is certain that the teacher must be at once a wise guide and a discerning disciplinarian; otherwise chaos descends upon the classroom. As we have had occasion to observe before, the pampered and unruly among our youth constitute a threat to democracy itself. These barbarians that we have reared may some unhappy tomorrow become the storm troopers of some would-be dictator, and, after they have climbed to positions of power, may destroy the heritage which the "sweat, blood, and tears" of many generations have built. Today, at any rate, the falsity of a romanticism that neglects discipline is clear from its fruits, namely, the deterioration of character and the lack of skill in certain basic subjects.

Two kinds of authority are, in fact, necessary. The first springs from that mature wisdom which some possess even though they have little formal education. The second consists of the special training, knowledge, and skill of the expert. Needless to say, both are necessary if the teacher is to inspire that respect which helps to reduce the discipline problem to a minimum. This, of course, in-

11. *The Coming Caesars* (New York: Coward-McCann, 1957), p. 341.

volves a mastery of subject matter as well as methods and techniques.

Moreover, if the wrong kind of authority is to be avoided, underlying and undergirding all, there must be a genuine respect for truth. Truth is really the final authority.[12] Whenever a false authority arises—such as a dictator—truth is always the first casualty.

If the basic freedoms are to be secure, two important facts must be constantly kept in mind. The first is the obvious fact that, regardless of what relativists may say, some things are actually true or real. The second is no less obvious: that none of man's concepts of truth are ever infallible or final. While the experts are much more likely to be right in matters pertaining to their own fields than laymen are, yet even *they* may be mistaken. This is evident from the very fact that they are so often in violent disagreement.

In short, we must aim at a conception of authority that does not involve authoritarianism—the setting up of an infallible system or institution. Nor must it be forgotten that freedom is just as much in jeopardy when we recognize no authority whatsoever as when we go all out for authoritarianism. Indeed, it has become clear that the first usually leads to the second.

5. Freedom Without License and Anarchy

The trouble with many who glibly mouth the word freedom is that they have never taken the time to define the term properly. In other words, they have never tried to distinguish it carefully from license. For them it simply means the "emancipated man," that is, the individual who is free from all inhibitions—who does as he *likes* or *feels*.

Under the influence of a false psychology even some educators, who should know better, have gone astray. They too are victims of that false, uncritical fear of repression preached by a popular

12. On this point, see Ch. V, pp. 86-87, and Ch. VIII, pp. 172-73. The strongest argument for the objectivity of truth is the fact that it cannot be denied without being affirmed.

brand of Freudianism. Hocking, in criticism of this popular brand of Freudianism, makes the valid distinction between an "abnormal" type of repression which brings havoc, and a normal form which is "inseparable from personality" and the achievement of the good life. The real "liberator" is also "the disciplinarian"; for experience has shown that there is no greater bondage known to man than that which comes from the failure to control and direct impulse and desire.[13] Only as reason stands in the chariot, as Plato told the world long ago, can there be true self-realization.[14] Those of us who teach can testify that we have seen many a gifted student wreck his career through the lack of a sense of direction, of determination, and of sustained effort.

The genius, with his unusual sensitivity, above all people, must learn discipline. Without it, in spite of his high I.Q. and in spite of his apparent success—with little effort—in high school and perhaps even in college as an undergraduate, he is likely to fail when the great and final test of his academic career comes—that is, when he enters graduate school. He is likely to fail for not less than three reasons: his failure to master vital background material; his failure to acquire effective study habits—including certain techniques and methods; and because, perhaps for the first time in his life, in a highly selective situation, he will be forced to compete with minds as gifted and, in many instances, more gifted than his own. He may, in fact, find himself surpassed by many with a lower I.Q., who have made up the difference through well-nigh superhuman efforts. It is the old story of Hercules and the tortoise all over again.

True freedom, then, is the child of inner discipline. That individual is truly free who, in accordance with the goal of the educative process as presented in Chapter VI, attempts to develop his highest creative capacities in accordance with excellence.

13. William Ernest Hocking, *Human Nature and Its Remaking*, pp. 36-39. Even Freud did not sanction license; see Ch. V, p. 101, n. 33, and also Ch. VII, p. 150, n. 20.
14. See his *Phaedrus*, 253-54.

6. A Universal Outlook

Finally, any philosophy of education adequate for these times must be dominated by nothing less than a universal outlook. It has already become evident that philosophy, by its very nature as the highest and most comprehensive expression of reason, can only be universal. Truth knows no frontiers and no barriers of race or nationality or color or creed: it is the same everywhere no matter how much men in totalitarian countries or in degenerate democracies may try, unsuccessfully, to twist it to their own selfish ends.

Yet, perhaps the greatest single weakness of most of the education of the past, especially on the lower levels, has been its narrow nationalistic and even chauvinist spirit. Instead of challenging youth to the highest possible creativity in terms of excellence and a global outlook, the chief aim of the various educational systems has been to indoctrinate students with the poison of a selfish nationalism—to seduce them to prostrate themselves before this Moloch. Thus, everything in the curriculum, from science and history and even to religion, was twisted to meet the momentary needs of nationalism. Is there any wonder that the nations literally bled themselves white?

In this, the Nuclear Age, the nation (which the philosopher Hobbes glorified as "that great Leviathan," and as "that *mortal god*"), as a self-sufficient absolute, is as archaic as it is dangerous. Nations can no more provide security for their citizens than they can live to themselves; for, in the very act of trying to protect themselves by means of their apocalyptic weapons, they endanger themselves as well as the entire human race. It is this fact—made so graphic by the Cuban crisis so that everyone, except the most benighted reactionary, could see it—which is behind the present more favorable turn of events, namely, the test ban agreement. The truth of the whole matter is that the only security still possible is that which can come through the society of nations, the federation of the world.

7. The Educator's Role Today and Tomorrow

Paradoxical as it may seem, while science has all but banished the crude apocalypticism that made our grandfathers tremble in their pews, in splitting the atom it has produced an apocalypticism all its own. However, unlike the old form, instead of the decision being in the hands of an anthropomorphic and somewhat erratic Deity sitting on a throne somewhere above the earth, this fateful decision now rests in the puny hands of man himself. Thus, men in our time, since they have the destiny of the race in their keeping, have fulfilled the serpent's ancient prophesy, "You will be like God."

Yet, in spite of the great danger in times such as this when the future trembles in the balance, there is also the possibility of a far greater creativity than in less perilous ages—a creativeness so great as to make that of other ages pale before it. With all his capacities at their very highest tension—like the strong man with his back against the wall—Homo sapiens may respond in such an extraordinary manner that history will indeed take a new direction. Even now, in truth, one can already see on the horizon the cloud of promise—though it is still only the size of a man's hand.

Moreover, it may well be that educators, whether they realize it or not, have the power in their hands to tip the scales in the right direction. This certainly places a heavy responsibility upon them; but it may also serve to awaken them—as the scientists are beginning to awaken.

Important as the educator's task undoubtedly is in this age of transition, nevertheless, even when this time of crisis passes, his task is not finished. In fact, as long as the stream of human life continues, his task is forever unfinished. Each new age will bring new problems, new responsibilities, and new opportunities.

There is also the problem of each person as a unique individual. The wonder of man is that he is twice-born. The first is the natural and physical as he enters this strange, mysterious world— not human yet for the most part, but certainly *potentially* human in the full sense of the word. The second is when the long process of *humanization* begins: that is, as the live coals of potentiality burst into flame, as the child responds to his environment not merely mechanically and biologically, but meaningfully and rationally. Truly this moment, when the child begins to make his first real human response, constitutes the greatest of miracles. If no individual had ever made this response, there would be nothing but the unreflective brute world.

The conclusion of the whole matter then is simply this: the educator's great opportunity as well as his forever unfinished task consists in furthering this process of *humanization* by doing everything in his power to direct it toward *excellence* and a deep sense of *social responsibility*. In short, in a confused world where the great danger is the *brutalization* and the *barbarization* of man, the *humanization* of man is the *one goal* on which all men of good will—regardless of creed—can and must concentrate.

Annotated Bibliography*

JOURNALS

Bulletin of the Atomic Scientists: The Magazine of Science and Public Affairs. For all who are interested in trying to keep up with what leading scientists think about the nuclear crisis and related problems, this journal is superb. Published at 935 East 60th Street, Chicago 37, Illinois.

Harvard Educational Review. This is probably the best educational journal in this country. Among other things, many excellent articles dealing with the philosophy of education and related problems have appeared in its pages. Published at 8 Prescott Street, Cambridge 38, Massachusetts.

The Journal of Philosophy. This fortnightly journal is essential for anyone who is interested in keeping up with what is going on in philosophy. Occasionally it has an article dealing with matters related to the philosophy of education. Published at 720 Philosophy Hall, Columbia University, New York 27, N.Y.

The Journal of Teacher Education. Although more specialized than the others, this journal (an organ of the National Education Association) is valuable as a source of information concerning the problems which the modern teacher faces and many other related matters. Published at 1201 Sixteenth Street, N.W., Washington 6, D.C.

Religious Education. This journal (the organ of the Religious Education Association) is the best in this field—at least so far as the United States and Canada are concerned. It is essential for anyone interested in keeping abreast of the best that is going on in religious education. Published at 545 West 111th Street, New York 25, N.Y.

* In this annotated bibliography only a few of the most outstanding journals and books are listed. Other journals and books are mentioned in the many footnotes in connection with the various subjects discussed. Both this bibliography and the footnotes are for the convenience of the student and other interested readers who want to pursue the various problems further.

BOOKS

Allport, Gordon W. *Personality: A Psychological Interpretation.* New York: Henry Holt & Co., 1937. Although this book appeared some years ago, it is still one of the most important studies in the field of personality.

Bagley, William C. *Education and Emergent Man.* ("Nelson Educational Series.") New York: Thomas Nelson & Sons, 1934. This is an important book by an outstanding essentialist and realist who follows a naturalistic and humanistic point of view.

Bereday, George Z. F., *et al*, editors. *The Changing Soviet School.* Boston: Houghton Mifflin Co., 1960.—by the Comparative Education Society. This book is especially valuable if supplemented by Fred Ablin (ed.), *Education in the USSR* (New York: International Arts & Sciences Press). The latter consists of actual articles from Soviet journals.

Brameld, Theodore. *Education for the Emerging Age.* New York: Harper & Row, 1961. With its strong social emphasis, this book of Brameld's is especially relevant to the present situation.

Breed, Frederick S. *Education and the New Realism.* ("Modern Teachers' Series.") New York: The Macmillan Co., 1939. For an understanding of essentialism from the standpoint of realism, this book is superb.

Brubacher, John S., editor. *Modern Philosophies of Education.* Second edition. New York: McGraw-Hill Book Co., 1950.

————. *Eclectic Philosophy of Education.* ("Prentice-Hall Educational Series.") New York: Prentice-Hall, 1951. These books supplement each other. The first deals with the nature of the various educational philosophies plus an attempt at synthesis, while the second is a book of readings arranged under various topics.

Butler, J. Donald. *Four Philosophers, and Their Practice in Education and Religion.* Revised edition. New York: Harper & Row, 1957.

————. *Religious Education: The Foundations and Practice of Nurture.* New York: Harper & Row, 1962. These books also supplement each other: while the first deals with naturalism, idealism, realism, and pragmatism and their relations to education and religion, the second casts light both on the background and on contemporary trends in religious education.

Callahan, Raymond E. *An Introduction to Education in American Society: A Text with Readings.* Second edition. New York: Alfred A. Knopf, 1961. This book, with a foreword by the famous educationist, George S. Counts, is one of the best of its kind. Part VI dealing with the American teacher is especially outstanding.

Cunningham, William F. *The Pivotal Problems of Education*. New York: The Macmillan Co., 1940. The author, as a Roman Catholic, criticizes other philosophies and defends supernaturalism.

Defferrari, Roy J. (ed.). *The Philosophy of Catholic Higher Education*. Washington: Catholic University of America Press, 1947. This constitutes a valuable source of information on Roman Catholic higher education.

Dewey, John. *Democracy and Education; An Introduction to the Philosophy of Education*. Paperback. New York: The Macmillan Co., 1961.

————. *Philosophy of Education*, paperback. Ames, Iowa: Littlefield, Adams & Co., 1956. While the first is Dewey's greatest book on philosophy of education, the second (originally published as *Problems of Men*) sheds additional light—especially since it contains an introduction written in 1946.

Dierenfield, Richard B. *Religion in American Public Schools*. Washington, D. C.: Public Affairs Press, 1962. This is perhaps the best recent report on the subject.

Eby, Frederick. *The Development of Modern Education: In Theory, Organization, and Practice*. Second edition. New York: Prentice-Hall, 1952. This constitutes a very helpful source of information. It is also well written— with real insight.

Farber, Seymour M. and Roger H. L. Wilson, editors. *Man and Civilization: Control of the Mind; a Symposium*. New York: McGraw-Hill, 1961.

————. *Man and Civilization: Conflict and Creativity; a Symposium*. New York: McGraw-Hill, 1963. These books comprise symposia by various experts dealing with the problems of mind control and creativity.

Getzels, Jacob W. and Philip W. Jackson. *Creativity and Intelligence: Explorations With Gifted Students*. New York: John Wiley & Sons, 1962. This book is important both in its analysis of creativity and its conclusion that IQ tests are inadequate means for the discovery of real creativity in individuals.

Graves, Frank Pierrepont. *A History of Education*. New York: Macmillan Co., 1909, 1910, 1915. Though written over fifty years ago, this three-volume work is still outstanding.

Hook, Sidney. *Education For Modern Man: A New Perspective*. Enlarged edition. New York: Alfred A. Knopf, 1963. This book is important for two reasons: it constitutes a new and stimulating evaluation of modern education from a pragmatic standpoint; and the last chapter—"The Good Teacher"— is nothing short of excellent.

Horne, Herman Harrell. *The Democratic Philosophy of Education*. New York: The Macmillan Co., 1932. This still remains one of the outstanding criticisms of John Dewey's philosophy.

Hutchins, Robert Maynard. *The Higher Learning in America.* ("Storrs Lectures.") New Haven: Yale University Press, 1936. This book contains both Hutchins' criticisms of higher education and his own proposals.

Jacob, Philip E. *Changing Values in College: An Exploratory Study of the Impact of College Teaching.* New York: Harper & Row, 1957. This interesting study discloses many facts about American colleges. Chief among these are: the general attitude of social conformity, and the fact that students seem to be "gloriously content" with things as they are. This book was written, of course, before the Cuban Crisis and before many students became seriously involved in the race problem.

Jaspers, Karl. *Man in the Modern Age.* Translated by Eden and Cedar Paul. Garden City, N. Y.: Doubleday & Co., 1957.

————. *The Future of Mankind.* Translated by E. B. Ashton. Chicago: University of Chicago Press, 1961. While in the first (which is available in paperback) this great philosopher expresses his fear that man may become dehumanized through the machine, in the second he reflects on the dangers of the Nuclear Age and what must be done to avoid the final catastrophe.

Jung, Carl G. *The Development of Personality.* Translated by R. F. C. Hull. Vol. 17 of his *Collected Works,* edited by Sir Herbert Read *et al.* ("Bollinger Series.") New York: Pantheon Books, 1954. This constitutes a collection of papers by the great psychologist. His criticisms of psychology, his discussion of the gifted child, of the significance of the unconscious in education, etc., make it important.

Kneller, George F. *Existentialism and Education.* New York: Philosophical Library, 1958. This book is important chiefly because so little has been written on the subject.

Koerner, James D. *The Miseducation of American Teachers.* Boston: Houghton Mifflin Co., 1963. Although this book is highly controversial, every educator should read it.

Korol, Alexander G. *Soviet Education for Science and Technology.* New York: John Wiley & Sons, 1957. For perspective on this phase of Russian education, this volume is important.

Maritain, Jacques. *Education at the Crossroads.* ("Yale University Terry Lectures.") New Haven: Yale University Press, 1943. Besides being by one of the outstanding contemporary Thomist philosophers, this book is important for its exposure of some of the weaknesses of modern education.

Meyer, Adolph E. *The Development of Education in the Twentieth Century.* ("Prentice-Hall Educational Series.") Second edition. New York: Prentice-Hall, 1949. This constitutes an excellent survey of education across some fifty years.

Moberly, Sir Walter. *The Crisis in the University*. New York: The Macmillan Co., 1950. Fully conscious of the world crisis, the author views the British system of higher education from a broad Christian perspective. Chapter III, "Some Causes of Our Present Discontent," is especially worth reading carefully.

Mulhern, James. *A History of Education: A Social Interpretation*. Second edition. New York: The Ronald Press Co., 1959. This is one of the best recent over-all surveys of education. The student will find it useful.

Peterson, A. D. C. *A Hundred Years of Education*. Paperback. Second revised edition. New York: Collier Books, 1962. Written by the Director of Education at Oxford University, this excellent little book gives the thoughtful inquirer both an illuminating survey of modern and contemporary education and also helpful criticisms of American education by a friendly critic.

Phenix, Philip H. *Philosophy of Education*. New York: Henry Holt & Co., 1958. Although the author (who is a professor at Teachers College, Columbia) may be attempting too much, this is certainly one of the best recent philosophies of education. The approach is broad and comprehensive.

Russell Bertrand. *Education and the Good Life*. New York: Boni & Liveright, 1926. Published in paperback by Avon Book Division of the Hearst Corporation. Although written some years ago, this provocative Nobel Prize Winner is still worth reading.

Taylor, Marvin J., editor. *Religious Education*. Nashville: Abingdon Press, 1960. This book contains thirty-seven brief articles dealing with various aspects of the problem. This, along with Butler's book, gives the student the needed perspective.

Toynbee, Arnold J. *Reconsiderations*, Vol. XII of *A Study of History*. New York: Oxford University Press, 1961. With this outstanding volume, Toynbee brings his monumental work, *A Study of History*, to a close. This book is especially important for perspective.

Ulich, Robert. *Philosophy of Education*. New York: American Book Co., 1961. Written by a leading educational philosopher and from a definitely *ethical* point of view, this book is important because it seeks significant answers to some of the basic issues which modern man faces.

Whitehead, Alfred North. *The Aims of Education; And Other Essays*. New York: The Macmillan Co., 1929. Published in paperback by the New American Library of World Literature. Written by one of the greatest of contemporary philosophers, this little book is important for its synoptic approach and its stress on creativity and excellence.

Index of Persons

Abelard, 34, 181
Ablin, Fred, 76 *n.*, 153 *n.*
Adler, Felix, 55
Aiken, Henry D., 218 *n.*
Alcott, Bronson, 62
Albertus Magnus, 31, 181
Alcuin, 33
Alexander, Samuel, 73
Allport, Gordon W., 119 *n.*, 131 *n.*, 158 and *n.*, 163 *n.*, 164 *n.*, 167-68 and *n.*
Antz, Louise, 218 *n.*
Aquinas, St. Thomas, 31, 32 *n.*, 43, 63, 64, 66 and *n.*, 117, 123 and *n.*, 126
Arcesilaus, 226 *n.*
Archimedes, 147
Aristophanes, 217
Aristotle, 18, 22, 27-28, 45, 46 *n.*, 63, 70, 117, 123 and *n.*, 124, 126, 127, 180 and *n.*, 238, 241
Ashley, Benedict M., 68 *n.*
Asoka, King, 210
Augustine, St., 30, 31 and *n.*, 123
Averroës, 32
Avicenna, 32
Ayer, A. J., 79 and *n.*, 162 *n.*, 171 and *n.*, 172, 219 and *n.*

Bacon, Francis, 64, 167
Bacon, Roger, 32, 33, 181
Bagley, William C., 58 and *n.*, 59 and *n.*, 63, 64, 97 and *n.*, 101 *n.*, 119 *n.*
Bardis, Panos, 8
Barnard, Henry, 55
Barnett, A. Doak, 234 *n.*
Barr, Stringfellow, 38 *n.*
Barrett, William, 218 *n.*
Barth, Karl, 69, 77, 201, 204 and *n.*
Beck, Robert N., 60 *n.*
Beethoven, Ludwig van, 122
Bergmann, Gustav, 46 *n.*, 79 *n.*
Bergson, Henri, 61, 145, 146 and *nn.*, 165 *n.*, 166
Bereday, George Z. F., 76 *n.*, 153 *n.*
Berkeley, George, 60, 62
Bertocci, Peter A., 60 *n.*, 102 *n.*, 171 *n.*, 172 and *n.*, 173 *n.*, 223 *n.*
Blake, William, 143
Blanshard, Brand, 172 and *nn.*, 217 *n.*, 223

Bockenski, I. M., 73 *n.*
Bode, Boyd H., 92 and *n.*, 95 and *n.*
Bond, Earl D., 149 *n.*
Boniface, 31
Booth, Edwin D., 86 *n.*, 182 *n.*, 210 *n.*
Brameld, Theodore, 51 *n.*, 55 *n.*, 64 *n.*, 81-82, 90 *n.*, 92 and *n.*, 93 *n.*, 99 and *n.*, 101 *n.*, 108 and *n.*, 112 *n.*, 127 and *n.*, 129 and *nn.*, 130 and *n.*, 136, 144, 208 *n.*, 209 *n.*, 215 and *n.*, 224 *n.*, 228, 236 *n.*
Breed, Frederick, 58 and *nn.*, 60 *n.*, 64, 92 and *n.*, 101 *n.*, 240 *n.*
Bretail, Robert W., 201 *n.*
Brick, Alan, 240 *n.*
Bright, John, 29 *n.*
Brightman, Edgar S., 47 *n.*, 60 and *n.*, 61 and *n.*, 62 and *n.*, 63 and *n.*, 96, 98 *n.*, 102 *n.*, 115 *n.*, 150 *n.*, 191 *n.*, 192 and *n.*, 200 *n.*, 223 and *n.*
Brightman, Robert S., 223
Brodhead, Russell, 156
Browning, Robert, 143
Brubacher, John S., 50 *n.*, 67 *nn.*, 71 *n.*, 97 *n.*, 113 *n.*, 122 *n.*, 123 *n.*, 124 *n.*, 128 *n.*, 129 and *n.*, 158 *n.*
Bruno, Giordano, 175
Buddha, 25 and *n.*, 28
Bultmann, Rudolf, 28 and *n.*, 204 and *n.*
Burkill, T. Alec, 200 *n.*, 201-2 and *n.*
Bushnell, Horace, 197
Burtt, A. E., 25 *n.*, 201 *n.*
Butler, J. Donald, 20 *n.*, 30 *n.*, 35 *n.*, 51 *n.*, 55 *n.*, 62 *n.*, 64 *n.*, 68 *n.*, 69 and *n.*, 193 *n.*, 196 and *nn.*, 200 *n.*

Calvin, John, 69
Carnap, Rudolf, 79 *n.*
Carnell, E. J., 70 *n.*
Carrell, Alexis, 165 and *n.*
Cauthen, Kenneth, 200 *n.*
Chander, Albert R., 71 *n.*
Charlegmagne, 33
Cicero, Marcus Tullius, 35, 241
Coe, George Albert, 197
Columban, 31
Comenius, John Amos, 34 and *n.*, 35, 55, 63 *n.*, 64, 94, 117, 196
Comte, Auguste, 84

Conant, James Bryant, 101 *n.*, 158 *n.*
Confucius, 25 and *n.*, 28, 111, 144, 238
Copernicus, Nicolaus, 36, 175, 181, 194
Counts, George S., 72 *n.*, 74 and *n.*, 75 *n.*, 241 *n.*
Creel, H. G., 25 *n.*
Cunningham, William F., 51 *n.*, 67 *n.*
Cuvier, Georges, 27

Dampier, William Cecil, 23 *n.*, 147 and *n.*
Darwin, Charles, 27, 51, 100, 115, 125, 143, 181, 184, 194, 211
Davidson, Thomas, 20 *n.*, 23 *n.*
Defferrari, Roy J., 68 *nn.*
De Hovre, Franz, 67 *n.*
Descartes, René, 62, 64
Dewey, John, 34, 35 and *n.*, 37, 43, 51, 55, 56, 57 and *n.*, 63, 78 *n.*, 81, 82, 84-92, 98, 113 and *n.*, 126, 129, 134, 158 and *n.*, 159 and *n.*, 164, 182 and *n.*, 188 and *n.*, 197, 228, 243
DeWolf, L. Harold, 28 *n.*, 29 *n.*, 200 *n.*, 204 *n.*
Dickens, Charles, 29
Dierenfield, R. H., 199 *n.*, 207 *n.*, 208 *nn.*, 209 *n.*, 215 and *n.*
Dostoevski, Feodor, 107
Douglas, Harl H., 182 *nn.*, 198 *n.*
Ducasse, C. J., 192 *n.*
Du Noüy, Lecomte, 86 *n.*, 98 *n.*, 182 *n.*

Eby, Frederick, 20 *n.*, 34 *n.*, 36 *n.*, 43 *n.*, 44 and *n.*, 57 *n.*, 119 *n.*, 180 *n.*, 188 *n.*, 195 and *n.*
Eddington, A. S., 177 and *n.*, 182 *n.*
Edel, Abraham, 186 *n.*
Einstein, Albert, 115, 124, 132, 143, 149, 173, 190
Eliot, Charles, 128 *n.*
Engels, Friedrich, 73
Erasmus, Desiderius, 35
Euripides, 22

Fallow, Wesner, 208 *n.*
Farber, Marvin, 132 *n.*
Farber, Seymour M., 56 *n.*, 143 *n.*, 145 *n.*, 150 *n.*, 153 *n.*, 163 *n.*, 164 *n.*, 166 *n.*
Feigl, Herbert, 79 *n.*, 222-23 and *n.*
Ferm, Dean William, 200 *n.*
Ferm, Vergilius, 102 *n.*

Feuer, Lewis S., 73 *n.*, 220 and *n.*, 225 *n.*
Fichte, Johann, 62
Finegan, Jack, 192 *n.*
Finney, Ross L., 64
Fleshman, Arthur C., 128 *n.*
Flewelling, Ralph Tyler, 62, 102 *n.*
Frankel, Charles, 49 *n.*
Frankena, William K., 50 *n.*
Freud, Sigmund, 101 *n.*, 148 and *n.*, 150 *n.*, 159, 161 and *n.*, 168-70 and *nn.*
Friedrich, L. W., 86 *n.*
Froebel, Frederick, 34 *n.*, 35, 43 and *n.*, 52, 55 *n.*, 94, 196 and *n.*

Gaebelein, Frank E., 70 *n.*
Galilei, Galileo, 36, 175, 181, 194
Gamow, George, 184 *n.*
Garnett, A. Campbell, 222 and *n.*
Gentile, Giovanni, 71, 96
Getzels, Jacob W., 34 *n.*, 141 and *n.*, 144 and *n.*, 147 and *n.*, 148 *n.*, 158 and *nn.*
Giesse, Vincent J., 68 *n.*
Gilson, Étienne, 201
Goebbels, Joseph Paul, 136
Graves, Frank Pierrepont, 20 *n.*, 23 *n.*, 24 *n.*, 31 and *n.*, 180 and *n.*
Green, Thomas Hill, 86
Grieder, Calvin, 182 *nn.*, 198 *n.*
Grimes, Howard, 30 *n.*, 193 *n.*

Haeckel, Ernst, 183
Harris, Errol E., 32 *n.*, 61 *n.*, 163 *n.*, 223, 244 *n.*
Harris, William Torrey, 36, 43, 62
Hartmann, H. Gertrude, 56 *nn.*
Hastings, James, 24 *n.*
Hegel, G. W. F., 26, 43, 51, 62, 73, 95
Heidegger, Martin, 77 and *n.*, 78, 110, 219, 223
Heinemann, F. G., 77 *n.*
Heisenberg, Werner, 86 *n.*
Hemholtz, H. L. F., von, 170
Heraclitus, 85, 99
Herbart, Johann, 43, 52, 181
Hiero, King, 147
Hitler, Adolf, 71, 72, 111, 119, 136, 166, 174, 187, 199, 201
Hobbes, Thomas, 71

Hocking, William Ernest, 23 and *n.*, 58, 59 *n.*, 60, 62, 101 *n.*, 120 and *n.*, 192 and *n.*, 249 and *n.*

Hook, Sidney, 55 and *n.*, 88 *n.*, 167 *n.*

Hordern, William, 70 and *n.*, 200 *n.*

Horne, Hermann Harrell, 30 *n.*, 58 *n.*, 62, 86, 87 and *nn.*, 90 and *n.*, 92, 102 *n.*, 131 *n.*

Hoyle, Fred, 184 *n.*

Hume, David, 183 and *n.*

Hutchins, Robert Maynard, 116, 125-27 and *nn.*, 224 *n.*

Huxley, Aldous, 206

Huxley, Thomas H., 36, 64, 177, 181 and *n.*

Jackson, Philip W., 34 *n.*, 141 and *n.*, 144 and *n.*, 147 and *n.*, 148 *n.*, 158 and *nn.*

Jacob, Philip E., 16 *n.*, 156 and *nn.*

James, William 51, 54, 61, 112 and *n.*, 165 *n.*, 169 *n.*

Jarrett, James L., 218 *n.*

Jaspers, Karl, 77 and *n.*, 78 *n.*, 129, 152 *n.*, 223

Jefferson, Thomas, 198 and *nn.*

Jesus, Christ, 18, 25, 28-30, 35, 69, 74, 144, 199

John XXIII, Pope, 67, 104, 174, 203, 204

Johnson, Marietta, 55

Judd, C. H., 224

Jung, C. G., 148 and *nn.*, 149 and *n.*

Kant, Immanuel, 43, 51, 60, 62, 128 *n.*, 130, 228

Kaufmann, Walter, 77 and *n.*

Kegley, Charles W., 201 *n.*

Kemeny, John G., 177 *n.*

Kennedy, John F., 17

Kent, Charles Foster, 30 *n.*

Keppel, Francis, 237 *n.*

Kierkegaard, Sören, 77, 219

Kilpatrick, William H., 55

King, Martin Luther, Jr., 60 and *n.*, 205 and *n.*

King, Winston L., 191 *n.*

Khrushchev, N. S., 76 *n.*

Kneale, William and Martha Kneale, 179 *n.*

Kneller, George F., 38 and *n.*, 55 *n.*, 78 and *nn.*, 107 and *n.*, 219 *n.*

Knox, John, 195

Koerner, James D., 37 *n.*, 47 *n.*, 59 and *n.*, 135 *n.*, 157, 158 *n.*, 224 *n.*, 236 *n.*

Korol, Alexander, 76 *n.*, 175 *n.*

Kubie, L. S., 148 *n.*

Ladd, John, 186 *n.*

Langer, Susanne, 83 and *n.*, 113 and *n.*

Lapp, Ralph E., 153 *n.*, 182 *n.*, 187 *n.*, 190, 237 *n.*

Laslett, Peter, 221

Latourette, Kenneth Scott, 31 *n.*

Leach, James E., 8

Leibniz, G. W., 60, 62

Lenin, V. I., 73 and *n.*

Levi, Albert William, 87 and *n.*, 89 *n.*, 150 *n.*, 168-69 and *n.*, 170 *n.*

Levin, Deana, 76 *n.*

Lewis, Clarence Irving, 124 *n.*

Lilge, Frederick, 71 *n.*, 95 and *n.*

Linneaus, Carl, 27

Locke, John, 64

Lodge, Nucia, 72 *n.*, 75 *n.*

Lotz, Philip Henry, 193 *n.*, 199 *n.*, 207 *n.*

Luther, Martin, 69, 117, 195

McConnell, Gaither, 235 *n.*

McGill, V. J., 132 *n.*

Macmurray, John, 166 *n.*

McMurrin, Sterling M., 218 *n.*

Mach, Ernest, 170

Machiavelli, Niccolo, 71

Macquarrie, John, 200 *n.*, 204 *n.*

Malkani, G. R., 8, 239 *n.*

Mann, Horace, 55, 198

Mannheim, Karl, 172

Marcel, Gabriel, 77, 129

Margolis, Joseph, 220 *n.*

Maritain, Jacques, 32 *n.*, 67 and *nn.*, 104 and *n.*, 113 and *n.*, 201 and *n.*, 223 *n.*

Martyr, Justin, 31 *n.*

Marx, Karl. *See also* Marxianism, 73, 74, 105-6

Mayo, H. B., 73 *n.*

Mead, George Herbert, 87

Medlin, Brian, 220 *n.*

Meland, Bernard Eugene, 191 *n.*

Mencius, 111

Meriam, Junius L., 55

Meyer, Adolph E., 20 *n.*, 51 *n.*, 52 *n.*, 55 *n.*, 56 *n.*, 59 *n.*, 71 *n.*, 72 *n.*, 119 *n.*, 126 *n.*
Micklem, Nathaniel, 200 *n.*
Mill, John Stuart, 61, 151
Millard, Richard M., 171 *n.*, 172 and *n.*, 173 *n.*
Miller, Randolph Crump, 108 *n.*
Millikan, Robert Andrew, 183 *n.*
Moberly, Walter, 26 and *n.*
Montagu, Ashley, 21 *n.*
Montague, William P., 64 *n.*
Moore, G. E., 79
Moses, 29
Mo-tzu, 111
Mulhern, James, 20 *n.*, 23 *n.*, 33 *n.*, 117 *n.*, 180 *n.*
Munitz, Milton K., 184 *n.*
Munk, Arthur W., 29 *n.*, 44 *n.*, 62 *n.*, 72 *n.*, 86 *n.*, 92 *n.*, 103 *n.*, 112 *n.*, 171 *n.*, 182 *n.*, 186 *n.*, 192 *n.*, 193 *n.*, 209 and *n.*, 210 *n.*, 213 and *nn.*, 220 *n.*, 221 *n.*, 225 *n.*, 228 *n.*, 229 *nn.*, 237 *n.*, 239 *n.*
Munk, J. B., 8
Mussolini, Benito, 70, 71

Naumberg, Madame, 55 *n.*
Neusse, C. J., 68 *n.*
Newhall, Jannette E., 223 *n.*
Newman, James R., 179 *n.*
Newman, John Cardinal, 123 and *n.*, 135
Newton, Sir Isaac, 100, 115, 143, 147, 181
Niebuhr, Reinhold, 201 *n.*
Nietzsche, Friedrich, 71, 77
Nietmann, W. D., 229 *n.*
Noss, John B., 25 and *nn.*

Ockham, William of, 32, 33
Ogden, Schubert M., 28 *n.*
Orwell, George, 187, 206

Pap, Arthur, 80 and *nn.*, 108 and *n.*
Parker, Francis, 55
Pascal, Blaise, 226 *n.*
Patrick, St., 31
Patterson, Charles H., 128 *n.*
Pauling, Linus, 190

Pavlov, Ivan, 159
Pegis, Anton, 123 *n.*
Peirce, Charles, 51
Pericles, 241
Perry, Ralph Barton, 166 *n.*, 198 *n.*
Pestalozzi, Johann Heinrich, 15, 34 *n.*, 35, 52, 53, 55 *n.*, 64, 94, 196 and *n.*
Peterson, A. D. C., 20 *n.*, 35 *n.*, 199 *n.*, 237 *n.*
Petry, Ray C., 29 *n.*
Phenix, Philip H., 176 *n.*
Phidias, 22
Philo, 31 *n.*
Pinkevitch, Albert P., 74 *n.*, 75 and *n.*
Pius XI, Pope, 67 *n.*, 68
Planck, Max, 86 *n.*, 182 *n.*, 183 *n.*
Plato, 18, 19, 22, 24, 26-27 and *n.*, 43, 46 and *n.*, 55 and *n.*, 61, 70, 72, 87 *n.*, 96 and *n.*, 100, 123, 126, 127, 143 and *n.*, 149 and *n.*, 180, 194 and *n.*, 228, 238, 241, 249 and *n.*
Poincare, Henri, 147
Pratt, J. B., 64, 128 *n.*, 129 and *n.*, 171 *n.*
Praxiteles, 22
Price, Kingsley, 220
Price, Lucien, 88 *n.*
Pusey, Nathan M., 194

Radhakrishnan, Sarvepalli, 200 *n.*, 221
Raeymaeker, Louis de, 201 and *n.*
Raikes, Robert, 195
Ramsey, Ian, 223
Rand, Benjamin, 183 *n.*
Reichenbach, Hans, 171 *n.*
Reid, Thomas, 64
Rhine, Joseph Banks, 168 and *n.*
Riencourt, Amaury de, 247 and *n.*
Robinson, John A. T., 200 *n.*
Rogers, Carl, 166 *n.*
Rousseau, Jacques, 34 and *n.*, 52, 55 *n.*, 64, 94, 128, 181, 196
Royce, Josiah, 60, 62
Runes, Dagobert D., 32 *n.*, 64 *n.*, 67 *n.*, 73 *n.*, 102 *n.*
Russell, Bertrand, 18 and *n.*, 60, 79 and *n.*, 80 and *n.*, 136 *nn.*, 190
Ryle, Gilbert, 219 and *n.*

Sabatier, Auguste, 103 *n.*
Sankara, 210

Santayana, George, 85 *n.*, 89 *n.*
Santillana, Giorgio de, 23 *n.*
Sartre, Jean-Paul, 77 and *n.*, 78, 107, 110
Scheffler, Israel, 220
Schelling, F. W. J., 95
Schiller, J. C. Friedrich von, 128 *n.*
Schilpp, Paul Arthur, 52 *n.*, 85 *n.*, 221 *n.*, 222 and *n.*
Schlick, Moritz, 79 and *n.*
Schweitzer, Albert, 213 and *n.*
Sellars, Roy Wood, 60, 73, 132 *n.*
Sellars, Wilfred, 79 *n.*
Shakespeare, William, 122
Shane, Harold G., 90 *n.*
Shumaker, Ann, 56 *nn.*
Simkhovitch, Vladmir G., 28 *n.*
Skinner, B. F., 166 *n.*, 167 and *n.*
Smith, Daniel Eugene, 179 *n.*
Socrates, 18, 22, 25-26, 28, 29, 43, 144, 217, 228, 229
Somerville, John, 73 *n.*
Sophocles, 22
Sorokin, Pitirium A., 17 *n.*
Spencer, Herbert, 181
Spinoza, Baruch, 165 *n.*, 167
Sprague, Elmer, 44 *n.*
Stalin, Joseph, 73, 75 *n.*, 187, 199
Sullivan, J. W. N., 182 *n.*
Swabey, Marie Collins, 58 *n.*
Szczesny, Gerhard, 202 and *n.*, 211 and *n.*, 213 *n*

Taylor, A. E., 194 *n.*
Taylor, Marvin J., 30 *n.*, 193 *n.*, 196 *n.*, 200 *n.*, 207 *n.*, 208 *n.*, 210 *n.*
Thompson, Samuel M., 44 *n.*
Thorndike, Edward L., 64, 119
Thrasymachus, 26
Thucydides, 100, 241
Tillich, Paul, 194 and *n.*, 200 *n.*, 201 and *n.*, 202 and *n.*, 204, 219

Titus, Harold H., 64 *n.*
Tolstoy, Leo, 107
Toynbee, Arnold J., 17 and *n.*, 18 and *n.*, 22 *n.*, 100 and *n.*, 120 and *n.*, 144 and *n.*, 151, 154-55 and *n.*, 192 and *n.*, 234 *n.*, 235 *n.*, 240 and *n.*, 241 and *n.*, 247
Trever, Albert A., 22 *n.*, 23 *n.*
Tsanoff, Radoslav, 128 *n.*

Ulfias, 31
Ulich, Robert, 47 *n.*

Van Dusen, Henry P., 28 *n.*, 198 *n.*, 207 *n.*
Visser 't Hooft, W. A., 203 *n.*, 205 *n.*

Warbeke, John M., 26 *n.*, 180 *n.*
Watson, John B., 159
Weigle, Luther A., 199 *n.*
Werkmeister, W. H., 64 *n.*
Westermarck, Edward A., 171 *n.*
White, Morton, 79 *n.*, 218 *n.*
Whitehead, Alfred N., 16 *n.*, 32 *n.*, 43, 61, 84 and *n.*, 87, 176 *n.*, 181 and *n.*, 192 and *n.*, 214 and *n.*
Wieman, Henry Nelson, 191 *n.*
Wiener, Nobert, 160 *n.*, 164 *n.*
Wild, John, 64, 77 *n.*, 113 and *n.*, 114 and *n.*, 120 *n.*, 201 *n.*, 213 and *n.*, 222 and *n.*
Williams, J. Paul, 198 *n.*
Wilson, O. W., 199 *n.*
Wilson, Roger H. L., 56 *n.*, 143 *n.*, 145 *n.*, 150 *n.*, 153 *n.*, 163 *n.*, 164 *n.*, 166 *n.*
Wittgenstein, Ludwig, 79, 220
Wornom, Herman E., 8
Wynne, John P., 51 *n.*, 92 and *n.*, 142 *n.*, 144 and *n.*, 150 *n.*

Index of Subjects

Academy of Plato, 24
adequacy, need of, 236-37
aim, aims. *See* goal, goals
Alexandria, University of, 24
America, Americans, 37, 76, 155, 224, 233, 235-36, 247
American Association of University Professors, 153
American education
  crisis in, 235-36
  list of weaknesses, 157
American Philosophical Association, 107
analysts, analytical philosophies, 79-81, 108-9, 110, 219, 221, 222
anti-intellectualism, 59, 71, 154, 157
Assyria, Assyrian, 22, 193
Athens, Athenian, 22, 23, 24, 55
authoritarianism, 65-76, 103-7, 110
  authority without, 246-48
  religious types of, 65-70, 103-4
  secular types of, 70-76, 104-7

Babylonia, Babylonian, 22, 23, 193
Baptists, 198
becoming, process of, 164
behaviorism, behaviorists, 85, 87, 98, 159
Bible, 69, 195
birth control and population explosion, 68, 154, 188 *n.*, 204-5, 234
Bologna, University of, 33
Brahman, 23
Buddhism, 210, 211. *See also* Buddha

California, University of, 210
Cambridge University, 33, 194
Catholicism, Roman, 66-68, 104, 110, 195, 197, 201, 203-4
China, Chinese, Sinic,
  ancient, and pre-Marxian, 16, 22, 23, 24, 25
  Marxian, 153, 154, 234-35
Christian, Christianity, 31, 74, 121, 201, 210, 211
church, churches,
  National Council of, 203
  World Council of, 203, 205
citizenship, 117-18, 133

civilizations
  contributions of ancient, 22-30
  Greco-Roman, 22, 100
  Syriac, 22
  Western, 120
class struggle, 54
communism. *See* Marxianism
computers, 164
conferences, philosophical
  fifth Inter-American, 221
  third East-West, 221 and *n.*, 223
confusion, effects of, 152-53, 214, 217
creativity, 7, 94-95, 137, 141-51
  and intuition, 145-48
  and the unconscious, 148-51
  as aspect of goal, 137
  its nature, 142-45
  need of, 151
  in philosophy, 221-23, 225-29
  in religion, 210-15
  in science, 189-90
culture, cultures
  collision of, 212, 217
  for its own sake, 122-23, 134
  transmission of, 15-16, 116-17, 133

democracy, 17, 37, 52, 54, 81-82, 91, 95, 136, 154, 197, 211
"demythologization," 28 and *n.*
determinism, 73-74, 98, 160-61, 164-68, 211, 217
dialectical materialism. *See* Marxianism
dilemma, American, 197-99
discipline, 56, 59, 103-4, 118-20, 134, 247, 248-49

education
  aimlessness of modern, 113-14
  and philosophy, 43-44
  and religion, 193-97
  and science, 180-82
  aspects of, 15-17
  crisis in American, 235-36
  goal of. *See* goal, goals
  greatest need in, 236-37
  humanization of, 35
  in perspective, 20-39
  nature and significance of, 15-19
  philosophies of, 50-82

education—*cont'd*
  Plato's scheme, 26-27
  primitive, 20-22
  Soviet, 74-76
Egypt, Egyptian, 22, 23, 193
essentialism, 57-65, 95-103, 110
evil, problem of, 96
evolution, emergent, 98
excellence, 135-36
existentialism, 38, 77-79, 107-8, 110,
  218-19, 221-22
experimentalism, a daring, 242-44. *See also*
  pragmatism

fascism, fascistic, 70-72, 104, 199, 205
fragmentary thinking, 244-46
freedom, 248-49
fundamentalism, 68-70, 103

German, Germany, 31, 80
goal, goals of education, 78, 82, 91, 94,
  112-38, 186
  aspects of adequate, 130-37
  criterion of, 114-16
  critique of ten, 116-30
  humanization as, 130-37, 197
  need of, 112-13
  objections to general, 137-38
God, gods, 61, 63, 67, 71, 96, 97-98, 102,
  120, 121, 123, 142, 170, 191-93, 210,
  214
Greece, Greek, 22, 23, 24, 31, 64, 187,
  188, 189
growth, 53, 89-90 and *n.*, 92, 125

Harvard Report, 58
Harvard University, 194
Hebrews, 24. *See also* Judaism
Hebrew-Christian tradition, 94, 111, 120,
  121, 197, 239
Heidelberg University, 33
Hindu, Hinduism, 16, 210, 211
history, turning point, 233-34
humanism, 35
  ethical, 110, 111, 128-29, 131
  theological, 128
humanities, the, 37, 78
humanization. *See* goal or man

idealism, 35-36, 60-63, 95-96, 101-3,
  104, 110, 218, 241-42
  absolute, 60-61
  personalistic. *See* personalism
  realistic, 239-42
illusionism, 161-62, 168-70, 211, 217
India, 23, 25, 193
Industrial Revolution, 74, 194, 233
intelligence tests, 157-58
intuition. *See* creativity
Iowa State University, 210
Instrumentalism. *See* pragmatism

Japan, 152
Jericho, 22 and *n.*
Judaism, 74, 204

knowledge for its own sake, 123-25, 134

Latin America, 152
learning, learner, 57, 93, 94, 119
logical positivism, 162 and *n.*, 219. *See
  also* analysts

man. *See also* mind, self
  as *"fighter for ends,"* 112
  danger of dehumanization, 108, 221-22
  dignity of, 111, 131-33, 239
  his precarious situation, 17-18
  humanization of, 130-37, 197, 238, 246,
    252
  primitive, 20-22
Marxianism, Marxists, 26, 72-76, 105-7,
  110, 194, 233
Medieval, Middle Ages, 30-33, 194
mediocrity, danger of, 154
meliorism, 82, 91
memory, 93-94
metaphysical society, 223
metaphysics, metaphysical, 51, 73-74, 81,
  85, 88-89, 125-27, 134, 226-27
method, methods
  analytical, 45, 115, 219, 220
  of Jesus, 29-30
  synoptic, 84, 115-16
Michigan, University of, 210
militarism, 189
mind and self
  as clue to reality, 60, 102, 133, 173,
    145-151

mind and self—*cont'd*
  capacities of, 85-86, 131-32, 163-64
  Dewey's view of, 85, 87
  epiphenomenalism, 85
  unconscious. *See* unconscious mind
National Education Association, 59
naturalism, 34-35, 36, 52, 73, 85-86, 96-99
Negroes, 137, 214
North Carolina, University of, 210
Nuclear Age and crisis, 17, 36, 118, 211, 233-35, 250

objectivity, cult of, 157-58
obstructions to creativity, 152-74
  four dogmas, 159-74
  in modern cultures, 152-55
  within the schools, 155-59
Oklahoma State University, 210
outlook, religious, 200-5
Oxford University, 33, 194

Padua, University of, 33
Palestine, 193
Peace Corps, 137
perfectionism. *See* self-realization
Persia, 22
personalism, 60-61, 86, 101-3, 110, 133, 191-92, 214, 241-42
perspective, 7
  American lack of, 38
  education in, 20-39
  need of, 18-19
philosophy, philosophies
  conditions of creativity, 225-29
  cost of neglect, 223-25
  creative tendencies, 221-23
  eclipse of, 216-21
  education and, 43-49
  in high school, 228-29
  nature of, 44-47
  value of, 82
philosophy of education
  significance of, 47-49
  toward unity in, 83-111
  types of, 50-81
pragmatism, experimentalism, 35, 36, 51-55, 104, 109

progressivism, progressives, 27 *n.*, 34, 35, 55-57, 74, 92-95, 104, 109-10
Protestantism, Protestant, 34, 68-69, 195, 203-4
psychology, psychological
  animal, 163
  experimental, 119
  faculty, 118-19
  Gestalt, 184
  reductionism in, 163-64
public schools. *See* school
puritanism, 197-98

Quakers, 198

realism, realists, 34-35, 62-64, 73, 96-99, 110
reason, 82, 84, 115-16
reconstructionism, 81-82, 109, 110
reductionism, 98-99, 159-60, 162-64, 211, 217
relativism, 162, 171-74, 211, 217
religion, 191-215
  as goal, 120-21, 134
  as *"mother of the Arts,"* 23 and *n.*, 120, 192
  conditions for creativity, 212-15
  Freud's view of, 161, 169-70
  nature of, 191-93
  relation to education, 193-97
  three great challenges, 214-15
religious education
  association, 8, 208, 209 *n.*
  Plato's view of, 26
  problem of, 205-10
  "released time," 208 and *n.*, 209
  role of home in, 207-8 and *n.*
  synoptic approach to, 207-10
Renaissance, 16, 34, 35, 55, 194
responsibility, social, 136-37
Rome, Roman, 23, 24, 31, 210
Russia, Russian, 80, 106-7, 153, 243. *See also* Marxianism

Scholasticism, 33, 194
school, schools, 155-59
  Catechumenal and Catechetical, 33
  Cathedral Schools, 33
  Palace School, 33
  parochial, 206

school, schools—*cont'd*
  public, 206
science, scientists, scientific, 36, 175-90
  as indispensable, 187-89
  conditions for creativity, 189-90
  limitations and dangers, 182-87
  nature of, 176-80
  presuppositions of, 183
  relations to education, 180-82
scientism, 89, 190, 212, 224
Scotland, 195
sectarianism, 199
secularism, 121-22, 134, 194, 206
self-realization, perfectionism, 127-30, 134-35
"social-self-realization," 81, 129
Society for Study of Dialectical Materialism, 223
Sophist, 23-24
Sparta, Spartan, 23
specialization, 244-46
Sputnik, 235
Stoics, 22
Sumeria, Sumerian, 22, 23, 193
Sunday school, 195
supernaturalism, 67
Supreme Court, 203
synoptic, synopsis, synthesis, 7, 39, 46, 48. *See also* method

Talmud, 24
teacher, teachers, educators
  qualifications, 247-48
  role of, 251-52
  Russian, 75-76
  the great, 24-30
tests, objective, 158
theism, theistic, 61, 63, 86, 110, 191-93, 214, 242
theology, theologians, 32, 52, 197, 200-2, 212-14
totalitarianism, 154. *See also* fascism

unconscious mind,
  relation to conscious, 150-51
  relation to creativity, 148-51
UNESCO, 38
United Nations, 38, 111, 173
Universal Declaration of Human Rights, 111, 173
universal outlook, 38, 250

Virginia, University of, 198

Wayne State University, 156
wholeness or inclusiveness, 7, 46, 84, 111, 131, 133-35, 186. *See also* method, synoptic

Yale University, 194